THIS AGING SOCIETY

Second Edition

THIS AGING SOCIETY

William C. Cockerham
University of Alabama at Birmingham

Prentice Hall
Upper Saddle River, New Jersey 07458

Library of Congress Cataloging-in-Publication Data

Cockerham, William C.
    This aging society / William C. Cockerham. — 2nd ed.
      p. cm.
    Includes bibliographical references and index.
    ISBN 0–13–651092–2
    1. Aging—Social aspects. 2. Aging—Social aspects—United
  States. 3. Aged—Social conditions. 4. Aged—United States—Social
  conditions. I. Title.
HQ1061.C56   1997   96–41176
305.26—dc20   CIP

This book was set in 11/13 Times Roman by D.M. Cradle Associates
and was printed and bound by Courier Companies, Inc.
The cover was printed by Phoenix Color Corp.

Editorial director: Charlyce Jones Owen
Editor-in-chief: Nancy Roberts
Acquisitions editor: Fred Whittingham
Associate editor: Sharon Chambliss
Director of production and manufacturing: Barbara Kittle
Managing editor: Ann Marie McCarthy
Project manager: Fran Russello
Editorial/production supervision and interior design: Mary McDonald
Manufacturing manager: Nick Sklitsis
Prepress and manufacturing buyer: Mary Ann Gloriande
Cover design: Wendy Alling Judy
Electronic art creation: Asterisk Group Inc.
Marketing manager: Chaunfayta Hightower
Copy editor: Sue Gleason

Printed in the United States of America

10 9 8 7 6 5 4 3 2 1

ISBN 0-13-651092-2

Prentice-Hall International (UK) Limited, *London*
Prentice-Hall of Australia Pty. Limited, *Sydney*
Prentice-Hall Canada Inc., *Toronto*
Prentice-Hall Hispanoamericana, S.A., *Mexico*
Prentice-Hall of India Private Limited, *New Delhi*
Prentice-Hall of Japan, Inc., *Tokyo*
Simon & Schuster Asia Pte. Ltd., *Singapore*
Editora Prentice-Hall do Brasil, Ltda., *Rio de Janeiro*

To Eva Louise Mail Hunnicutt and
to Carl and Jewel Cockerham—
the best examples of successful aging

CONTENTS

PREFACE

The aging of human society worldwide is rapidly becoming one of the most distinct features of modernity. The fact that older people will exist on this planet in greater numbers than ever before means not only significant changes in the age composition of society, but a corresponding change in the norms, values, and attitudes concerning the elderly and the social policies affecting them. In the twenty-first century, approximately one in five persons will be age 65 or over, a demographic reality that has enormous implications. Today's elderly have attained higher levels of education and economic position, and are larger in number, than in the past, and the aged are becoming a major social and political force.

Consequently, it is the intent of this book to assess both the causes and the direction of social change in the modern world brought on by the aging of society. The focus is on the social aspects of the aging process, from the standpoint of both the individual and the wider society. In the social sciences, interest in and analysis of our aging society are likely to increase, such that social gerontology will become one of the most important fields of study and research in human social behavior. This book is an effort to provide an overall view of the literature that currently represents this growing specialty. The views expressed are those of the author. However, the author wishes to thank the reviewers of the first and second editions for their important suggestions: Henry M. Barlow (Cleveland State University), Richard Rogers (University of Colorado), Reba Rowe (McNeese State University), and Yvonne Vissing (Salem State College) for this second edition; Leonard D. Cain (Portland State University) and Dale A. Lund (University of Utah) for the first edition.

William C. Cockerham

Chapter 1

SOCIAL PERSPECTIVES ON AGING

The purpose of this book is to examine the social aspects of the aging experience. Growing old is not simply a biological process; it is also a social and psychological phenomenon that involves important changes in the aging person's perceptions, social roles, self-concept, behavior, and approach to daily living. Aging also has important effects on society, because the trend worldwide is toward increasingly larger numbers and proportions of aged persons; in fact, the twentieth century can be described as a period of rapid growth for aged populations. In the twenty-first century, this process will become even more accelerated. Improved nutrition, sanitation, housing, and health care have combined to help promote longer lives for most people. Increasing longevity has in turn fostered a growing interest in both the biological and the behavioral aspects of the aging process and the role of the aged person in society.

GROWTH IN AGED POPULATIONS

Overall life expectancy in the United States in 1993 was 75.5 years. This figure represents an increase in longevity of over 50 percent since 1900, when life expectancy was 47.3 years. The rise in life expectancy has brought a corresponding increase in the growth of the elderly population. In 1940 the elderly (those persons 65 years of age and over) constituted 9 million people, or about 7 percent of the total American population. By 1993 their number had increased to 33 million, or about 13 percent of the population.

Not only are more people living to reach older ages, but since 1958 the birthrate in the United States has been declining. The lower death rate coupled with the lower birthrate has resulted in a much higher proportion of older Americans in relation to the total population. Table 1–1 illustrates this trend by showing that in 1900 only 4 percent of the total U.S. population was age 65 or over. By 1993, as noted, older Americans constituted 13.0 percent of the total population, and by 2050 it is projected that 21.8 percent of all Americans will be in this age bracket. This means that persons over age 65 will make up more than *one-fifth* of the population in the twenty-first century. The point is obvious: Americans are living longer, and the percentage of elderly in the population is increasing significantly.

This trend will undoubtedly bring about a marked change in American society. The aged population will be healthier, better educated, and more affluent than any comparable cohorts of elderly persons in the past. They are likely to have not only a higher standard of living, but also increased political power because of their large numbers and experience with the political process. This means they will have the clout to bring about legislation for public services to meet their needs. Even though elderly Americans will be healthier than ever before, more pressure is likely to be put on health care delivery systems and public health insurance to keep them fit. Pressure will also be put on the Social Security system to maintain or increase payments for old age benefits. With the relatively fewer children resulting from the baby boom generation in the United States, which was born between 1946 and 1964 and is now headed toward late middle age, the financing of old age benefits will require increasingly more money from a smaller working population. In 1955, for example, there were 8.6 taxpayers per Social Security beneficiary; but by 2005 the ratio will be 2.7 taxpayers per retiree. By 2035 the ratio will drop to about 1.9 taxpayers for every retiree. A future crisis in

TABLE 1–1   Percentage of Total U.S. Population Age 65 and over for Selected Years

	1900	1930	1950	1980	1993	2000 (Projected)	2050 (Projected)
Percentage age 65 and over	4.0	5.4	8.1	11.2	13.0	13.1	21.8

Source: U.S. Census Bureau.

the financing and provision of services for the elderly in the United States appears certain.

These trends are important, because when people become very old they require a greater share of public services. In developed nations, the care of the elderly has generally shifted from being a family responsibility to being more of a societal responsibility. This change has come about for a number of reasons. One reason is the decline of the extended family, in which multiple generations of a single family continued to live with or near each other, and its replacement by the nuclear family; that is, a family consisting of one couple and their children. Other reasons include the high cost of health and nursing care, the type and degree of care required, and the increase in the number of persons needing such care. Although most old people will be relatively healthy in old age, there will come a time, particularly for the oldest of the old, when their health will fail, bringing about a need for extended care and greater public expenditures.

With larger numbers of active, well-educated, affluent, and relatively healthy elderly people in society, there may also be an adjustment in normative expectations for social roles and values pertaining to aged persons. Negative stereotypes about the elderly, which were common in the past, are in the process of changing. Past stereotypes of the elderly as unhappy, in poor health, and lonely do not match the reality of life for the majority of older Americans (Spacapan and Oskamp 1989). Images of the elderly in the media are changing as well. For example, a study of television shows with central elderly characters in the early 1990s (such as *Murder She Wrote, In the Heat of the Night, The Golden Girls,* and *Matlock*) found that earlier television stereotypes of older people as comical, stubborn, eccentric, and foolish had been replaced by more positive images of powerful, affluent, admired, and attractive individuals (Bell 1992). This process is likely to accelerate as the baby boom generation enters old age. The baby boomers number some 79 million Americans, about 30 percent of the total population, and have been the nation's primary consumers of goods and services. Advertising and marketing campaigns, as well as entertainment, will undoubtedly adjust to the aging of this financially powerful group by adapting to their needs, tastes, and attitudes in a positive way. Consequently, the emphasis on youth in Western society will likely decline as greater social value is assigned to the elderly, along with some features of older age, such as having experience or looking distinguished.

When the aged population of the United States was only 4 percent in 1900, the needs of the elderly were not as important in relation to the total population and could more easily be overlooked. But with one in every five Americans being aged in the twenty-first century, concerns of the elderly will

TABLE 1–2 Median Ages for Selected Countries, 1990 and 2010

Country	1990	2010 (Projected)
Germany	37.8	44.3
Italy	36.7	43.3
Japan	37.2	43.1
Great Britain	35.7	40.9
Canada	33.1	39.6
Australia	32.1	37.8
United States	32.8	37.4
South Korea	26.6	35.7
China	25.5	33.4
Brazil	22.1	28.1
Mexico	19.5	25.6
Nigeria	16.3	18.1

Source: U.S. Census Bureau.

be an increasingly important feature of social policy in the United States. The same circumstance exists to an even greater degree in other developed countries. For example, Table 1–2 shows that in 1990 the median age (half of the population is younger than this age, and the other half is older) in the United States was 32.8 and is projected to rise to 37.4 by 2010. However, the median age in 1990 was already 37.8 in Germany, 37.2 in Japan, and 36.7 in Italy. In 2010 the median age will be 44.3 in Germany, 43.3 in Italy, 43.1 in Japan, and 40.9 in Great Britain. Although the median age will be much younger in developing countries, such as Brazil, Mexico, and Nigeria, Table 1–2 nevertheless shows that the overall direction of aging in the world is toward progressively older populations.

SOCIAL GERONTOLOGY

With the increase in numbers and proportions of the aged, the study of gerontology, or aging, has correspondingly increased in scope and importance. At its current stage of development, gerontology is multidisciplinary, not a discipline by itself. However, those in the field tend to believe that the field's multidisciplinary approach is a major strength, for it attracts researchers from a variety of areas—medicine, biology, biochemistry, sociology, psychology, and the like. Social scientists tend to specialize in *social gerontology*, which is the study of aging as a social experience. Social gerontology is a rapidly growing subfield because of the demand for research that can be articulated into social policy and programs for the aged, due to the increase in the elderly population. The intent of this book is to review the subfield of social gerontology, especially from the standpoint of work in sociology and social psychology.

A social science focus on aging is important because it allows for a more complete understanding of what it means to be old in society; it is not limited by explanations that are strictly biological, biochemical, or psychological. According to Riley and her associates (Riley, Foner, and Waring 1988), there is a plasticity to aging, in which social processes interact with biological and psychological processes to influence the ways people change from childhood through adulthood and old age. Riley and her colleagues suggest that there is a diversity among individuals as they grow older, which is dependent on their socioeconomic position, their relationships with other people, and their concept of self. They conclude, along with others (Fennell, Phillipson, and Evers 1988), that understanding the process of aging is largely a sociological matter. It is not that biology and psychology are unimportant. Quite the contrary; aging is fundamentally a biological process with significant psychological implications for the individual. However, aging is also experienced socially, and to a large extent what it *means* to be aged in society is a sociological phenomenon. This book, accordingly, will discuss the social aspects of aging.

WHAT CAUSES AGING?

For centuries, people have wanted to know what causes biological aging, but the answer remains a mystery. Aging is known to occur as a result of changes in the cells of the body, yet what makes these changes take place is not clear. The two most widely accepted concepts of aging involve the idea that either (1) "wear and tear" on the body over time causes it to break down and age, or (2) we have genetic clocks ticking away within us, which are programmed to determine the manner and time in which we all age and die (Rosenfeld 1985).

The "wear and tear" view includes the notion that aging may be due in large part to deterioration in the links *(integratory homeostasis)* that exist between cells of the same tissue and those of other tissues. Although the body's DNA is known to have a self-repair capability, this capability apparently declines over time, and when this happens people begin to age. Another "wear and tear" perspective on aging is that it is due to a decline of immunity. In other words, over time, the body loses some of its ability to recognize and attack disease-causing agents and may even attack healthy cells, resulting in autoimmune diseases such as rheumatoid arthritis. When the immune system begins to wear down, the aging process may be accelerated.

The genetic clock approach maintains that aging is the result of some form of preset genetic program. In other words, as Albert Rosenfeld (1985: 101) suggests, we all have some sort of built-in timer that sets off aging at a preselected point in time. All species appear to have a specific life span that sets limits on how long they are likely to live. For example, some tortoises may live for 150 years, and people in developed nations average about 75 years. Thus aging may not be just a case of random wear and tear. Rather, a genetic clock may set certain limits beyond which no one is able to live. According to some researchers, the natural limit to the human life span is about 85 years on the average, and that limit is not likely to change very much (Fries 1980). S. Jay Olshansky and his colleagues (Olshansky, Carnes, and Cassel 1992) investigated the upper limits of human longevity by estimating the life expectancy that would result from hypothetical cures for all cardiovascular diseases, ischemic heart disease, diabetes, and cancer in the United States. They found that, even given cures for the major degenerative diseases, it was unlikely that life expectancy at birth would exceed age 85. Although findings like these are not conclusive, they nevertheless provide strong evidence that humans have life span limits and that further gains in life expectancy will be modest.

If people do indeed have a genetic clock in their physiological makeup, where is it located? One view is that the clock is cellular, because normal cells have been found to have a finite life span; however, cancer cells have been found to be immortal. It is not clear why normal cells age and abnormal cancer cells do not; it may be that there is a cellular genetic clock that can be disrupted by abnormal cells. Another view is that the clock is at the base of the brain, in the area housing the hypothalamus and the pituitary gland, which controls the release of hormones into the body. At some preset time, a hormone—currently unidentified—may be released into the body to produce aging. Or it may be that there is a relationship between cellular and brain triggers in the aging process, or there may be some combination of genetic clocks and the effects of wear and tear on the body.

Evidence supporting the importance of hormones in the aging process comes from the discovery by Daniel Rudman and his colleagues (1990) that the human growth hormone could reverse the effects of aging. In a clinical test involving 21 healthy men between the ages of 61 and 81, a genetically engineered version of the natural growth hormone reduced body fat, increased muscle bulk, and helped rebuild vital organs, such as the heart and kidneys, that shrink with age. Moreover, the men's skin regained a more youthful appearance and thickness. They looked more fit and in better over-all physical condition. These results suggest that a decline in the body's pro-duction of growth hormone is a major factor causing fat to accumulate, mus-cles to wither, and organs to become smaller as a person ages. Although the research by Rudman and associates is not conclusive, it strongly suggests that the growth hormone has a critical role in aging and can be used to help elderly people maintain muscles and increase strength.

Whatever the cause of aging, the interaction of various genetic and other biological factors is involved, and social-psychological influences, such as stress, also seem to be important. In addition, aging can be of a pri-mary or secondary nature. *Primary aging* occurs over time; *secondary aging* is usually due to disease or psychological trauma, and is premature. The most obvious indication of aging is the appearance of a person's skin, which tends to dry out and wrinkle. The person's capacity for sight and hearing is reduced, and the brain begins to shrink from loss of cells. Muscles also shrink and become weaker, joints stiffen and swell, while the heart, lungs, kidneys, and bladder begin to operate at reduced levels of effectiveness, and the body's output of hormones begins to diminish. The body thus becomes increasingly susceptible to infection, injury, and degenerative diseases, such as coronary heart disease, cancer, and diabetes.

According to Donald King, Neela Pushparaj, and Kathleen O'Toole (1982), illness and disability in the elderly result from a programmed process of deterioration (a genetic clock), and death involves stresses (wear and tear) on the body that are better tolerated at younger ages. "Indeed," states King and his colleagues (1982:109), "when one looks at morbidity and mortality in the very old, one ironically finds that the leading causes of disability and death are those seen in the very young—infection and trauma." The differ-ence is that younger people can cope with infection and trauma (injury) much better than older people. King and colleagues suggest that the oldest of the elderly should be viewed as resisting the genetic and environmentally derived pathologies that determine susceptibility to disease and death throughout the human life span. Genetically caused diseases are often responsible for death in the young, but if the individual survives early child-hood, the years to about age 40 are comparatively healthy. Between ages 40 and 80, illness and mortality begin to increase, and King and associates sur-mise that environmental factors are most responsible for this trend—in par-ticular, a detrimental personal lifestyle in previous years involving a lack of physical activity, smoking, heavy alcohol consumption, and poor diet. Such a lifestyle—especially if imposed on genetic mechanisms that predispose a person to obesity, diabetes, heart disease, cirrhosis, cancer, or other prob-lems—promotes death.

Therefore, King and colleagues maintain that those who survive well beyond the age of 80 are a select group by virtue of both genetic and environmental advantages. Nevertheless, the steady deterioration of the body, which seems part of a programmed process, ensures that any advantage in warding off signs of aging by the individual acts only to defer the final and irrevocable outcome.

What separates aging from other biological processes is that physical aging (1) comes on gradually from within the organism instead of from the external environment, (2) has a negative effect on physical functioning, and (3) is universal in that the physical changes that take place happen to everyone (Strehler 1977). If any one of these three criteria is missing with regard to a physical change in an individual, then that change is not part of aging. For example, cancer can come on gradually from within the body and have a negative effect on physical functioning, but not everybody gets cancer, and the onset of cancer can be influenced by factors in the external environment (such as radiation, biochemicals, or, in the case of lung cancer, cigarette smoking). Although aged people may be more likely to get cancer, cancer is not automatic with aging.

Who lives the longest? Rosenfeld (1985), while noting that most people in primitive societies age quickly and die young, suggests that the greatest longevity may nevertheless be among certain groups of people living in economically depressed mountain tribes. The Vilcabambans of Ecuador, the Hunzas on the border of China and Pakistan, and the Abkhasians in the Caucasus region have people claiming to be 120 years of age and older. Whether these claims are valid is not known, although the proportion of persons who say they are over 100 years old in these groups is unusually high. What is known is that they live a slow-paced rural life at high altitudes, work and exercise regularly even at old age, and eat a simple diet that is practically meat-free, omits sugar, and includes large amounts of fruits, vegetables, and yogurt. They also consume fewer calories (about 2,200 a day on the average) than Americans and Western Europeans, whose diet often exceeds 3,000 calories daily.

The American claiming the longest life, according to Rosenfeld, is Charlie Smith, who arrived as a slave from Africa in 1854 and died in 1979 in Florida, supposedly at the age of 137. The longest life that has been documented in the world, however, is for a French woman, Jeanne Calment, who was 121 years old in 1996 and lived in a nursing home in Arles in southern France. She was born in Arles in 1875, a year before Alexander Graham Bell invented the telephone. The second documented most long-lived person is Shigechiyo Izumi of Japan, who died in 1986 at 120 years of age. The oldest living male in 1996 was a white American, Christian Mortensen, who was

113 years old and lived in a retirement home in California. Mortensen was not the oldest American, however. That distinction in 1996 belonged to an African-American woman, Mary Thompson, living in a Florida nursing home at the age of 119.

What people with longevity have in common is that they tend to come from families whose members typically live a long time. For example, the father of Jeanne Calment, the oldest person in the world, lived to 93 and her mother lived to 86. This pattern is evidence that longevity is inherited, but to what degree is not known. Nor is much else known about why certain people reach the oldest ages and others do not. Persons at the upper end of the socioeconomic scale tend to live longer than members of lower socioeconomic groups, but an affluent lifestyle, involving a rich diet, heavy smoking, and lack of exercise, can also be detrimental to a person's health. Poverty clearly decreases an individual's life chances because it enhances exposure to crowded living conditions, poor diet, inferior housing, violence, alcoholism and problem drinking, and drug abuse. People who are relaxed and not greatly affected by stress; who have a family history of longevity; and who live a healthy lifestyle with respect to eating properly, getting enough rest, exercising, and avoiding practices like smoking, abusing alcohol, and taking drugs appear to be the most long-lived.

AGING AND THE LIFE COURSE

In the United States, age 65 has generally marked that point in life when a person is "officially" old. This is largely because of its selection by the Social Security Administration in 1935 as the age of eligibility for old age benefits. Except for its bureaucratic significance, however, being age 65 has no other particular relevance. Chronological age is an inconsistent indicator of the aging process. Just as physical and intellectual capabilities mature at different times in different people, so can aging be said to begin at different points in time for different people. It is possible to be a "young" 65 or an "old" 55.

Not only do individuals vary in relation to aging, but the concept of old age itself is relative and differs between societies. The more primitive the society, the earlier in life people are defined as being old (Cowgill 1986). Modern societies select a chronological age, like 65, as the point of old age, whereas less-developed societies tend to rely more on a particular event, such as becoming a grandparent, to mark a person as old.

One way to organize the social and psychological aspects of the aging experience is to categorize that experience into stages that denote the human life course. Although the stages of the life course are based on chronological age and do not account for variations among individuals, they are indicative of the general life cycle most people follow. Implicit in the idea of a life course is a common set of social experiences through which members of a society are expected to pass. For instance, childhood is the time when a person generally receives a primary education; adolescence and young adulthood are usually the time of courtship and marriage; the period of later maturity is typically the time of retirement.

Age is an important dimension of social organization, because the divisions of the life course are those prescribed by the culture to lend stability and predictability to the typical sequence of life events. Implied in this arrangement is the idea that individuals also undergo a change in behavior as they pass from one stage of life into a subsequent stage. Others expect infants, children, young adults, middle-aged adults, and older persons to behave in a manner characteristic of their age group; social judgments of their maturity depend on how closely their behavior approximates the corresponding age-related norm. Furthermore, at each stage of life, a person takes on new social roles and the responsibilities that accrue to those roles, and the person's status and relationships with other people are modified accordingly.

The typical stages of the human life course and the approximate ages they represent are shown in Table 1–3. Although a person can be regarded as aging from the moment of conception or from the moment of birth (there is some disagreement on this point), for the purposes of our discussion, the stages of middle age, later maturity, and old age are the most relevant. Although not everybody necessarily experiences the life course in neatly packaged phases, stage theories are useful in highlighting the general pattern of aging.

TABLE 1–3   The Life Course

Stage	Approximate Age
Infancy	2
Preschool	2–5
Childhood	5–12
Adolescence	12–17
Early maturity	17–25
Maturity	25–40
Middle age	40–55
Later maturity	55–75
Old age	75

While this book focuses on the period of late maturity and old age, the path to these stages starts in infancy and continues through the life course. Aging is usually not a concern of adolescents and young adults who are in the prime of their life with respect to their appearance and physical capabilities. Rather, it is middle age (ages 40 to 55) when people initially sense that they are being affected by biological aging (Atchley 1994).

Middle age is the time when the person recognizes a reduction of energy and often begins to favor less strenuous activities. Usually the person's work career more or less reaches a plateau, and the great majority of a couple's children will have left home to lead their own lives. This is a time of life when parents or other older people close to the individual die. As Robert Atchley (1994) explains, middle age is also when most people realize that they themselves are aging and that death is very real, not just something that happens to somebody else. Robert Kastenbaum (1971, 1992), for example, found that a characteristic of old age is a foreshortened time perspective. The older person avoids thought of the future because of the limited time left and instead dwells on the past. Kastenbaum suggests that a majority of people are past oriented by age 40, and virtually all people are by age 55.

Later maturity (ages 55 to 75) is characterized by a marked reduction in energy, vision, and hearing. Chronic health disorders are commonplace, and poor health can join with reduced income, retirement, and the deaths of friends and relatives to curtail social interaction. By their midsixties, many women are widows. But, as Atchley notes, the period of later maturity can be a pleasant one for those people who plan for it, retain a good measure of physical vigor, and perhaps wish to enjoy a time of lessened responsibilities. The aged individual may also continue to be a highly productive member of society. Charles Bowden and Alvin Burstein (1974:212) point out, for example, that the "myth that age necessarily involves an inability to produce is challenged by the numbers of second careers and examples of influence maintained by prominent individuals late into their lives." Both Ronald Reagan and George Bush were elected president of the United States while in their sixties; many members of Congress and most members of the U.S. Supreme Court serve in office while elderly. In fact, Richard Posner (1995:180) refers to the judiciary as "the nation's premier geriatric occupation." "The remarkable thing about judges," states Posner (1995:181), "is not that they hang on to their jobs to such advanced ages but that they perform them creditably, and indeed sometimes with great distinction, at advanced ages."

Old age (75 and over), in contrast to other stages of life, is more likely to be a less pleasant period, for there is a higher probability of loneliness and physical decline. It can also be a time when mental processes are diminished. Whereas it seems clear that the aged brain takes longer to respond to a stimulus, and the recall of recent events may be impaired, remote memory of past events is usually quite good. If there is considerable memory loss, it can be a sign of dementia. But it should be realized that, although dementia is likely to occur with increasing age, it does not occur in most elderly people. Besides reduced mental activity in very old age, another problem peculiar to the elderly is physical frailty and the possibility of being so disabled that physical mobility is highly restricted or denied.

Physical and mental infirmities and the reality of being tired, ill, and less able to cope with problems—all set in a framework of recognition of impending death—can and do produce severe problems of adjustment and depression for the elderly. With reduced resources, the elderly person is less able to cope with stress and adapt to new conditions. Old age is thus a period in life many people wish to avoid; yet, as in the period of later maturity, the key to success in old age is to maintain an optimal level of physical strength, mental awareness, and happiness.

However, to be old in a modern society often means assuming a devalued status. Despite the fact that a majority of aged persons are not sick, lonely, poor, insecure, or mentally deficient, many of them are, and the negative stereotype of the elderly results from this situation. But it must be pointed out that the transition from middle to old age is not always negative and that added years of life now mean added opportunities. Older people today differ markedly from the aged of earlier periods, in that they are more healthy, alert, vigorous, and younger in outlook (Pifer and Bronte 1986). In modern societies, it is typically only after the age of 75 that most people begin to decline physically, and some mentally, whereas others remain relatively healthy past the age of 75. Many people may not be extremely sick or disabled, on the average, until the very end of their lives.

Consequently, there is now a blurring of the life cycle periods between middle age and later maturity for many people, for it is becoming less apparent when middle age ends and later maturity begins. As Bernice and Dail Neugarten (1986) observe, it is a new historical phenomenon that a very large group of elderly are healthy, vigorous, financially secure, well integrated into the lives of their families and communities, and politically active. What seems to be emerging among the elderly are new divisions of "young-old (from approximately 65–75 years of age)," "old-old (75–85 years)," and the "oldest-old (85 and over)," with the young-old being both active and youthful in their approach to life. The majority of the young-old would not be appreciably different from younger persons in the early part of the late maturity stage (55 to 75 years) of the life cycle.

According to Matilda White Riley and John Riley (1986), the implications of added years for the individual's life cycle are only now beginning to be comprehended. What increased longevity means for the individual, state Riley and Riley (1986:53), is (1) prolonged opportunity for accumulating life experiences; (2) maximized opportunities to complete or change the roles of early and middle life—such as changing careers or marriage partners, or taking on new roles in the later years; (3) prolonged relationships with others—spouse, family, children, and friends, who also live longer; and (4) increased potential complexity of a person's social networks—kinship, friendship, and community—as all members survive longer. As Riley and Riley (1986:53–54) explain, "All these consequences of longevity mean that people now have unprecedented opportunity to accumulate experience, to exercise new and expanded options, to respond to social change, and to influence it."

In the final analysis, although growing older means stability and can include the potential for personal growth, aging also means physical and perhaps mental decline. The last part of the life cycle is both a period of opportunity and a period in which death is an increasing reality.

SUMMARY

Social gerontology is the study of the social experience of aging. This field has gained in importance and scope in recent years because of the significant worldwide increase of aged persons during the twentieth century. In 1993 life expectancy had reached 75.5 years for Americans, and the elderly constituted 13 percent of the population. By 2050, it is projected that over 20 percent of the population, or one in five Americans, will be age 65 or older. This trend is likely to bring important changes, because the aged population will not only be larger, but also healthier, better educated, and more affluent than comparable cohorts of elderly persons in the past.

Currently, it is not known what causes physical aging. The two most widely accepted theories are (1) that wear and tear on the body over time causes it to break down and age, or (2) that all of us have genetic clocks ticking away within us that are programmed or preset to determine the manner and time at which we age and die. Either theory may be correct, or there may be some combination of wear and tear and genetic clocks that triggers aging. One way to view the social experiences associated with physical aging is to organize those experiences into stages denoting the human life cycle. Such stages are indicative of the general life course that people follow. This book focuses on the stages of later maturity (ages 55 to 75) and old age (age 75 and over). However, in recent years there has been a blurring of life cycle periods between middle age and later maturity. The ages from 65 to 75 are beginning to represent a category of "young-old" persons, because many people in this age group remain relatively active and healthy. Old age is becoming both a period of increased opportunity and a time in which death is near.

Chapter 2

THE DEMOGRAPHY OF AGING: NORTH AMERICA

As discussed in the previous chapter, the greatest change in the age structure of most societies in the twentieth century has been the growth of the population over the age of 65. Because of its strong social implications, this demographic trend is not something that younger people today can consider unimportant or irrelevant. The significant increase in numbers and proportions of older people will impact heavily on future patterns of employment, taxation, health care delivery, and other aspects of daily life. Unless there is a global war or some widespread epidemic or natural disaster that takes millions of lives, the increase in elderly people will intensify in the twenty-first century. At present, the world's elderly population is growing faster than the world population as a whole. If the current rate continues, the U.S. Census Bureau (1994) estimates that there will be 426 million elderly worldwide by the year 2000 (compared with 332 million in 1991). Moreover, the increase in numbers of the aged will be taking place not just in the most advanced nations, but throughout the world. The result is that there will be a greater proportion of elderly people in the twenty-first century than ever before in human history.

In this chapter we examine this situation by first discussing the demography of aging in the United States and then comparing the U.S. pattern with that for Canada. To put this discussion in perspective, it should be pointed out that large numbers of elderly persons are a very recent occurrence in human society. As Donald Cowgill (1986) explains, life expectancy in prehistoric times averaged only about 20 years per person; thus old people were very rare during humankind's earliest periods. Longevity increased little during the time of ancient Greece and Rome, and actually declined somewhat after the fall of Rome. There was not a noticeable improvement until the seventeenth century in Europe, when the average life expectancy reached just under 30 years of age. Yet this modest increase was not enough, as Cowgill observes, to produce any significant change in the age structure of even the most developed countries at that time.

Consequently, for most of the history of the world, human populations have tended to consist largely of children and young adults. Relatively few persons reached middle age, and only very few reached old age. It was not until the middle of the nineteenth century that the average life expectancy in a developed nation finally reached 45 years. The greatest extension of longevity has occurred in the twentieth century, especially since World War II, with the most advanced nations now showing life expectancies in the mid-seventies or higher. In 1991 the highest mean for life expectancy in the world was 82.8 years for Japanese women. For the first time ever, large populations of old people are becoming common throughout the world.

DEMOGRAPHIC PATTERNS IN THE UNITED STATES

The demographic pattern of aging in the United States has followed a course similar to that of other major industrialized countries. Life expectancy for Americans, as noted in the last chapter, increased from 47.3 years in 1900 to 75.5 years in 1993. In 1900 persons 65 years of age and over in the United States numbered 3.1 million and constituted 4 percent of the total population; in 1993 some 33 million, or 13 percent, of all Americans were 65 or older. As shown in Figure 2–1, the proportion of the elderly is expected to increase even more significantly in the future. The growth of the older population will be relatively slow during the 1990s because of the decline in the birthrate during the Great Depression of the 1930s. From 33 million in 1993, Figure 2–1 shows that the number of older Americans will reach 34.9 million in the year 2000. However, the most rapid increase in the elderly population will take place in the twenty-first century; Figure 2–1 shows the aged population reaching 39.4 million in 2010, 52.1 million in 2020, and 65.6 million in 2030. By 2000, persons 65 years and older are expected to be 13.1 percent of the total population, and this percentage may reach 21.8 percent by 2050.

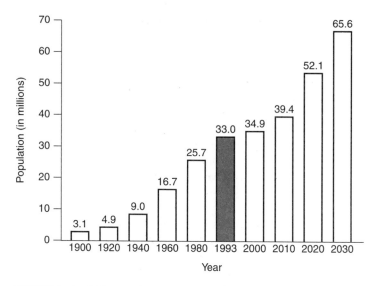

FIGURE 2–1   U.S. population age 65 and over, 1900–2030

Source: U.S. Census Bureau.

Declining mortality rates and the rise in life expectancy have also meant that the older population itself is getting older. Thus it may not be unusual in the future to see 70-year-old daughters caring for their 95-year-old mothers. We see this potential in statistics like those for the period 1960–1990. During this 30-year period, the overall population of the United States increased 39 percent. By age group, the population under 25 years increased only 13 percent compared to 89 percent for those over 65. However, the fastest growing segment of the aged population is the oldest-old—those persons age 85 and over. The oldest-old age cohort increased by 231 percent in the United States between 1960 and 1990. In terms of actual numbers, Figure 2–2 shows that the oldest-old will grow from 3 million in 1990 to 4.3 million in 2000; by 2050 some 17.7 million Americans are expected to be age 85 and over. Not shown in Figure 2–2 is the projection that some 1.3 million Americans will be 100 years or older by 2040. From about 1 percent of the U.S. population in 1990, the oldest-old will constitute over 5 percent of the population by the midtwenty-first century, which is the largest gain of any age group during this period.

As the fastest-growing age group in the United States, the oldest-old are generally healthier than the old-old (those 75 to 85 years of age). Heart disease and stroke are the most frequent among men in their fifties through eighties and for women about ten years later. Those who make it through

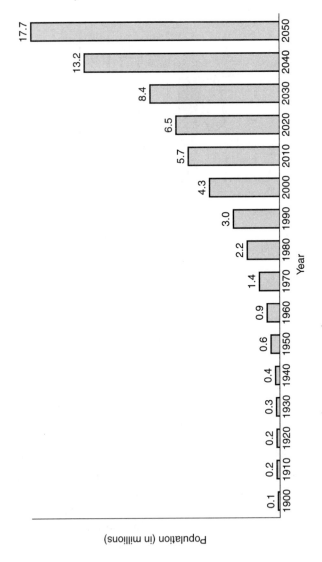

FIGURE 2–2 U.S. population age 85 and over, 1900–2050

Source: U.S. Census Bureau.

these age-specific danger zones for cardiovascular death are less likely to be stricken with these afflictions at all. Alzheimer's disease typically affects the elderly by their mideighties. Thus those aged persons who pass 85 years tend to be especially healthy in the United States—perhaps even healthier than their age counterparts in Japan and Europe (Manton and Vaupel 1995). The oldest-old appear to have increasingly better health and less physical disability, and are likely benefiting from the rapid reductions in smoking, hypertension, and cholesterol levels in American society, as well as other factors, such as higher national expenditures on health care for the elderly, long-term care facilities, and rehabilitation services.

Gender

Although the life expectancy of the elderly in the United States has increased significantly in the twentieth century, the greatest increase has been among women and whites. Females tend to live much longer than males, and this fact is true both in the United States and worldwide. Male exceed female death rates at all ages and for the leading causes of death, such as heart disease, cancer, stroke, accidents, and pneumonia. Women do suffer from illness and physical disability more often than men, but their usual health problems are not as serious or life threatening as those men typically encounter. Although, later in life, women also die from the same illnesses as men, what distinguishes the sexes, as Lois Verbrugge (1985) observes, is the frequency of those problems and the pace of death. Men, for example, are 1.5 times more likely than women to die from cancer. Coronary heart disease is the leading cause of death for women after age 66 but becomes the number one killer of men after age 39. In sum, women are sick more often (with less serious health problems), but live longer; men, in contrast, are sick less often, but die sooner from more life-threatening diseases.

There is also evidence that women have a biological advantage in life expectancy over men from the earliest periods of life. Males have higher mortality rates than females from the prenatal and neonatal stages of life onward. Although percentages vary from year to year, males die at about a 12 percent greater rate than females during the prenatal stage, and rates are 130 percent greater during the neonatal (newborn) stage. Consequently, males appear to be weaker physiologically than females as the two sexes begin life, and their biological disadvantage seems to continue over the life span.

Social and psychological factors also play an important role in influencing life expectancy for males. Men are generally expected to be more aggressive than women in their roles in society. At least this seems to be the case, for men have significantly greater participation in violent sports and exposure to high-risk occupations, such as motorcycle racing, structural steel work, lumbering, munitions, coal mining, and police work. More men than women are killed or injured in accidents. In addition, men and boys drink alcohol more frequently and consume more when they drink than do women and girls. High alcohol use has been identified as a risk factor for some diseases (such as cirrhosis of the liver) and for death from automobile accidents. Another factor contributing to excess male mortality may be occupational competition and the pressure associated with a job. For instance, middle-aged business executives and professionals who emphasize their career and display a strong drive toward success as part of their lifestyle are noted by insurance companies as a high-risk group for heart disease. This is particularly true if they smoke, are overweight, or tend to overwork. It would seem, therefore, that both the male sex role and the psychodynamics of male competitiveness have an effect on male longevity.

The result is that, as of 1993, the average life expectancy in the United States for females was 78.8 years compared with 72.2 years for males. Overall, women outnumber men in the United States, 130.5 million to 124.5 million, with the greatest disparity at the oldest ages. U.S. Census figures for 1993 show that of the 33.0 million elderly persons in the United States, 19.8 million were women and 13.2 million were men. For every 100 women 65 years of age and older, there were 67.8 men in the same age group.

What this pattern signifies for most women is a highly decreased likelihood of being married in old age. This situation is depicted in Figure 2–3,

FIGURE 2–3   Number of unmarried men per 100 unmarried women in 1992

Source: U.S. Census Bureau.

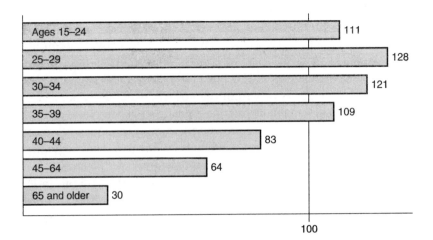

Ages 15–24	111
25–29	128
30–34	121
35–39	109
40–44	83
45–64	64
65 and older	30

100

which shows U.S. Census Bureau statistics for unmarried adults in 1992. As Figure 2–3 indicates, for every 100 unmarried women, there were 111 unmarried men in the 15–24-year-old age group, 128 men in the 25–29 age group, 121 men at 30–34, and 109 men at 35–39. The figures are reversed, however, beginning at ages 40–44, where Figure 2–3 shows that, for every 100 unmarried women, there were 83 unmarried men; at ages 45–64, there were 64 eligible men per 100 unmarried women; and, finally, for age 65 and older, there were only 30 male bachelors for every 100 unmarried women.

There is some evidence that the U.S. population may be shifting toward greater equality in mortality between the sexes. If this is the case, the ratio of men to women at the oldest ages could change somewhat. This possibility is based on data, as Verbrugge (1985) explains, that shows sex differences for some major causes of death have either become stable, decreased, or only slowly widened. Considerable speculation exists with respect to the possible effects on female longevity of their increased participation in the labor force and changes in lifestyle, but it will be several years—until the present cohort of middle-aged and young adult women die—before these effects can be fully determined.

However, we are already seeing such changes as a decline in lung cancer among males because of reduced smoking, whereas lung cancer has increased significantly among women as a result of greater numbers of females taking up smoking in the 1940s. Between 1960 and 1983, death rates from lung cancer increased at an average annual rate of 6.2 percent for women. Lung cancer ranked eighth among cancer deaths for women in 1961, was second to breast cancer by 1979, moved into first place as the leading cancer killer of women by 1986, and continues to be so today. Male death rates from lung cancer are still higher than those of women, but the dramatic increase in deaths from lung cancer for women has reduced the differences between the sexes for this cause of death. Patterns like these may produce a greater balance in mortality between men and women in the future and may affect aging trends. For instance, life expectancy for men increased from 70.9 years in 1982 to 72.2 years in 1993, an improvement of 1.3 years; for women, life expectancy improved six-tenths of a year (from 78.2 to 78.8) during the same period. But, for the time being, the imbalance between males and females in overall mortality remains weighted heavily in favor of women.

This imbalance is reflected in the much greater proportion of elderly females than elderly males in the total population. Figure 2–4 shows the distribution by age and sex for the United States for 1980, 1990, and 2000. Figure 2–4 is a *population pyramid*, a method used to depict graphically the

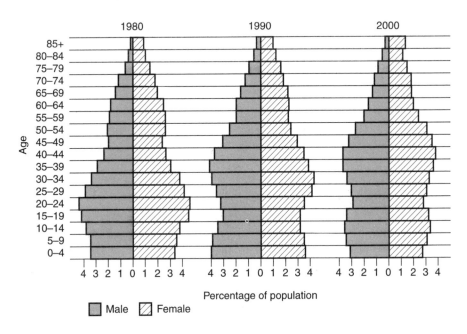

FIGURE 2–4 Distribution of U.S. population by age and sex, 1980, 1990, and 2000

Source: U.S. Census Bureau.

overall age structure of a society. Figure 2–4 shows that the largest proportions of people (as indicated by the largest bulges in the pyramid) in 1980 were in age groups spread between 15 and 34 years of age. In 1990 the shape of the pyramid had changed with the aging of the population; the bulges were greatest for age groups between 25 and 44 years. For the year 2000, Figure 2–4 shows the shift in population continuing toward older age groups, with the largest proportion of people located in the 35- to 49-year-old age brackets. Figure 2–4 also shows increasingly larger proportions of persons in the oldest age categories and an increasing preponderance of women at the oldest ages.

Race

An important reflection of social inequality in the United States is the difference in life expectancy between whites and blacks. Table 2–1 shows that life expectancy for both whites and nonwhites has significantly increased since 1900. By 1993, the average life expectancy of white females is shown in Table 2–1 to have increased to 79.5 years compared with 73.1 years for white males. For blacks, females had an average life expectancy of 73.7 years in 1993 compared with 64.6 years for males.

TABLE 2–1   Average U.S. Life Expectancies by Race and Sex

Birth Year	White Males	White Females	Black Males	Black Females
1900	46.6	48.7	32.5[1]	33.5[1]
1950	66.5	72.2	58.9	62.7
1960	67.4	74.1	60.7	65.9
1970	68.0	75.6	60.0	68.3
1980	70.7	78.1	63.8	72.5
1990	72.7	79.4	64.5	73.6
1993	73.1	79.5	64.6	73.7

[1]Includes all nonwhites.

Source: U.S. National Center for Health Statistics, *Health, United States, 1995* (Washington, D.C.: U.S. Government Printing Office, 1996).

Although Table 2–1 shows that gender produces a strong difference in life expectancy, race is still important. The black female has a definite advantage in longevity over the black male, but white females outlive black females, black males, and white males by a wide margin. The most disadvantaged individual is the black male, whose life, on the average, is 8.5 years shorter than that of the white male and 14.9 years shorter than that of the white female. Thus, despite the female advantage, life expectancy in the United States is strongly affected by racial background and the manner in which this background can be translated into a healthy life. Unfortunately, the conditions of poverty restrict the life chances of many racial minorities. For a long life in the United States, it is best to be female and white.

The disadvantage in life expectancy among blacks is greater than not only that of whites, but also any other racial group in the United States. This has happened despite the significant increase in longevity for the African-American population during the twentieth century. Several sources report that blacks have higher death rates than non-Hispanic whites, Hispanics, Asians, Pacific Islanders, and native Americans for heart disease, all forms of cancer, and other major causes of mortality—including homicide and AIDS (Braithwaite and Taylor 1992; National Center for Health Statistics 1995). Prior to the 1980s, native Americans had the worst health profile in the United States, but today that position has been taken by African Americans, who are at greater risk because of smoking, high blood pressure, high cholesterol levels, alcohol intake, excess weight, and diabetes (Braithwaite and Taylor 1992; Otten et al. 1990; Sorlie et al. 1992). Low income appears to be an important risk factor as well, because of its association with stress and the manner in which stress promotes high blood pressure and poor health habits such as smoking, excessive drinking of alcohol, and overeating. Lack of physicians and medical facilities in low-income neighborhoods, poverty, and adverse living conditions in slum areas are also important barriers to higher life expectancy for economically disadvantaged African Americans.

Strong evidence exists that overall differences in the life expectancy of blacks and whites can be explained almost entirely by differences in socioeconomic status (Cockerham 1995b; Mutchler and Burr 1991; National Center for Health Statistics 1993; Sorlie et al. 1992). The adverse impact of socioeconomic factors on the life expectancy of blacks is greatest for those under the age of 75. African Americans 75 years of age and older have approximately the same life expectancy as white Americans in the same age group (Sorlie et al. 1992).

In 1992 the overall racial composition of the population 65 years of age and older in the United States was about 90 percent white, 8 percent black, and 2 percent other races (namely, native Americans, Eskimos, Aleuts, Asians, and Pacific Islanders). Hispanics, whose racial origin may be either white, black, or native American, constituted some 3 percent of the older population. For the future, the proportion of the elderly population that is black, Hispanic, or Asian is likely to increase, whereas the proportion of whites will decline somewhat, and the proportion of other races will remain about the same. However, in terms of total numbers, the elderly population in the United States will be predominantly white.

Socioeconomic Status

Age does not determine a person's socioeconomic position in the United States. That is, simply being old in itself does not confer enhanced social prestige unless the individual is 100 years of age or older, which is generally viewed as an accomplishment (Baker 1985). Typically, an individual's income, level of education, and occupational prestige are the major determinants of his or her socioeconomic status. Usually, the elderly do not have great incomes or high occupational status because they are retired. Also, in the past many of the elderly were not highly educated. Therefore, elderly persons have not generally filled roles associated with the highest socioeconomic status. There have been some exceptions, however, such as Ronald Reagan, who served as president of the United States from 1980 to 1988 while in his seventies. Yet Reagan's high status in American society was determined by his role as president, not his age. But, with persons now surviving to the oldest ages with greater financial resources and higher levels of education than in the past, the socioeconomic position of the aged as a cohort needs to be reexamined.

The term *socioeconomic status* is a reflection of the work of the German sociologist Max Weber (1864–1920), who maintained that wealth alone does not determine a person's social standing; rather, it is a combination of social class position, status, and power that serves to mark an individual's position in society. It was Weber's (1958) contention that, although social class is an objective dimension of social life, signified by how much money and property a person has, status is subjective in that it consists largely of how much esteem a person is accorded by other people. A person's status is derived particularly from his or her lifestyle, but also from educational attainment and occupational prestige. Persons belonging to the same status group share similar material circumstances, prestige, levels of education and occupation, and political influence and power; they also display the same lifestyle and the social perspectives associated with it.

Weber's influence on analyses of social stratification is seen mainly in the use of socioeconomic status as a variable to determine social position. Typically, socioeconomic status consists of measures of income, occupational prestige, and level of education. It not only reflects a person's economic situation but also allows for status differences that are not necessarily based on wealth. A drug dealer, for example, can be wealthy but will have low socioeconomic status, whereas a university professor may not be wealthy but can have relatively high status because of his or her education and academic accomplishments.

As for the socioeconomic status of the elderly in American society, it is important to note that the aged are a diverse group from all walks of life. To be over the age of 65 does not automatically confer a low socioeconomic rank on an individual; the aged are found in every social class. The elderly may enjoy upper-class status because of their wealth, prestige, and power, or be lower class because of their relative lack of such attributes. Consequently, age alone does not cause an individual's level of social standing. However, old age is usually a negative factor in determining current status—wealth, power, and past statuses can be more important determinants. Nevertheless, some general statements can be made about the overall position of the elderly in society from the standpoint of income, occupation, and education.

Income   The median income (half of all persons have incomes higher than the median, and half have incomes that are lower) in 1993 in the United States was $21,102 for men and $11,046 for women. Among the elderly, median incomes in 1993 were $14,983 for men and $8,499 for women. On an individual level, the incomes of aged men and women are about one-third less than that of persons below age 65. Among families generally, regardless of size, the median 1993 income was $30,291 ($32,960 was the median for whites, $22,886 for Hispanics, and $19,533 for blacks); among families headed by persons age 65 or over, the median 1993 income was $25,965 ($26,761 for whites, $20,459 for Hispanics, and $17,782 for blacks). Overall, families headed by an elderly person had incomes from one-fourth to one-third lower than those of families headed by younger persons.

The major source of income for older families and individuals in 1992 was Social Security (40 percent), followed by income from assets (21 percent), earnings (17 percent), pensions (20 percent), and other payments, such as Supplemental Income Security, unemployment compensation, and veterans' benefits (2 percent). In the 1960s, about 60 percent of all elderly people lived solely on Social Security, but currently most retired people have some income in addition to Social Security from pension plans. However, for those persons age 65 and over with the lowest incomes, Social Security remains the largest source of money. As shown in Table 2–2, 81 percent of the income for the lowest income group in 1992 came from Social Security, compared to 20 percent for the highest income group. The clear pattern shown in Table 2–2 is that, the higher a person's income, the lower the percentage of income from Social Security. Persons in the highest income group received the highest percentage of their income from assets (29 percent) and earnings (27 percent), followed by pensions (22 percent). The lowest group, in contrast, received only 3 percent of its income from pensions, 3 percent from assets, and less than 0.5 percent from earnings. Public assistance (welfare) provided 11 percent of the income for the lowest income group.

TABLE 2–2   U.S. Distribution of Income for Persons Age 65 and over, 1992

| Source | Percentage of Income | | | | |
	Lowest Fifth	Second Fifth	Third Fifth	Fourth Fifth	Highest Fifth
Social Security	81	77	62	46	20
Pensions	3	8	17	24	22
Assets	3	6	12	16	29
Earnings	*	3	6	11	27
Public assistance	11	3	1	*	*
Other income	2	3	3	3	2

*Less than 0.5 percent.
Source: U.S. Department of Health and Human Services.

Some 3.7 million elderly persons lived below the poverty line in 1993, which ranged from $7,363 or less annually for one person to $29,529 for a family of nine or more persons. A family of four was considered poor with an income of $14,763 or less. Some 12.2 percent of persons age 65 and over lived below the 1993 poverty line. However, the percentage of elderly living below the poverty line is not disproportional when it is recognized that the proportion of all Americans living in poverty that year was 15.1 percent, or 39.3 million. Furthermore, 12.2 percent is a vast improvement over 35.2 percent, which was the percentage of elderly persons living below the poverty line in 1959. Although poverty remains a serious problem for many aged Americans, it is clear that the trend is toward lessened numbers of the elderly in the ranks of the poor.

Yet it should be noted that there are groups within the older population that still confront very high rates of poverty. Some 10.7 percent of all elderly whites were poor in 1993, compared with 28 percent of African Americans and 21.4 percent of Hispanics. Aged persons living alone or with nonrelatives were much more likely to be poor (24.1 percent) than older persons living in families (6.5 percent). Older women had a higher poverty rate (15 percent) than older men (9 percent).

Occupation   In 1994, some 3.9 million elderly persons, representing 12 percent of the total population age 65 years or older, were in the labor force, either working or actively seeking employment. Some 2.2 million men (16.8 percent of all elderly men) and 1.7 million women (9.2 percent of all elderly women) constituted the aged labor force; these persons represented some 2.9 percent of the entire U.S. labor force. Over half (53 percent) of these workers were employed part time. Some 26 percent of all older workers in 1994 were self-employed, and three-fourths of them were men. Because most elderly persons (88 percent) are not employed or seeking work, the prestige of one's current occupation is not a major factor in determining the socioeconomic status of the aged. However, the prestige associated with their former occupation can still be important.

Education   The educational level of the elderly has been consistently increasing. The median level of education for the aged in 1980 was 10.3 years for males and 7.4 years for females; by 1991, the median level of education for elderly males had risen to 11.8 years and to 9.5 years for older females. It is projected by the U.S. Census Bureau that 20 percent of all aged persons will hold college degrees by the year 2010. The trend is clearly toward higher levels of educational attainment for future generations of the aged.

Overall, it would appear that the elderly are becoming more affluent and reaching old age with higher levels of education than in the past. As a group, it would appear that the socioeconomic status of the elderly in society

is improving because the aged have more money and education. Consequently, the loss of socioeconomic status in general that old age brings may
not be so pervasive in the future.

This does not mean that being old now enhances one's socioeconomic
status. Older persons still tend to have lower status than younger persons in
the same socioeconomic group because of the effects of retirement on
income and occupational prestige. However, Robert Atchley (1994) reminds
us that these changes do not necessarily bring lessened status among the
elderly themselves. According to John Henretta and Richard Campbell
(1976), factors such as education and occupation, which determine income
in retirement, are the same ones that determined income before retirement.
Those elderly with high incomes before retirement tend to have relatively
higher incomes during retirement, even though everybody may "take a pay
cut." Therefore, among the elderly, a person's preretirement socioeconomic
status usually carries over into retirement among his or her age peers. The
elderly may lose socioeconomic status in the wider society, but among themselves their former status tends to be preserved.

It should be noted that, as Gordon Streib (1984) points out, research on
social stratification and aging in the latter part of the life cycle requires a shift
in analytical perspective. Typically, such research focuses on social mobility
and status attainment. In the case of the aged, it is highly unlikely that they
will be upwardly mobile; rather, they will tend to maintain their status, especially among their age peers, or will be downwardly mobile. Moreover, Streib
points out that biological factors associated with aging complicate patterns of
stratification among older people. The physical and mental decline of the aged
can have a major effect on their social status—regardless of their income, education, power, lifestyle, or former occupation. Status is altered significantly if
a person is physically or mentally disabled as well as old. Streib suggests that,
instead of employing the same stratification rankings that apply to younger
persons, such as occupational prestige, perhaps new concepts and measures to
determine the status of those beyond the working years should be developed.

Marital Status

With women living to old age in greater proportions than men, it is not surprising that in 1990 there were nearly five times as many widows (13.3 million) as widowers (2.8 million) in the United States. Among all women age 65
and over in 1990, 34.7 percent were married, 54.3 percent were widows, 6.1
percent were separated or divorced, and 4.9 percent were never married. For
elderly men, 72.3 percent were married, 16.9 percent were widowers, 0.7 percent were separated or divorced, and 0.1 percent were never married. The

notable difference in marital status between aged men and women is that men are significantly more likely (nearly twice as likely) to be married in old age than are women.

Living Arrangements

Most elderly Americans, about 94 percent, live in a noninstitutionalized environment. The remaining 6 percent, some 1.9 million people, in 1990, live in nursing homes or homes for the aged. The idea that most aged persons are institutionalized is clearly a myth, for the great majority live in ordinary households. However, the percentage of older people living in long-care facilities for the elderly increases with age; and over the life course, about 20 percent of those over age 65 will eventually live in a long-term care facility. For the oldest-old (those over age 85), one in four is eventually institutionalized.

Most elderly, as noted, live outside institutions in family settings. U.S. Census data for 1994 show that 82 percent of older men and 57 percent of older women lived either with their spouse or other relatives. More specifically, 75 percent of the men lived with their spouse and 7 percent with other relatives, whereas 39 percent of the women lived with their spouse and 18 percent lived with other relatives. These living arrangements are depicted in Table 2–3, which also shows that 16 percent of older men and 41 percent of older women lived alone. The remaining 2 percent of noninstitutionalized men and women lived with nonrelatives. Living alone in old age is much more common for women.

Geographic Distribution

Table 2–4 shows the distribution of the elderly by state in the United States for 1990. In numbers, California has the largest number of aged persons (over 3 million), followed by Florida and New York, each with over 2 million. About half (49 percent) of all elderly persons are concentrated numeri-

TABLE 2–3   U.S. Living Arrangements of Noninstitutionalized Persons Age 65 and over, 1994

	Men	*Women*	*Overall*
Living alone	16%	41%	30%
Living with spouse	75	39	55
Living with other relatives	7	18	13
Living with nonrelatives	2	2	2

Source: U.S. Census Bureau.

TABLE 2–4 Population 65 Years and over, by State, 1990

Rank, State	Population 65 Years and over	Percentage 65 Years and over
United States	31,241,831	12.6
1 Florida	2,369,431	18.3
2 Pennsylvania	1,829,106	15.4
3 Iowa	426,106	15.3
4 Rhode Island	150,547	15.0
4 West Virginia	268,897	15.0
6 Arkansas	350,058	14.9
7 South Dakota	102,331	14.7
8 North Dakota	91,055	14.3
9 Nebraska	223,068	14.1
10 Missouri	717,681	14.0
11 Kansas	342,571	13.8
11 Oregon	391,324	13.8
13 Massachusetts	819,284	13.6
13 Connecticut	445,907	13.6
15 Oklahoma	424,213	13.5
16 New Jersey	1,032,025	13.4
17 Montana	106,497	13.3
17 Wisconsin	651,221	13.3
17 Maine	163,373	13.3
20 New York	2,363,722	13.1
20 Arizona	478,774	13.1
22 Ohio	1,406,961	13.0
23 Alabama	522,989	12.9
24 District of Columbia	77,847	12.8
25 Tennessee	618,818	12.7
25 Kentucky	466,845	12.7
27 Illinois	1,436,545	12.6
27 Indiana	696,196	12.6
29 Minnesota	546,934	12.5
29 Mississippi	321,284	12.5
31 North Carolina	804,341	12.1
31 Delaware	80,735	12.1
33 Idaho	121,265	12.0
34 Michigan	1,108,461	11.9
35 Washington	575,288	11.8
35 Vermont	66,163	11.8
37 South Carolina	396,935	11.4
38 Hawaii	125,005	11.3
38 New Hampshire	125,029	11.3

(continued)

TABLE 2–4   *(continued)*

Rank, State	Population 65 Years and over	Percentage 65 Years and over
40 Louisiana	468,991	11.1
41 Maryland	517,482	10.8
41 New Mexico	163,062	10.8
43 Virginia	664,470	10.7
44 Nevada	127,631	10.6
45 California	3,135,552	10.5
46 Wyoming	47,195	10.4
47 Texas	1,716,576	10.1
47 Georgia	654,270	10.1
49 Colorado	329,443	10.0
50 Utah	149,958	8.7
51 Alaska	22,369	4.1

Source: U.S. Census Bureau.

cally in eight states, with California, Florida, and New York followed by Pennsylvania, Texas, Illinois, Ohio, and Michigan. When it comes to percentage of the total state population, a higher percentage of elderly persons (18.3 percent) live in Florida than any other state. The elderly population in Pennsylvania, Iowa, Rhode Island, and West Virginia is 15 percent or higher. Alaska has the lowest percentage of elderly (4.1 percent), and Utah has the next lowest (8.7 percent).

The percentage of elderly in the total population for each state is illustrated in Figure 2–5. States with over 14 percent of their total population age 65 and over are concentrated in the central United States in a band stretching from North Dakota down to Arkansas, clustered in the eastern states of Rhode Island, Pennsylvania, and West Virginia, and in the South in Florida. Higher proportions of elderly tend to be found in Florida because of the warm climate and the lack of a state income tax and in the central U.S. because older residents have tended to remain while younger persons have moved to other parts of the country. Therefore, in the case of Florida, the elderly have migrated in; while in the central U.S. the young have migrated out and caused a higher concentration of the old.

DEMOGRAPHIC PATTERNS IN CANADA

Aging patterns in Canada generally resemble those in the United States, but there are two important differences. First, the U.S. elderly population (33.0 million) for 1993 is larger than the entire Canadian population (28.5 million).

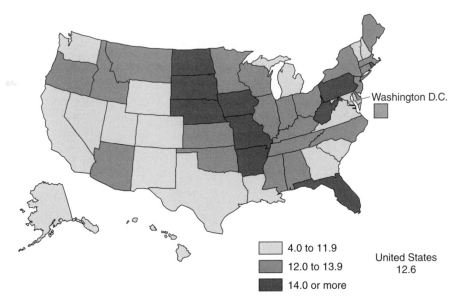

FIGURE 2–5   Percentage of total state population age 65 and over, 1990

Source: U.S. Census Bureau.

Second, Canada's population, on average, is somewhat older than that of the United States, and the gap is increasing. In 1990 the difference in median age between Canada (33.1 years) and the United States (32.8 years) was three months. By 2010, the median age in Canada is projected to reach 39.6 years contrasted with 37.4 years for Americans—a difference of 2.2 years. So, although both countries are moving toward increasingly older average ages, Canada is moving at a faster rate.

Three major factors account for this development: (1) immigration, (2) increased life expectancy, and (3) a declining birthrate. First, Canada experienced a major population increase of young adults early in the twentieth century, through immigration. These persons are now aged. Second, life expectancy has risen steadily for both men and women during the twentieth century. For example, in 1931 Canadian men lived on average to age 60 and women to age 62.1; by 1991, the average life expectancy for men was 74.8 years (fifth highest among the world's major countries or regions) and 81 years for women (fourth highest). Life expectancy in 1991 in the United States, in comparison, was 72 years for men (24th highest) and 78.9 for women (16th highest). Third is the decline in birthrate. Canada's birthrate in 1960 was 31.4 births per 1,000 persons in the general population, but by 1994 it had dropped to 13.4 births per 1,000. This development has led to a decrease in the number of young people and is the most important factor in the increase in Canada's aging population (Novak 1993).

The proportion of aged persons in Canadian society is still somewhat less than that of the United States, with 1992 figures showing that 12 percent of Canada's population of 28.5 million was age 65 and over compared to 12.6 percent of the United States population of 255 million. However, by the year 2000, the proportion of elderly in the total population of both countries will be about the same (around 13 percent) as a result of Canada's more rapid aging.

Other population characteristics of the aged in Canada, as shown in Table 2–5, are similar to those of the United States. Table 2–5 shows that in Canada, as in the United States, (1) men are more likely to be married than women in old age; (2) most older persons live with a spouse, until the oldest ages, when a significantly higher proportion of women are widows; (3) the great majority of elderly live in houses and apartments; and (4) most perceive their health status as good or excellent. An exception is education, in that older Canadians tend to have less schooling than Americans, other than the percentage of college graduates, which slightly favors Canadians.

Other data likewise show Canadians and Americans to have similar aging patterns. In a comparison of aging attitudes and experiences in five nations—the United States, Canada, Great Britain, West Germany, and Japan, Diane Rowland (1992) found that Americans and Canadians had the greatest similarity. For example, they expressed the highest satisfaction with their lives and reported the best health status compared with those in the other nations. The most notable difference between Americans and Canadians was the great fear held by Americans of the possible financial consequences of serious illness. Canada has a national health insurance program, which provides comprehensive coverage for health costs, unlike Medicare for the elderly in the United States, which has limits and requires some out-of-pocket costs.

Canada is facing an aging situation common to advanced societies generally. The proportion of elderly is increasing, and this is particularly true of the oldest-old. The number of males age 90 and over doubled between 1966 and 1986, and the number of females in this age group tripled. The pattern is continuing in the 1990s as the population aged 66 to 74 is expected to double by 2010. This means that, in the future, the aged will need greater financial and health resources. As Mark Novak (1993:96) points out, Canadian society has its own history, economics, and values, and will have to discover its own responses to population aging.

TABLE 2–5 Percentage Distribution of Persons 65 Years and over by Selected Characteristics, According to Age, 1991

Characteristic	65 Years and over		65–74 Years						75 Years and over					
	Both Sexes		Both Sexes		Men		Women		Both Sexes		Men		Women	
	Canada	United States	Canada	United States	Canada	United States	Canada	United States	Canada	United States	Canada	United States	Canada	United States
Marital Status														
Married	57.1	54.7	64.0	63.3	80.4	80.3	50.0	50.3	45.1	40.9	67.1	70.4	31.5	23.8
Widowed	31.4	34.1	24.1	25.0	8.5	8.3	37.3	37.8	44.2	48.8	23.2	21.6	57.2	64.5
Divorced or separated	3.9	6.3	4.1	6.9	3.3	6.2	4.8	7.4	3.7	5.4	4.6	4.4	3.2	6.0
Never married	7.5	4.4	7.8	4.4	7.8	4.8	7.9	4.0	7.0	4.4	5.1	3.1	8.2	5.2
Family Size														
1 person	31.0	32.2	26.1	26.4	15.7	13.9	34.9	36.0	39.7	41.4	23.5	21.3	49.7	53.1
Alone	28.2	30.5	23.6	24.8	14.8	12.3	31.1	34.4	36.2	39.7	20.7	20.6	45.8	50.7
With a nonrelative	2.8	1.7	2.5	1.6	0.9	1.7	3.8	1.6	3.5	1.8	2.8	0.7	3.9	2.4
2 persons	52.0	53.0	55.3	58.1	62.1	67.0	49.4	51.2	46.2	44.9	62.3	65.9	36.3	32.9
Spouse	45.1	46.0	49.5	52.2	59.8	63.8	40.9	43.3	37.3	35.8	54.3	62.0	26.8	20.8
Other relative	6.9	7.1	5.7	5.8	2.4	3.2	8.6	7.8	8.9	9.1	8.0	3.9	9.5	12.1
3 or more persons	17.0	14.8	18.6	15.5	22.1	19.1	15.7	12.8	14.1	13.6	14.2	12.9	14.0	14.1
3 persons	9.8	8.9	11.3	9.6	13.4	12.1	9.5	7.6	7.3	7.7	8.7	8.4	6.4	7.3
4 or more persons	7.1	5.9	7.3	6.0	8.7	6.9	6.2	5.2	6.8	5.9	5.4	4.4	7.6	6.8
Education														
0–8 years	46.9	34.6	41.7	29.7	43.8	32.1	39.8	27.9	56.1	42.5	62.8	45.1	52.0	41.0
9–11 years	22.4	16.8	24.1	17.6	21.9	16.8	25.9	18.2	19.6	15.6	16.6	15.5	21.5	15.7
12 years	9.9	28.1	11.1	31.7	10.0	26.9	12.1	35.4	7.7	22.4	7.0	19.7	8.1	23.9
13 years or more	19.5	18.6	21.9	19.6	23.0	22.8	21.0	17.2	15.4	17.0	12.8	17.3	17.0	16.9
Housing														
House or apartment	95.5	93.5	95.9	93.5	95.9	94.5	94.3	92.8	96.3	93.3	96.5	92.3	96.2	94.0
Other	3.3	6.5	3.4	6.5	2.8	5.4	3.9	7.3	3.2	6.7	2.4	7.7	3.8	6.1
Perceived Health Status														
Good to excellent	62.0	66.7	66.9	67.6	66.9	66.7	63.3	68.3	56.9	65.2	60.3	64.2	54.8	65.6
Fair	28.9	21.4	27.4	21.4	24.7	20.6	29.7	22.1	31.5	21.3	29.2	21.3	32.9	21.2
Poor	8.9	11.5	7.4	10.6	8.1	12.5	6.8	9.2	11.6	13.0	10.5	13.8	12.3	12.5

Source: U.S. Department of Health and Human Services.

SUMMARY

The focus of this chapter has been to describe demographic patterns of aging in the United States and Canada. The pattern of aging in the United States is much like that of other developed nations in that the proportion of the aged in society is significantly increasing. Life expectancy for Americans rose from 47.3 years in 1900 to 75.5 years in 1993. The percentage of elderly in the total population increased from 4 percent to 13 percent between 1900–1993. By 2050, the percentage of older Americans may reach as high as 21.8 percent, or one-fifth of the entire population. The largest increase in the elderly population has been among women, whites, and the oldest-old (85 years and older). Women currently outnumber men three to two in the United States, with the greatest disparity at the oldest ages.

Being elderly does not confer enhanced social status on an individual by virtue of his or her age alone (unless the person is 100 years of age or older). Rather, a person's position in society is determined by his or her socioeconomic status or attributes: income, occupational status, and level of education. The elderly are at a particular disadvantage in this regard because they are most likely to have a reduced income and be retired. However, with the significant increase in numbers of elderly persons who are more affluent and better educated than older generations in the past, the status of the aged appears to be improving somewhat in American society. The percentage of elderly living below the poverty line in 1992 was 12.2 percent.

As for living arrangements, most older Americans (95 percent) live in ordinary households. The idea that a majority of aged persons are institutionalized is a myth. Most elderly men (75 percent) live with their spouse, whereas 39 percent of the women live with their spouse and 41 percent live alone. Elderly women are much more likely than elderly men to live by themselves. The state with the largest proportion of elderly is Florida (18.3 percent).

The major differences between Canada and the United States in the overall pattern of aging is that the U.S. has more elderly than Canada has people and a more rapid growth of the aged population is taking place in Canadian society. The drop in the birthrate, more than any other demographic change, has led to the greater growth rate of the aged in Canada. Otherwise, the general characteristics of older people are similar to those in the United States.

Chapter 3

THE DEMOGRAPHY
OF AGING WORLDWIDE

This chapter discusses aging patterns worldwide. Each nation is part of an interdependent world system linked with other countries through trade, banking and finance, communications, and international politics. The ties that countries have with each other do not necessarily mean a growth in world unity. In fact, since the collapse of the former Soviet Union, there has been considerable disunity, civil war, and revolt in several parts of the former Soviet bloc and the former Yugoslavia. Nevertheless, capitalism has emerged in the late twentieth century to thoroughly dominate the world economy and link nations in a single world system (Wallerstein 1983). As *modernization*, (the process by which societies move to a more technologically advanced level of existence) and *globalization* (the links that tie societies together) continue, people will find their daily lives increasingly influenced by events and trends happening elsewhere in the world (Cockerham 1995a). This situation is particularly true when it comes to aging. Older populations are increasing on a global basis; therefore, the issues and problems associated with aging are worldwide.

THE INCREASED AGING POPULATION

The extent of global aging for the 1990s is depicted in Table 3–1, which shows the world's population by age and sex for 1991 and 2000. Table 3–1 shows that the world's population in 1991 was over 5.4 billion, of whom 332

TABLE 3–1 World Population by Age and Sex, 1991 and 2000

Year and Age	Population (millions)			Percentage			Males per 100 Females
	Both Sexes	Male	Female	Both Sexes	Male	Female	
1991							
All ages	5,422	2,730	2,692	100.0	100.0	100.0	101.4
Under 15 years	1,750	894	856	32.3	32.7	31.8	104.4
15 to 64 years	3,340	1,693	1,646	61.6	62.0	61.2	102.9
65 years and over	332	142	190	6.1	5.2	7.0	75.0
2000							
All ages	6,283	3,163	3,120	100.0	100.0	100.0	101.4
Under 15 years	1,953	996	957	31.1	31.5	30.7	104.1
15 to 64 years	3,904	1,980	1,924	62.1	62.6	61.7	102.9
65 years and over	426	187	240	6.8	5.9	7.7	77.9

Source: U.S. Census Bureau.

million people were 65 years of age and over. Some 142 million elderly were males and 190 million were females, for a ratio of 75 older males for 100 females. By 2000, Table 3–1 indicates that the world's population will increase to about 6.3 billion, with 426 million age 65 and over. In 2000 some 187 million elderly are projected to be male and 240 million, female—for a ratio of 77.9 males for every 100 females in the oldest age group. During this ten-year period, we see the world's elderly increasing from 6.1 percent of the globe's population to 6.8 percent. The percentage of people under age 15 is shown to decline from 32.3 in 1991 to 31.1 in 2000. The pattern of population change shown in Table 3–1 illustrates the fact that an increased aging population is a worldwide phenomenon.

To illustrate further the worldwide increase in elderly persons, Table 3–2 shows that, in 1991, 27 countries had aged populations of 2 million or more people, but by 2020, some 49 nations will have reached this level. As

TABLE 3–2   Countries with More Than 2 Million Elderly in 1991 and 2020

1991		2020 (Projected)	
Country	*Population Aged 65 and over (in thousands)*	*Country*	*Population Aged 65 and over (in thousands)*
China	67,967	China	179,561
India	32,780	India	88,495
United States	**32,045**	**United States**	**52,067**
Japan	15,253	Japan	33,421
Germany	12,010	Indonesia	22,183
United Kingdom	9,025	Brazil	18,800
Italy	8,665	Germany	18,396
France	8,074	Italy	13,078
Brazil	6,680	France	12,119
Indonesia	5,962	United Kingdom	12,108
Spain	5,378	Mexico	10,857
Pakistan	4,734	Pakistan	9,678
Poland	3,851	Nigeria	9,152
Mexico	3,522	Bangladesh	9,057
Bangladesh	3,492	Spain	8,162
Vietnam	3,196	Turkey	7,990
Canada	3,140	Thailand	7,828
Argentina	3,012	Poland	7,243
Turkey	2,789	Vietnam	6,707
Nigeria	2,676	Philippines	6,646
			(continued)

TABLE 3–2 *(continued)*

	1991		2020 (Projected)	
Country	*Population Aged 65 and over (in thousands)*		*Country*	*Population Aged 65 and over (in thousands)*
Romania	2,489		South Korea	6,550
Philippines	2,380		Canada	6,404
Thailand	2,350		Egypt	5,680
Yugoslavia	2,328		Iran	5,235
South Korea	2,135		Yugoslavia	4,933
Egypt	2,077		Argentina	4,862
Iran	2,052		Romania	4,588
			Colombia	4,464
			South Africa	4,084
			Australia	3,956
			Ethiopia	3,920
			Taiwan	3,500
			Netherlands	3,461
			Burma	3,425
			Czechoslovakia	3,149
			Morocco	2,972
			Venezuela	2,912
			Saudi Arabia	2,867
			North Korea	2,734
			Zaire	2,643
			Peru	2,580
			Sri Lanka	2,527
			Algeria	2,450
			Greece	2,237
			Hungary	2,186
			Malaysia	2,139
			Chile	2,133
			Belgium	2,071
			Portugal	2,053

Source: U.S. Census Bureau.

seen in Table 3–2, China and India have and will continue to have the largest number of elderly of any nations on earth. This is because both countries have larger overall populations than other nations, and both have experienced lower birth and death rates than in the past. Consequently, the aged population in China and India will increase dramatically between 1991 and 2020. In

2020, Table 3–2 shows, China will have over 179 million elderly (up from almost 70 million in 1991) and India, over 88 million (from nearly 33 million in 1991). The United States will be a distant third in 2020 with some 52 million elderly, followed by Japan with over 33 million and Indonesia with over 22 million. Overall, the greatest increase in absolute numbers of the aged will be in Asia.

Figure 3–1 shows the percentage increase in the elderly populations of selected countries between 1985 and 2025. By 2025, the percentage of older persons will more than triple in Guatemala, Singapore, Mexico, the Philippines, and Indonesia. What is indicated in Figure 3–1 is that the expansion of the world's elderly population is going to be greatest in developing nations. In none of the developed nations will the proportion of the elderly increase by 200 or 300 percent. Figure 3–1 shows that the proportion of elderly in Canada will increase by 135 percent by 2025, but this percentage (the highest for a developed nation shown in Figure 3–1) is far below the 357 percent projected for Guatemala or even the 201 percent for Bangladesh. In fact, the elderly populations of many developing Asian countries—Singapore, the Philippines, Indonesia, India, China, Hong Kong, and Bangladesh—will more than double between 1985 and 2025. Although not shown in Figure 3–1, the lowest overall increases will be recorded in Africa; but there are some exceptions to this trend, particularly for Kenya, where the aged population is also expected to nearly triple by 2025. In the year 2000, some 41 percent of the world's elderly will live in developed nations and 59 percent in developing countries; by 2025, only 31 percent will live in developed nations, compared with 69 percent for the developing nations. By the first quarter of the twenty-first century, more than two-thirds of the world's old people will reside in developing areas.

Although the greatest increases in the percentage of older persons will be in developing nations, the greatest percentages of elderly in relation to the total population are currently found in developed nations. For example, Figure 3–1 shows that the percentage of the elderly will increase in Guatemala by 357 percent and in Sweden by only 21 percent between 1985 and 2025. Sweden's growth rate for elderly persons is small because the country's population has already aged. Sweden, in fact, is the world's "oldest" country because it currently has the largest percentage of elderly persons of any country in the world. According to Table 3–3, which shows the 20 countries with the greatest percentage of elderly in 1992, Sweden is ranked first at 17.7 percent. Norway is second, with some 16.3 percent of its population age 65 or older, followed by Great Britain with 15.7 percent. The United States is ranked 20th with 12.6 percent.

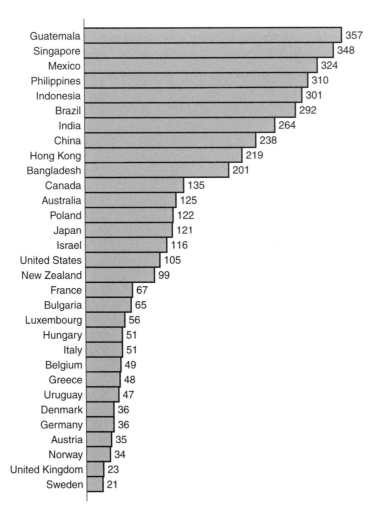

FIGURE 3–1 Percentage increase in elderly population, selected countries, 1985 to 2025

Source: U.S. Census Bureau.

While Asia has the most older persons in terms of absolute numbers and is expected to show the greatest increases in both numbers and percentages of the aged by 2025, Table 3–3 shows that Western Europe is the world region with the highest percentages of aged at present. As Table 3–3 indicates, the only non–Western European countries ranked in the top 20 for the highest percentage of elderly are Bulgaria, Hungary, Japan, and the United States. However, Western Europe's aged population will increase only mod-

TABLE 3–3   **The 20 Countries with the Greatest Percentage of Persons Age 65 and over, 1992**

Country	Percentage
Sweden	17.7
Norway	16.3
United Kingdom	15.7
Belgium	15.4
Denmark	15.4
Austria	15.3
Italy	15.2
France	15.0
Germany	15.0
Switzerland	14.9
Greece	14.8
Spain	14.1
Finland	13.9
Luxembourg	13.8
Bulgaria	13.8
Hungary	13.7
Portugal	13.6
Netherlands	13.2
Japan	12.8
United States	12.6

Source: U.S. Census Bureau.

estly in the immediate future, because they are already among the world's oldest populations. By 2025, Sweden will have an older population of 22.2 percent, which will still be the highest percentage of older people in any one country in the world. But other countries will be catching up. Japan, with 12.8 percent of its population age 65 and over in 1992, will see its proportion of the elderly increase to 20.3 percent by 2025. This increase will occur because the aging of the population in Japan is taking place more rapidly than in any other nation in the late twentieth century. Between 1985 and 2005, the 65- to 74-year-old age group in Japan is expected to experience an average annual growth rate of 2.7 percent, and the 75 and older age group will average a 2.9 percent annual increase. Japan will have literally doubled (from 7 to 14 percent) the proportion of its older population in just 25 years between 1970 and 1995. It will take the United States 66 years (1944–2010) to increase its aged population from 7 to 14 percent, and it took France 115 years (1865–1980) to accomplish the same thing. In 1992, as noted, the elderly constituted 12.8 percent of Japan's population. By 2005, they will reach 16.5 percent, and by 2025, the elderly population will have increased to 20.3 percent—one of the world's highest percentages.

In the twenty-first century, however, China is likely to age faster than any other country. China has an official policy of one child per married couple. This policy has resulted in fewer children relative to the adult population; and if it continues into the twenty-first century, projections are that some 40 percent of the population will be 65 or older by the midtwenty-first century.

Asia has been the most successful region of the world in reducing fertility (Hermalin 1995; Martin 1988). Reductions in fertility reduce the proportions of younger people and raise the proportions of older people. Consequently, Asian nations will be the first among the developing nations to have to accommodate large elderly populations, including highly developed Japan. By 2025, several Asian countries—Japan, Singapore, China, Sri Lanka, and South Korea—will have more than 10 percent of their population age 65 or over. Therefore, Asia is beginning to view aging as not just a concern of the West but as its own problem as well.

GENDER

Table 3–4 depicts life expectancy at birth and at age 65 by sex in major countries and regions of the world in 1991. It shows that Japan has the highest life expectancy for both males (76.4 years) and females (82.8 years). Israel is second in life expectancy for males, at 75.1 years, followed by Sweden (74.9), Greece (74.7), and Canada (74.4). The United States is ranked 24th in life expectancy for males, at 72.0 years. For females, France is second after Japan, with a life expectancy of 82.0 years, followed by Switzerland (81.4), Canada (81.0), and Sweden (80.6). Table 3–4 shows American females are 16th in life expectancy at 78.9 years.

Even though men and women in the United States do not rank especially high in overall life expectancy compared to Japan, Western Europe, and a few other countries (Table 3–4), there is evidence that the oldest-old in the United States have a particularly long life. Kenneth Manton and James Vaupel (1995) found that life expectancy for Americans between the ages of 80 and 95 was higher than for similarly aged persons in Sweden, France, England, and Japan. Manton and Vaupel suggest that the greater socioeconomic disparities account for much of the disadvantage in life expectancy for Americans prior to age 65. Socially and economically disadvantaged Americans tend to die at earlier ages, thereby reducing the average life expectancy. However, once the remaining Americans reach age 65, differences in life

TABLE 3–4   Life Expectancy at Birth and at Age 65, According to Sex, 1991

	Male Life Expectancy in Years			*Female Life Expectancy in Years*	
Country	*At Birth*	*At 65 Years*	*Country*	*At Birth*	*At 65 Years*
Japan	76.4	16.6	Japan	82.8	21.0
Israel	75.1	15.8	France	82.0	20.9
Sweden	74.9	15.4	Switzerland	81.4	20.1
Greece	74.7	15.9	Canada	81.0	20.0
Canada	74.4	15.7	Sweden	80.6	19.2
Switzerland	74.2	15.6	Spain	80.5	19.2
Norway	74.2	14.9	Netherlands	80.4	19.2
Netherlands	74.2	14.6	Norway	80.3	19.0
Italy	73.7	15.1	Greece	80.1	18.4
England and Wales	73.5	14.4	Israel	79.8	17.7
France	73.5	16.2	Finland	79.5	18.2
Spain	73.4	15.5	Austria	79.3	18.3
Costa Rica	73.3	15.2	Germany (West)	79.2	18.2
Australia	73.2	15.0	Belgium	79.1	18.4
Cuba	72.9	15.9	England and Wales	79.0	18.1
New Zealand	72.9	14.9	United States	78.9	19.1
Singapore	72.7	14.6	New Zealand	78.7	18.6
Germany (West)	72.7	14.3	Italy	78.5	19.1
Austria	72.7	14.9	Northern Ireland	78.3	17.7
Denmark	72.6	14.4	Denmark	78.2	18.1
Belgium	72.3	14.0	Singapore	78.1	17.7
Northern Ireland	72.2	13.7	Puerto Rico	77.9	18.3
Ireland	72.2	13.4	Ireland	77.9	17.1
United States	72.0	15.3	Costa Rica	77.8	17.6
Scotland	71.5	13.3	Portugal	77.3	17.1
Finland	71.4	14.1	Scotland	77.2	17.0
Portugal	69.8	13.4	Cuba	76.8	17.8
Chile	69.4	14.0	Chile	76.5	17.6
Germany (East)	69.3	12.8	Australia	76.4	19.1
Puerto Rico	68.8	15.1	Germany (East)	76.4	16.2

Data for Australia, Belgium, and Chile are for 1989. Data for Cuba, Germany (West), Germany (East), Italy, Israel, Spain, and Sweden are for 1990. Rankings are from highest to lowest life expectancy based on the latest available data for countries or geographic areas with at least 1 million population. This table is based on official mortality data from the country concerned, as submitted to the *United Nations Demographic Yearbook* or the *World Health Statistics Annual.*

Source: U.S. National Center for Health Statistics, *Health, United States, 1994* (Washington, D.C.: U.S. Government Printing Office, 1995).

expectancy begin to diminish until age 80 when they surpass the Swedes, French, English, and Japanese in the average number of years left to live. Thus, the oldest-old in the United States appear to be especially healthy compared to other countries with long-lived populations. Manton and Vaupel (1995:1232) conclude that mortality in the United States is relatively high before age 65, but relatively low at age 80 and thereafter.

Although the general trend in worldwide life expectancy is toward increasingly longer lives, there are exceptions. Life expectancy in some countries remains relatively low and in others is declining. The lowest life expectancies in the world are found in some African countries south of the Sahara. These are countries such as Sierra Leone, where life expectancy in 1990 was 37.5 years for males and 40.6 years for females, Gambia (43.4 for males, 46.6 for females), Niger (44.9 for males, 48.0 for females), and Angola (44.9 for males, 48.1 for females).

The only region of the world where life expectancy is declining is the former Soviet Union and Eastern Europe. For example, Table 3–5 shows that, in 1960, males in the former Soviet Union had a life expectancy of 65.3 years which dropped to 61.3 years in 1980. Table 3–5 shows male life expectancy briefly rose to 65.1 years in 1987 as the central government's anti-alcohol campaign—virtually the only public health change in the former Soviet Union during the mid-1980s—had a positive effect on reducing male mortality (Shkolnikov 1995). However, the campaign was cancelled in 1987 because of its widespread unpopularity. By 1989, life expectancy had fallen

TABLE 3–5   Life Expectancy at Birth in the Former Soviet Union and Russian Republic, Selected Years, 1960–1994

	Male	*Female*
Soviet Union		
1960	65.3	72.7
1980	61.9	73.5
1987	65.1	73.9
1989	64.2	73.9
Russia		
1991	63.5	74.3
1992	62.0	73.8
1993	59.8	72.0
1994	57.3	71.0

Source: Population of the USSR, 1962; U.S. National Center for Health Statistics, 1991, 1993; and Russia State Committee on Statistics, 1994, 1995; and Shkolnikov, 1995.

64.2 for males. After the collapse of the Soviet Union in 1991, the decline continued for males in the new Russian Republic and stood at 57.3 years in 1994. For females, Table 3–5 shows that life expectancy increased in the former Soviet Union until 1987–1989, but fell for Russian women from 74.3 years in 1991 to 71 years in 1994. A similar pattern has occurred in Eastern Europe, where life expectancy has fallen in Bulgaria, Hungary, Poland, and elsewhere.

The decline in life expectancy in the former Soviet Union and Eastern Europe is an unusual trend for industrialized societies. Such nations typically have longer life spans because of higher standards of living and improved health care. The downturn in life expectancy in this region began in the mid-1960s prior to the collapse of communism during 1989–1991 and accelerated in the early 1990s with the transition toward capitalism. The reasons generally cited for the drop in life expectancy are poor-quality medical care, alcoholism and industrial accidents, and environmental pollution in some areas (Mezentseva and Rimachevskaya 1992). However, the primary social determinant of the upturn in deaths may be poor health lifestyles—reflected especially in increased alcohol consumption, and also in smoking, lack of exercise, and high-fat diets. The decline in life expectancy has been much greater for males than for females—which forecasts significantly smaller cohorts of men at the oldest ages.

In virtually every developed nation, women live longer than men. In North America and most European countries, women outlive men some seven years on the average. Only in a few developing nations of South Asia and the Middle East, where females have low social status and strong preferences exist for male offspring, is there equality in life expectancy or higher life expectancy for males. In Bangladesh, for example, the most recent available figures show men living to an average age of 56.9 compared to 56.0 years for women in 1988, whereas life expectancy in Nepal was 50.8 years for men and 48.1 years for women in 1981. Life expectancy in India was about even, at 55.4 years for men and 55.7 years for women in 1985. In other countries, such as Afghanistan, Iraq, Pakistan, and Yemen, women typically outlive men by only a few months on the average.

With females outliving males in practically all countries, it is not surprising that elderly women greatly outnumber elderly men. Therefore, as a population grows older, the usual pattern is for the percentage of women in each cohort to become larger. This is especially true in developed nations, where a majority of the oldest-old are women. For example, in Western Europe, population data for 1990 show that, at age 80 and over, for every 100 women there were 39 men in Germany, 41 in Austria, 42 in Belgium, 43 in Great Britain, and 45 in France. Greece has the most favorable male-to-female ratio at age 80 in Western Europe, with 69 men per 100 women. Overall, there is a preponderance of women at the oldest ages in Western Europe, and this is especially true of the most developed countries in that region.

In Japan in 1990, there were 53 men for every 100 women at age 80 and over, and 56 men per 100 women in China. In Asia generally, as in North America, Latin America, and Western Europe, there is a relative surplus of women at the oldest ages. Exceptions are found in South Asia, where the sex ratio is more balanced in the elderly population and in some countries is reversed because, as noted, men have a somewhat higher or equal life expectancy compared to women. In Bangladesh, for example, in 1990 there were 189 men age 80 and over for every 100 women, in India the ratio was 117 men per 100 women, and in Pakistan the difference was 105 men per 100 women.

In most developing nations, other than in some countries in South Asia, older women outnumber men, and the differential increases sharply with age. And, in the majority of developing states, the female proportion of future older populations is expected to increase even further. Therefore, when the world as a whole is considered, there are significantly more older women than older men. Widowhood is a fact of life for a majority of women worldwide after the age of 65. Most elderly men, in contrast, are married, because women usually live longer than men and men often marry younger women, which increases the likelihood of the wife's outliving her husband.

LIVING ARRANGEMENTS

Historically, the family has provided for the needs of its aged members. With life expectancy relatively low until the nineteenth century, family assistance for the aged was typically of short duration. In modern society, conditions for the care of the elderly have clearly changed, with people living longer and the elderly increasingly requiring support, especially medical treatment, which is beyond the capability of families to perform for themselves. Moreover, urbanization and modern economic development have contributed to the decline of the extended family, with its large network of mutually supporting relatives, and promoted the rise of the nuclear family, consisting only of an adult couple and their children. The nuclear family is less able to sustain long-term care of the elderly, and the importance of the aged in such a family is also diminished, because adult children typically will not be living in the same household with their elderly parents or grandparents. Consequently, living alone is becoming more common for the elderly in developed countries; and, in developing nations, family support for the aged is beginning to erode as the need for long-term care for the oldest-old becomes increasingly necessary.

In the United States, as discussed in Chapter 2, about 30 percent of all persons 65 years of age and older (41 percent of all older women and 16 percent of all older men) lived alone in 1994. Half of all women age 75 and over lived alone. In Canada in the late 1980s, 17 percent of men and almost 35 percent of women age 75 and over lived alone (Novak 1993). In some parts of Western Europe, the proportion of elderly people living alone is much higher. For example, in Austria, urban France, Germany, Great Britain, and the Scandinavian countries, the elderly are especially likely to live apart from their children (Hugman 1994). This pattern is seen particularly in Great Britain, where only 6 percent of people age 65 and over lived with their children in 1991 (Pilcher 1995). Some 80 percent of all British women age 75 and older lived alone. The elderly are less likely to live alone in rural France, Italy, Portugal, and Spain, but the general Western European pattern is nevertheless toward separate living arrangements for the aged and their children (Hugman 1994; Simons 1992).

A major exception to this pattern in developed nations is found in Japan, where less than 10 percent of the elderly lived alone in 1989. Of those living alone, most are women (Martin 1988). The majority of aged persons in Japan still live with an adult child and their family, although this living arrangement is changing. For example, 60 percent of Japanese elderly lived with children in 1989 compared to 77 percent in 1970 (Hermalin 1995). However, in the remainder of Asia, aged persons traditionally live with families or spouses, and it is rare to live alone. According to Albert Hermalin (1995), the majority of Asian and South Asian elderly live with children, as seen in the percentages for Singapore (88 percent), Sri Lanka (84 percent), rural India (83 percent), China (82 percent), South Korea (78 percent), Thailand (77 percent), Taiwan (71 percent), Malaysia (69 percent), the Philippines (68 percent), and Indonesia (67 percent).

Consequently, the family still provides most of the support for the aged in developing nations, where the norm is for the parent or parents to live with children in old age. This pattern includes countries not only in Asia, but also in Africa, the Middle East, and Latin America. However, Martin (1988) suggests that, in Asia, this norm may be changing somewhat because of migration, urbanization, and increased female labor force participation, which may mean that generations of the same family may live apart or female caregivers may not be available for full-time care of elderly family members. Yet Martin also explains that, given the traditional role of the family in Asia in the care of the elderly, institutionalization of older persons is seen as undesirable and infeasible. Homes for the aged in Asia have a bad reputation because they are primarily homes for the aged poor. At present, as noted, families play a larger role in caring for the elderly in developing countries than in developed nations, and this is especially true in Asia.

SUMMARY

This chapter discussed demographic patterns of aging worldwide. Western Europe has the greatest proportion of elderly at present. Sweden is considered the world's oldest country, with 17.9 percent of its population age 65 or older. However, in the future, the greatest increases in both absolute numbers and percentages of older people will take place in developing countries—especially in Asia. China and India have the largest populations in the world, and these two countries will see the greatest gains in numbers of the aged. Although developed nations currently have the greatest proportions of the elderly, this will change in the future as the proportions of aged increase in developing nations. In the year 2000, some 41 percent of the elderly will live in developed countries and 59 percent in developing nations; by 2025, only 31 percent will live in developed nations, compared with 69 percent for developing countries. Some 40 percent of China's population, potentially the largest of any country, may be age 65 and older by midtwenty-first century.

At present, the proportion of older persons in Japan is expanding more rapidly than in any other country and is projected to reach 20.3 percent by 2025. Sweden will still have the highest percentage of elderly (22.2 percent) at that time. Japan also has the highest overall life expectancy in the world (76.4 years for males and 82.8 years for females). Israel is in second place for males and France for females. Women outlive men worldwide and do so in practically every nation, with the exception of a few countries in South Asia and the Middle East. Thus elderly women outnumber elderly men in the world, and elderly women are significantly more likely to live alone. Unlike those in developed nations, families in developing nations are more likely to be responsible for the care of older family members and to have those family members as part of the household.

Chapter 4

SOCIAL THEORIES OF AGING

This chapter examines selected theories intended to explain aging as a social experience. *Theories* specify relationships between concepts and provide a framework for explaining why certain things happen the way they do. When it comes to the social aspects of aging, no single theoretical approach is dominant. Social gerontology is a relatively new field that marks its beginning in the late 1940s. The development and testing of theoretical statements have largely taken place only since the 1960s. Nevertheless, a considerable amount of theoretical work has been accomplished, and several viewpoints have emerged to provide the field with a variety of theories and a solid foundation for the future.

The objective of this chapter is to review those theories in social gerontology that have been the most influential to date in explaining the relationship between society and the aging process. The theories are (1) disengagement, (2) activity, (3) continuity, (4) age stratification, and (5) modernization. Two other important theoretical approaches, symbolic interaction and conflict theory, whose potential for studying aging has not been realized, will also be discussed.

DISENGAGEMENT THEORY

Disengagement theory is based on the structural-functionalist perspective in sociology, especially the work of France's Émile Durkheim (1858–1917) and

America's Talcott Parsons (1902–1979). Disengagement theory was attractive to many sociologists concerned with explaining the social aspects of aging, because structural-functionalism was a particularly important theoretical approach in sociology in the mid-1950s and 1960s when social gerontology was developing into a specialized field. Disengagement theory also had the merit of providing a link to classical sociological theory, because its orientation could be traced to such major works in structural-functionalism as Durkheim's *The Division of Labor in Society*, originally published in 1893, and Parsons's *The Social System*, which appeared in 1951. Consequently, disengagement theory had a strong claim to academic legitimacy when it was initially proposed and was readily accepted by sociologists who were advocates of structural-functionalism in general and the work of Parsons in particular. This section will therefore begin with a brief introduction to structural-functionalism, for it provides the theoretical foundation for disengagement theory.

The Structural-Functionalist Perspective

Structural-functionalism, often called simply "functionalism," portrays society as a self-regulating system made up of interdependent parts operating together to generate stability and social order. The components of this system consist of various social institutions such as religion, the family, medicine, the economic system, politics, and the like, which function to maintain society in a state of harmonious balance or equilibrium. Because functionalist theorists perceive social systems as composed of these various interconnected parts, they argue that changes, decisions, and events that take place in one part of the system inevitably affect all other parts of the system to some degree. What makes social life possible is the expectation that people will typically behave in accordance with the norms and values common to their particular social system. This process is "functional" because it results in social harmony and counterbalances dysfunctional processes, such as crime and mental illness, that disrupt the social order. Functionalist theory thus provides a view of society that emphasizes stability, integration, and order.

When social problems arise, they are handled within the system as society's various components adjust to the dysfunctional situation in order to control, reduce, or eliminate it. Individuals are pressured by society to conform to the prevailing norms, with punishment or isolation from the social mainstream falling to those who are found deviant. For example, for those who are criminals, society develops a criminal justice system intended to apprehend, bring to trial, and remove to prisons those persons who disrupt the social order by breaking laws. Medicine, as Parsons (1951) observes, is also an institution of social control, in that the mentally and physically ill are likewise sent to hospitals; this institutionalization lessens their dysfunctional impact on society. Society generally distinguishes between criminals and the sick by punishing lawbreakers and providing therapeutic care for the ill. But both processes require the intervention of social agencies, law enforcement, or medicine in order to control deviant behavior and maintain social stability and cohesion.

The tendency of a society toward self-maintenance through equilibrium is very similar to the biological concept of homeostasis, in which the human body attempts to regulate physiological (internal) conditions within a relatively constant range in order to maintain bodily functioning. A person may suffer from indigestion, migraine headaches, or a broken leg and still be generally healthy. Likewise, a social system is viewed in the functionalist perspective as maintaining social functioning through the regulation of its various parts within a relatively constant range. A social system may have problems with crime, delinquency, and mental illness, but still be "healthy" because of its overall capacity to function effectively.

Functionalism was a dominant theoretical perspective in sociology until the late 1960s, when its influence was significantly curtailed. Conflict theorists (Dahrendorf 1959), whose intellectual roots lie in Marxist theory, argued that functionalism was too conservative in its emphasis on stability and order. Conflict theorists insisted that functionalism failed to explain adequately such important processes in society as social change, conflict, and alienation. Symbolic interactionists (Blumer 1969), whose focus is on small-group processes, objected to the functionalist view that individual human behavior is largely determined by society. These theorists claimed that human beings determine their own behavior by defining their particular social situation and acting on the basis of that definition, instead of always acting in a certain way simply because society requires it. Functionalist theory, in their view, needed to give more credit to the individual's ability to think and decide on his or her own course of behavior.

Nevertheless, functionalist theory still has some merits. The theory can explain why various components of a social system exist and why they persist (because they provide certain functions for society that result in certain consequences). Functionalism also provides insight into how large-scale social processes can create situations in which people are more or less forced to respond to conditions not of their own choosing. Being required to disengage from society through retirement, not because of choice but because of age, is an example of the latter.

The Disengagement Perspective

Disengagement theory is an application of functionalism to the study of aging. According to its proponents, Elaine Cumming and William Henry (1961), disengagement theory has three basic propositions: (1) a process of mutual withdrawal of aging individuals and society from each other is natural; (2) this process of withdrawal is inevitable; and (3) it is also necessary for "successful" aging. Disengagement theory tells us that, although all people eventually die, society's institutions need to survive if they are to maintain social stability. It follows then that it is necessary to have an orderly means of transferring power from older members of society to the younger. Disengagement theory supports the notion that it is to society's benefit to phase out those individuals whose deaths would disrupt the smooth functioning of the social order. The process of phasing out older people from the mainstream of society thus becomes institutionalized, as stable and routine norms are developed to indicate which individuals should be disengaged and what forms of behavior should occur at this time. Accordingly, societies develop norms requiring that an individual retire from work at a certain age, and a rite of status passage—usually a retirement ceremony—often marks the occasion. When the ceremony is over, the person honored sees his or her status change from being employed to being retired. However, disengagement is typically not a single event, but is instead a gradual process that involves the separation of the individual from several of his or her regular social roles and activities over time.

Disengagement theory is consistent with the Kingsley Davis and Wilbert Moore (1945) functionalist theory of social stratification. Davis and Moore held that, to attract the best-qualified people to compete for the positions that meet society's most important needs, it is necessary to offer such people society's greatest rewards and inducements (money, power, status, and prestige). Differential rewards are therefore required as a means of ensuring that essential tasks are accomplished. The extent of the rewards is related to the social importance of a particular position and the relative availability of qualified persons to fill that position. The greatest rewards are associated with those roles that (1) have the greatest importance for society and (2) require the greatest training or talent.

Disengagement theory extends the Davis-Moore thesis by explaining that the work of people in key positions must also continue uninterrupted if the social order is to be preserved. Society must be able to replace people whose ability to perform adequately in an important position becomes questionable as a result of old age. Therefore, the continuous functioning of social institutions can be enhanced through a disengagement process. Such a process allows for an orderly transition of younger persons into the positions of older persons, while avoiding the disruptions that might occur if all workers stayed in their jobs until they died. Of course, the disengagement of elderly people is more likely in a developed, industrialized society, where a continuous replacement of older workers by younger ones is needed to maintain modern work skills. In developing societies, the aged do not typically disengage from society as much, because the elderly are more likely to continue to work and remain as the head of the family.

Yet the disengagement of society from the individual is only half of disengagement theory. The other half of the theory is that individuals themselves select to withdraw from particular social roles when they become old. The more roles an older person withdraws from, the less involved that person is in mainstream activities. He or she is no longer preoccupied with work, career, raising children, and the like. The disengaged person is thus able to fill a particular social role (the retired person) that allows him or her to become increasingly more self-centered and focused on personal interests, such as hobbies, clubs, travel, and sports like fishing and golf.

There are, however, some important shortcomings to disengagement theory. The theory assumes that people will desire to be disengaged in order to pursue their own interests and does not explain what happens if this is not the case. The assumption of disengagement theory—that people naturally want to disengage as they get older—is not necessarily true of everyone. Some people may disengage only because an institution's rules and regulations force them to or because of poor health. But with the opportunity, means, and continued capacity for work, they might well choose to continue. Furthermore, disengagement does not seem to occur in all social institutions. U.S. Supreme Court justices, for example, are appointed for life, and the majority continue in the position when they are elderly. If disengagement were a functional necessity for society, it should apply to everyone—including members of the Supreme Court. Consequently, disengagement theory does not apply to all people, nor to all situations. As Alfred Lindesmith and his colleagues explain:

> The theory does not account for the "nondisengaging" behaviors of certain groups and of certain individuals. Elderly rural Americans, for example, are still commonly absorbed into the fabric of the extended family; those persons who do not leave the labor market at age 65 often have been observed to lead healthy, involved, and politically influential lives into their late 80s. Both Charles de Gaulle and Winston Churchill were in their mid-80s when they died; Pablo Casals was 93, and Picasso was 86.[1]

1. Alfred R. Lindesmith, Anselm L. Strauss, and Norman K. Denzin, *Social Psychology*, 6th ed. (Englewood Cliffs, NJ: Prentice-Hall, 1988), 351.

In a review of 25 years of research findings, Robert Atchley (1994) determined that disengagement is not natural or inevitable. Most cases of disengagement were found to result from a lack of opportunity for continued involvement. Gordon Streib and Clement Schneider (1971) noted earlier that disengagement, if it occurred, was more likely to be partial than total. Older people may withdraw from some activities because of age, but may maintain or simply decrease participation in other things they do.

Why, then, is disengagement theory important? Chiefly because it is able to describe the social processes that occur when older people withdraw from their usual roles as a result of age. The theory is particularly applicable to situations of forced disengagement according to predetermined rules of an institution or organization and to situations of mutual disengagement, in which both society and the individual define disengagement as positive. The strength of disengagement theory lies in the realization that, at some point in time, the interests of society intersect with the role performance of older people in their positions, and the result is often the disengagement of that older person. By setting a specific age, usually 65, as the time of retirement, disengagement becomes institutionalized, orderly, and inevitable—just as aging itself is inevitable. Some degree of disengagement appears to be inherent in the aging process for many (perhaps most) people, and disengagement theory helps to explain what happens when this is the case.

It is precisely for this reason—the transition from work to retirement, regardless of the desires of the individual, that disengagement theory remains important. Many elderly people are forced to retire, whether they want to or not, and disengagement theory explains why this happens in modern societies.

ACTIVITY THEORY

As formulated by Robert Havighurst (1963), *activity theory* is primarily an action theory for successful aging. It has three basic premises: (1) that the majority of normally aging people will maintain fairly constant levels of activity; (2) that the amount of engagement or disengagement will be influenced by past lifestyles and socioeconomic factors, rather than by some inevitable process; and (3) that it is necessary to maintain or develop substantial levels of social, physical, and mental activity if the aging experience is to be successful.

What constitutes successful aging? According to Havighurst, the norms for old age are the same as those for middle age; therefore, successful aging is based on how closely an elderly person approximates the norms and activities of middle-aged persons. In other words, activity theory is an approach to understanding the social behavior of elderly people in terms of how well they deny the fact that they are elderly. Successful aging consists of being or behaving as much as possible like a middle-aged person. If certain roles are lost because of retirement or poor health, Havighurst points out that other activities can be substituted in their place so that the individual remains active.

There is research that supports the basic propositions offered by activity theory. In a major longitudinal study carried out at Duke University over a ten-year period, Erdman Palmore (1968, 1969) found that older men tended to show almost no overall reduction in their activities or in life satisfaction, whereas older women tended to have a small but statistically significant reduction in both activities and life satisfaction. Temporary decreases in the men's activities due to illness were usually followed by subsequent increases so that there was little or no overall change.

Palmore noted that his data were obtained from people who were relatively healthy and that therefore disengagement may be more typical of the less healthy. His point was, however, that disengagement by the elderly is not an inevitable result of aging. The respondents showed consistently high levels of activity throughout the ten-year period of the study. Furthermore, it was found that activity was strongly related to high morale and life satisfaction. The more active a person was, the more likely that person was to be happy. Palmore concluded that continued engagement rather than disengagement was typical of the normal, healthy older person, and the amount of that person's activity was consistent with his or her past lifestyle. If disengagement occurred, it usually did so only just prior to death.

In another study, Andrea Fontana (1977) investigated what it meant to the individual to grow old among a group of elderly persons at a senior citizens' center in a small, affluent community in southern California. Fontana found that activity was strongly related to high morale and life satisfaction. The more active a person was, the more likely that person was to be happy. Fontana found that these persons tended to deny that they themselves were old, although they were more able to give reasons why someone else might be old. Among many of these aged individuals, a person had to be at least 80 years old to be considered beyond middle age. The respondents indicated that to keep active was to stay young and that to become passive and relinquish one's activities and associations was to become old. Thus successful aging was to be active and to be active was to be young. Fontana concluded:

> Americans may have succeeded in freeing themselves from the work ethic, but the dying monster has sprung many new heads: activities. Work no longer pro-

vides the central identification of life for many, but activities do. Thus, older individuals find new ways to give their lives meaning, by being a bridge player, a canasta-club member, a shuffleboard contestant, going fishing, watching television, writing postcards, or walking in the woods. Not only do activities provide meaning, but they are seen as the panacea to cure the plague of old age: to be active is to keep old age at bay.[2]

What activity theory essentially tells us is that most people do not disengage from society when they become old. If they do retire from their occupational role, they compensate for it by substituting some other type of activity that provides satisfaction. Bernice Neugarten (1971), for example, cites the case of a 75-year-old schoolteacher who made the most money of his life selling insurance after retirement. This is not to forecast, however, that most elderly persons seek a second career, but rather that they are likely to remain active in some fashion if their past lives were characterized by being active.

Yet, as a theory explaining the social behavior of the aged in general, activity theory suffers from two basic inadequacies. First, it rests on the assumption that older people judge themselves according to norms common to middle-aged activity and behavior, but it does not explain what happens when the elderly do not subscribe to such norms. And, second, it does not explain what happens to those older people who cannot, for physical, mental, or socioeconomic reasons, maintain a middle-aged standard of living regardless of how they judge themselves. The older a person gets, the more difficult it is to be active according to middle-aged standards. Activity theory does account for the manner in which some (perhaps a majority) of the aged cope with aging through activity, but, like disengagement theory, it cannot explain the behavior of all elderly.

Also, it should not be presumed that being active prolongs an older person's life. Activity may promote life satisfaction among the aged, but there is no conclusive evidence that activity also leads to a longer life. In an eight-year study of a population of Mexican-American and non-Hispanic elderly in Texas, David Lee and Kyriakos Markides (1990) attempted to determine whether there is a significant relationship between being active in old age and living longer. The popular notion that an active life among the elderly leads to extended longevity was not supported. Whether a person was active or inactive in old age made little or no difference in living longer. Activity theory's strength rests in its assertion that elderly people generally desire to

2. Andrea Fontana, *The Last Frontier: The Social Meaning of Growing Old* (Beverly Hills, CA: Sage, 1977), 176.

be active when they are old, and, if this is possible, they feel better about themselves and their lives as a result.

CONTINUITY THEORY

Continuity theory is based on the premise that people retain a high degree of consistency in their personality over the various stages of the life cycle. As a person grows to maturity and passes on into old age, continuity theory holds, that individual develops rather stable values, attitudes, norms, and habits, which become an integral part of his or her personality. The manner in which an individual reacts to the aging process will thus be influenced by that person's personality traits and predispositions. Successful aging is thought to occur when people are able to maintain or continue having the traits, interests, and behaviors they have always had while aging.

Continuity theorists do recognize, however, that predispositions to act in certain ways are subject to change or modification because of the ongoing and sometimes complex forms of interaction people have with others and their social environment during all stages of the life cycle. Although there will be a tendency toward consistency, continuity theory admits that people also change by adapting to new situations. For instance, a person who looked forward to retirement might not like it after all, and might instead be forced to accommodate to an unwelcome situation and to adjust his or her expectations and behavior. Continuity theory thus maintains that a wide range of reactions to the aging experience is possible, but that, on balance, the aged person will generally respond to situations in a manner consistent with his or her basic personality over the life cycle.

According to Neugarten (1964), continuity theory is based on two central propositions: (1) people tend to maintain their own particular personality over time; and (2) the only major internal dimension of the personality that changes with age is the tendency to experience greater introversion by turning one's attention and interest inward on the self. Other studies support the notion that a person's personality tends to remain stable after middle age as mature adults typically respond to situations in a consistent manner and deal with their social world in habitual ways (McCrae and Costa 1982; Streib and Schneider 1971). According to Vern Bengston and his associates (Bengston, Reedy, and Gordon 1985), there is a global aspect to the personality, which is stable and reflects a person's general character throughout life. Beneath this global orientation, there can be changes in certain features of someone's personality without inducing an overall personality change.

Continuity theory contributes to our understanding of the aging process by showing that the personality of people in old age tends to be much the same as it was in middle age. This finding is of great use in predicting the behavior of old people and provides both practical and theoretical insight to researchers studying how aging is experienced. However, continuity theory is not a full-blown theory in the research literature on aging, because it is concerned with only one particular and limited aspect of aging—that of personality effects.

However, compared with the social theories of aging discussed previously in this chapter—disengagement and activity theory—continuity theory presents a micro, rather than a macro, orientation. Macro-level social theories explain how large-scale social processes, such as disengagement and a normative emphasis on activity, influence individual behavior. Micro-level views, like continuity theory, allow us to see how individuals, not the wider society, construct their own behavior. What continuity theory tells us is that people tend to respond to social situations in their old age in a fashion that is consistent with their past adult personality. Although there is much more to the aging process than simply its effect on the personality, continuity theory nevertheless provides an important perspective on behavior among the elderly.

AGE STRATIFICATION THEORY

Age stratification theory is a relatively recent theory based largely on the work of Matilda White Riley (1971, 1987; Riley, Foner, and Waring 1988; Riley, Johnson, and Foner 1972). It takes the position that society is stratified into various age cohorts. Each age cohort has both life course and historical dimensions. The life course dimension refers to stages of the life cycle. People belong to a particular age group depending on how long they have lived, and, as a result, they share similar social roles and experiences. At approximately the same point in their lives, they have all been children, students, workers, perhaps parents and grandparents, were retired, and so forth. Thus they have had similar roles in their respective pasts, are occupying similar roles in the present, and are likely to have similar roles in the future as members of the same age cohort moving through the life cycle. As they grow older, everyone else grows older as well, and younger people fill their former roles, while they move on with others of their age to assume roles consistent with their age cohort. As Anne Foner (1974, 1986) notes, people of similar ages have similar roles and confront similar life cycle circumstances that foster common attitudes and interests. Belonging to a particular age cohort is not only a characteristic of a person beginning at birth but also has consequences for that person at every age.

The historical dimension pertains to the fact that people experience distinct periods of history together and share particular events on the basis of age. For example, the Vietnam War is likely to have had a different meaning for Americans who were children at the time, or who were eligible for military service, or who were older and had experienced World War II and the Korean War. Each shared an event but brought a different perspective to it that was influenced by age.

Riley (1987) argues, however, that different age cohorts also age differently as the societies they live in change; that is, both similarities and differences can be found between age cohorts. Similarities stem from younger people replacing older people in the same roles, whereas differences emerge not only because of historical events but because society itself changes over time. Riley explains:

> People who were young earlier in this century learned from the age norms and patterns of behavior prevalent in that period; most learned from their parents that only a few years of schooling suffice for most jobs; and from their grandparents that old age can be bleak. But now that these people have themselves grown old, they have outdistanced the world for which they were initially prepared. Similarly, cohorts of people who are young today are perceiving the entire occupational ladder as it is now—before it has time to be further transformed by fast-breaking technological innovations and accompanying changes in the age structure of the future. These young people will not be old in the same society in which they began. In short, while individuals within a particular cohort are aging, the society is changing around them.[3]

But age stratification theory holds that not only are new patterns of aging caused by social change, they also contribute to it. At every level of the social system, society and the process of aging influence each other sequentially over time. The link between the aging of individuals and the larger society, in Riley's view, is the flow of age cohorts. Cohort flow affects the numbers and kinds of people in a particular age strata, as well as the capacities, attitudes, and activities of people in that strata. Riley (1987:4) points out that, as society moves through time, the age structure and people within that structure are altered. People in a particular age strata are no longer the same people, in that they have been replaced by younger people with more recent life experiences as they themselves have replaced older people. Meanwhile,

---

3. Matilda White Riley, "On the Significance of Age in Sociology," *American Sociological Review* 52 (1987): 5.

various roles, institutions, and norms may have been affected as changes in retirement age, patterns of leisure for older persons, the composition of the workforce, and perhaps even tax burdens for younger people take place. Riley states:

> In response to social change, millions of individuals in a cohort begin to develop new age-typical patterns and regularities of behavior (changes in aging); these behavior patterns then become defined as age-appropriate norms and rules, are reinforced by "authorities," and thereby become institutionalized in the structure of society (social change); in turn, these changes in age norms and social structures redirect age-related behaviors (further changes in aging). Through such a dialectical sequence, the members of each cohort, responsive to social change, exert a collective force for further change as they move through the age-stratified society: they press for adjustments in social roles and social values, influence other people throughout the age strata, contribute to continuing alterations in both aging and social structure.[4]

Consequently, age stratification theory provides a view that emphasizes a continuing interplay—generated by cohort flow—between social change and individuals as they age. Though interdependent, the processes of aging and social change are not synchronized. People follow a predictable and sequential life cycle, but social change moves along its own axis of historical time and according to its own rhythm. Some periods of history witness greater social change than other periods, but people follow the same life course. As a result, the degree of difference between age cohorts because of social change can vary from great to small.

In sum, Riley claims that society is composed of successive cohorts of individuals who are aging and continually forcing older cohorts into and out of particular social roles. "This flow of cohorts," states Riley (1987:5), "forms the channel that connects the two dynamisms of aging and social change: it ties them both to the forces of history, creates the asynchrony between them, and presses for still further alterations." The larger society, institutions, groups, social networks and strata, and individuals are all affected by the aging process of particular cohorts, as these cohorts are affected, in turn, by them.

Age stratification theory does offer a method by which most characteristics of age cohorts can be analyzed. An age cohort can be seen as a particular generation in relation to other living generations and one that brings its own attitudes, beliefs, and values to bear on situations held in common. Individuals can also be seen as members of a generation living within the con-

4. Ibid., 4–5.

text of particular historical circumstances. People can, accordingly, be viewed as living in a world already constructed for them and as active participants in shaping that world to meet their needs. Aging is not passive; the individual's aging process is influenced at the macro level by the wider society and at the micro level by other people and the person's own characteristics and personality. Age stratification theory is attractive because it is logical, appears comprehensive, and points the way toward researchers' analyzing the interplay between macro- and micro-level social processes as they relate to aging.

Unfortunately, this theory is somewhat difficult to put to use for testing and empirical research because of its complexity. Moreover, an important critique of age stratification theory by Gordon Streib and Carroll Bourg (1984) calls attention to the need for some additional considerations. Streib and Bourg seriously question whether age stratification theory actually qualifies as a theory of stratification, because it does not account for social inequality. Rather, they maintain that differences within age cohorts, especially socioeconomic differences, can be as great or greater than differences between age cohorts. The Vietnam War, for example, would have been experienced differently by people not only on the basis of age, but also (and perhaps of just as much or even more importance) in relation to their socioeconomic situation. Socially and economically disadvantaged young adult males were much more likely than their affluent counterparts to serve in the war, especially in combat units. Parents in low-income families were likewise more likely to have their sons drafted for military duty or volunteer as a means to escape poverty. More advantaged young adult males could gain deferments from military service if they were in good standing as college or university students; thus affluent families had a different experience with the war than the less affluent, even if they belonged to the same age cohort.

Streib and Bourg thus reject the notion that a person's experience of historical events is so strongly determined by age. Although age clearly constitutes a major division of society and biological aging is the principal force behind the aging experience, other variables, such as socioeconomic status, affect responses to aging in powerful ways. A weakness of age stratification theory is that differences within, not just between, age cohorts are not given sufficient consideration. Besides socioeconomic factors, gender, race, and ethnicity may also shape the aging experience within cohorts, and age stratification theory does not account for such differences. However, despite its critics, including Streib and Bourg (1984) and others (Cain 1987), age stratification theory remains a highly influential theoretical perspective.

MODERNIZATION THEORY

Modernization theory is a macro-level sociological theory of global social change, which has been adapted by Donald Cowgill (1986) to explain aging. As a theory of social change, modernization theory takes the position that underdeveloped societies will gradually be transformed by industrialization to resemble North America and Europe. The theory depicts the world as divided into either wealthy industrial nations (about one-fifth of the world) or poor preindustrial countries (the remaining four-fifths), with poor countries in various stages of evolution toward modernity. According to Walt Rostow (1978), there are four stages to modernization: (1) the traditional stage, in which mortality and population growth decline and life expectancy increases as a result of improved health care and living conditions; (2) the takeoff stage, consisting of growth in a market economy and an increased achievement orientation among the population; (3) the drive to technological maturity, which includes a growing industrial economy, urbanization, and mass education; and (4) the high mass consumption stage, in which a wide range of consumer goods and services appears.

Modernization theory is consistent with the foreign policy of industrial nations with respect to providing assistance for economic development and introducing Western culture. However, the theory has some important criticisms: (1) it tends to view technological advances as positive only; (2) it has only one path to modernization; (3) it is largely ahistorical; (4) foreign aid is seldom simply a case of altruism on the part of developed nations (they want something in return); and (5) the causes of poverty in developing nations are not found just in underdeveloped regions of the world, nor are solutions to these problems found only among industrialized countries. Many nations have experienced modernization as suggested by modernization theory, but the theory remains controversial because it seems to favor a privileged position for developed societies as a model in the world economy and overlooks issues of conflict and exploitation.

How, then, does modernization theory explain aging? According to Cowgill (1986; Cowgill and Holmes 1972), there is a systematic relationship between aging and modernization. Cowgill explains that the concept of old age is relative to a society's degree of modernization. People in primitive societies, as compared to modern ones, are classified as old at earlier chronological ages; have the onset of old age determined more by an event (such as becoming a grandparent) than by age; and live shorter lives but have higher status and are more likely to hold positions of political and economic power. In modern societies, in contrast, the elderly are likely to live longer but have low status and hold less important positions in society. Therefore, the aged have relatively high status in developing societies where they are able to continue useful and valued functions, but have low status in technologically advanced societies where the most important work is done by younger people. Moreover, there can be differences within countries; for example, old men living in Turkish provinces characterized by low urbanization and industrialization are more likely to head a household and hold a job than elderly men living in industrial centers (Gilleard and Gurkan 1987). Even modern education appears to promote devaluation of the elderly. As Cowgill explains:

> Certainly one of the most salient aspects of modernization relative to the status of [the] aged is the development of specialized institutions of formal education. These, along with libraries, voluminous printed material, and recent revolutionary techniques for storing and retrieving information, have all but completely abolished a formerly highly significant role of older people—that of repositories and transmitters of vital information to the younger generation. Schools, both general and technical, are always viewed as an essential part of any modernization effort. But the main targets and beneficiaries of mass education efforts are the young. One consequence of such efforts is that very shortly the younger generation has command of more information, especially technical information, than the elderly. Certainly the elderly no longer have a monopoly on such information, as they have in nonliterate societies, and with the loss of that monopoly, they lose a vital status-according role.[5]

With a lessened position in education and the workplace, combined with urbanization and the decline of the extended family, modernity appears to have adversely affected the status of the aged. Retirement, notes Cowgill, is a modern invention found chiefly in modern high-productivity societies. A system of retirement based on age has been adopted by all industrialized societies and is a means to ensure that younger and more recently trained workers have jobs available. Consequently, the basic premise of the modernization theory of aging is that the processes that cause societies to change from a rural and agrarian system to an urban and industrial economy also change the roles of the elderly and reduce the status and esteem they are accorded. A tendency toward disengagement of the aged, states Cowgill, appears to accompany modernization.

Therefore, modernization would seem to be an especially negative process for the status of old people. Yet Cowgill suggests that this is not necessarily the case in the mature modern state. He cites research (Palmore and Manton 1974) showing that, whereas the status of the aged is generally low in modernized societies, the trend in the most modernized countries is toward

---

5. Donald O. Cowgill, *Aging Around the World* (Belmont, CA: Wadsworth, 1986), 197.

somewhat higher status. In other words, among modern nations, the most advanced societies accord greater esteem to the elderly than do the less advanced. Other research (Pampel 1981), for example, shows considerable improvement in the quality of life available to older people in the United States. Cowgill suggests that perhaps modern societies were unprepared for large numbers of elderly persons, and it is not surprising that there were temporary dislocations—including an overvaluation of youth. The most modern societies, according to Cowgill (1986:200), "are now beginning to come to terms with their aged populations and are achieving appropriate cultural and institutional adaptations." James Dowd (1984) likewise agrees that the status of older people is higher in modern societies than it was earlier and cites the extension of old age pensions and benefits in the late twentieth century as evidence of this change.

There are critiques of the modernization perspective on aging, such as the fact that a concept of retirement for aged workers is not new and can be found in some premodern societies (Quadagno 1982), or that the theory does not adequately account for differences in gender and socioeconomic status in the aging of modern populations (Dowd 1980; Williamson, Evans, and Powell 1982). Furthermore, when it comes to the effects of modernization on aging, culture appears to be an important intervening variable. Japan is one of the most modern and industrialized nations in the world, yet the status of the aged has remained quite high. Elderly Japanese tend to remain strongly integrated into both family and community life in a manner consistent with Japanese culture in particular and Asian culture in general (Morgan and Hirosima 1983; Palmore 1975a, 1975b, 1985). The effects of modernization on the status of the aged may therefore be strongly influenced by culture.

SYMBOLIC INTERACTION THEORY

One promising theoretical approach in sociology that has not seen extensive use in studies of aging is symbolic interaction. This is surprising, because symbolic interaction is a major theoretical perspective and has considerable potential for aging research, especially in regard to explaining the self-concepts and social relationships of the elderly.

Symbolic interaction theory views society from the micro-level standpoint of the individual person, not in terms of personality but in the nature of the interaction that person has with other people. It regards the individual as a creative, thinking entity able to choose his or her behavior instead of reacting more or less mechanically to the influence of large-scale social forces, as implied by functionalist theories. Central to the symbolic interaction conception of human behavior is the assumption that all behavior is self-directed on the basis of symbolic meanings that are shared, communicated, and manipulated by interacting human beings in social situations (Denzin 1970a). The process of such interaction between people forms behavior in a creative fashion, rather than being merely a means by which behavior is expressed. Therefore, society is seen as a human product, and people are seen as a social product, because both are formed in a continuing dialectical process in which human beings and their social environment act and react toward each other (Berger and Luckmann 1967).

Although the symbolic interaction tradition in sociology can be traced to the ideas of William James, John Dewey, William I. Thomas, and Charles Cooley at the beginning of the twentieth century, George Herbert Mead (1863–1931) is generally regarded as the individual most responsible for its development. Mead, an American philosopher who taught social psychology at the University of Chicago between 1894 and 1931, published little; yet his book *Mind, Self, and Society* (1934), based on student notes from his courses and unpublished manuscripts, is a sociological classic. A major interpretation of Mead's work, however, is found in the writings of Herbert Blumer, one of Mead's students, who has drawn together much of the material that is the basis of contemporary symbolic interactionist thought.

Blumer (1969), for example, explains Mead's analysis of social action by denoting its five central features: (1) the self, (2) the act, (3) social interaction, (4) the object, and (5) the joint act. Mead believed that the *self* of a person is formed and developed as a result of social interaction and experience with other people; thus the self is a social product derived from a person's relationship with others in society. In this context, the human being is able to perceive, have conceptions of, communicate with, and act toward himself or herself as a social object in relation to other people. Second is Mead's concept of the *act*. Mead insisted that human beings do not just respond more or less automatically to a given social influence but are able to interpret and define their own particular situation and organize their behavior to meet their circumstances. Blumer states:

> In order to act the individual has to identify what he wants, establish an objective or goal, map out a prospective line of behavior, note and interpret the actions of others, figure out what to do at other points, and frequently spur himself on in the face of dragging dispositions or discouraging settings.[6]

6. Herbert Blumer, *Symbolic Interaction* (Englewood Cliffs, NJ: Prentice-Hall, 1969), 64.

Third is the concept of *social interaction,* which consists of two forms: the nonsymbolic and the symbolic. Nonsymbolic interaction is essentially the stimulus-response paradigm in which a person makes a nonthinking response to a certain stimulus, such as stepping back from a growling dog or raising a hand to catch a baseball. Symbolic interaction, in contrast, is a situation in which human beings interpret and define actions and objects based on symbolic meanings shared with other people. Fourth is the notion of the *object,* which maintains that objects do not possess inherent meaning but become what they are defined as by human beings interacting with each other. Thus human beings act toward an object on the basis of the meaning that object has for them. Humans define gold as valuable and act toward it accordingly. Yet there is nothing intrinsic to gold that makes it valuable; the social meaning of gold depends on how humans define it. Fifth is the *joint* act, which is the focal point by which symbolic interactionists judge group behavior. Each participant in a social gathering brings his or her own individual social act or line of behavior to a situation. By fitting together all of these separate acts or lines of behavior into a single collective or joint act involving each person present, it is possible to ascertain the overall direction of group behavior. The result is that group activities are socially constructed by individual people coming together and interacting with each other with respect to the overall group enterprise. Joint acts may be open to many outcomes; once started they may be interrupted, abandoned, modified, or continued as expected. What happens depends on what those involved decide to do and how they act on their decisions.

Joint acts contribute a sense of stability to social situations, because they require a participant to identify that activity and orient himself or herself in that direction prior to engaging in behavior that is appropriate to the scene. Blumer (1969:71) states, "Thus, to act appropriately, the participant has to identify a marriage ceremony as a marriage ceremony, a holdup as a holdup, a debate as a debate, a war as a war, and so forth." However, as pointed out by Norman Denzin (1970b), it is necessary to go beyond the surface of social situations and extend analysis of the joint act to the more subtle nuances of social relationships between people; for example, those verbal and nonverbal acts and gestures between two persons that signify particular interpretations of a situation.

We can see in the above analysis of social interaction that human behavior is regarded as an ongoing process of definition of, interpretation of, and calculated response to the actions of others and the conditions of the environment. *Reality is therefore socially constructed as it emanates from the perceptions and actions of those involved.*

The merit of symbolic interaction for aging studies is its capability to analyze micro-level, or small-scale, forms of human interaction. Symbolic interaction theory is unique in its ability to explain the subjective meaning of social experiences and the manner in which reality is socially constructed between individuals. But, in general, symbolic interactionists have tended to ignore aging. Existing work, however, includes analysis of the formation of a "sisterhood" by elderly women living in a housing project (Hochschild 1973); the self-feelings of widows in relation to the social support provided them by their adult children (Mutran and Reitzes 1984); and the impact of bereavement on the self-concepts of elderly surviving spouses (Lund et al. 1986).

The housing project study by Arlie Hochschild (1973) took place in San Francisco. Hochschild discovered that the widowed residents formed sibling bonds (a sisterhood) that provided support and a social life independent of the family. This was a positive adjustment to an old age situation in which social isolation and loneliness were the alternative. The study by Elizabeth Mutran and Donald Reitzes (1984) involved a nationwide survey investigating the forms of support provided by adult children to their widowed mothers. Receiving help from their children was found to be an important factor in allowing the widows to feel positive about themselves. In Salt Lake City, Dale Lund and his colleagues (1986) studied the self-concepts of older persons whose spouses had died. They found that the surviving spouses expressed significantly lower levels of social anchorage; that is, the death of their spouses deprived them of their identity as part of a "couple." Thus they had not only lost a spouse, they had also lost part of their sense of self.

A limitation of symbolic interaction theory, however, is in linking individual and small-group behavior to the larger social order. Micro-level theories like symbolic interaction often do not adequately acknowledge the influence of larger social structures and organizations or account for relationships between them. The strength of this approach, on the other hand, lies in the capability of explaining how people perceive situations, events, and people, and define a course of action. It also helps to explain individual variations and the role of culture in providing symbolic meanings.

CONFLICT THEORY

Conflict theory has sometimes been used to help explain the disadvantaged situation of older people in relation to employment problems and retirement, but it has not seen extensive application in studies of aging in Western society. As its name indicates, *conflict theory* views society as a social system characterized by inequality and conflict. It traces its intellectual origins to Karl Marx (1818–1883) and Max Weber (1884–1920). Conflict theory rejects the view put forth by functionalism that society is held together by shared norms and values. Instead, it claims that true social consensus does not exist; rather, society's norms and values are those of the dominant group, which imposes them on the less privileged in order to maintain its advantage. Social processes are therefore essentially struggles over resources. All social systems contain inequality, which causes conflict, which in turn causes reorganization of the social system.

Marx argued that social relationships between people are determined by their relative positions in regard to the means of economic production common in their society. These relationships were characterized historically as a class struggle between various groups of "haves" and "have nots" until eventually a classless society based on economic, political, and social equality evolves from the conflict. Class consciousness (an awareness of common interests with others in the same socioeconomic circumstances) was viewed by Marx as the key element in how a person interprets reality and organizes his or her behavior.

Marx focused on how particular social relationships and means of production, during specific historical periods, allowed the economically and politically powerful to shape the social order to their advantage. The poor, of course, would be disadvantaged; their social reality would tend to be alienating and oppressive. Class struggle and revolution would eventually lead to socialism, which would evolve into communism and bring about improved conditions for those at the bottom of society. In the meantime, the disadvantaged would remain in an exploited state.

For workers, scientific and technological advances under a capitalist system would not improve their lives. Workers would find themselves in an even more marginal economic position as new machinery and automation took the place of human labor. Those that remained employed would be subjected to greater stresses as they became tied to machine production and inflexible schedules. In this situation, older persons would be more likely to be fired and least likely to be hired. For example, William Graebner (1980) found, in his study of retirement in the United States, that many older workers were phased out of their jobs or simply fired when speed of production became a central feature of factory work in the late nineteenth and early twentieth centuries. In the printing business, for example, Graebner describes how older workers at the turn of the century were phased out for younger ones with better eyesight, speed, and endurance. Age limits in hiring became commonplace, and some firms were willing to take the more unpopular action of simply releasing older employees. Laying off workers once they became old was a clear case of age discrimination, and, until retirement programs were established on a widespread basis in the 1920s and Social Security benefits were authorized in 1935, many workers found themselves destitute in old age.

Marxism underestimates the elderly's capability to mobilize for political action in capitalist societies and to bring reform, such as old age pensions and government-sponsored health insurance for the aged. Consequently, a conflict theory explanation of the social aspects of aging, grounded in Marxism, appears to have serious limitations and to be confined to the manner in which work affects the elderly. Work is a major determining factor in the quality of life, and Marxist theory provides a background for understanding this situation. But whether or not a Marxist perspective has more to offer as an explanation of social aging has yet to be determined.

Weber (1958), like Marx, found the basis of social conflict residing in socioeconomic differences between groups. However, Weber suggested that social divisions are based not only on money and property, as a Marxian analysis would indicate, but also on prestige or status and political influence. Varying degrees of status (from high to low) can be assigned to people by other people for reasons other than income, such as level of education or age. Therefore, Weber's concept of social stratification—the allocation of people to different levels of society—is more extensive than Marx's. Moreover, the conflicts that socioeconomic differences generate, according to Weber, are permanent features of social life. Although Weber did not analyze the social aspects of aging, his concept of status helps us recognize that age can be a status variable independent of one's finances and a basis for conflict as older and younger generations compete for social resources.

A Marxist view of the situation of people considered too old to be effective in the workplace places the blame for their circumstances on the general problems of capitalist society. Exploitation by the capitalist system through low wages or layoffs would produce a sense of alienation, not only among older workers, but among workers generally, as they found little satisfaction in their lives and felt individually powerless to deal with the situation. The centrality of work in a person's life rests in the Marxist claim that work is the means through which people come to realize themselves in relation to others. According to Vicente Navarro (1986:34), it is obvious that "in our consumer society today what *you have* depends on what *you do,* but even more important, that one's psychological framework—which determines one's level of expectations—is very much determined by one's work." But, under capitalism, work is controlled by the upper class and organized to protect their socioeconomic advantage. This situation promotes alienation, and Marx maintained that, the more alienated people are from their work, the less able they are to conceive of themselves as other than they are in the present (Lichtman 1982).

All of this points to a particularly disadvantaged situation for the elderly, as they are less in demand as workers and their status as unemployed or retired places them in a highly marginal and devalued position in a capitalist society. However, Bryan Turner (1987) points out that there are some difficulties with this perspective. For instance, being socially and economically disadvantaged when old is not peculiar just to capitalism, but is found throughout human history in various types of societies. Marxist theory also underestimates the capability of the elderly to mobilize for political action and bring reform—which has been the case in Western countries.

One contemporary approach to conflict theory in the United States has been to move away from notions of class struggle and to concentrate instead on competition among interest groups such as those representing labor, management, geographical regions, political parties, and professional and other organized pressure groups, including agencies within the government itself. Laws and government regulations, as well as social and economic advantages, are viewed as outgrowths of power struggles among interest groups. In this context, the elderly clearly qualify as an interest group in American society and have organized effective political action groups, like the American Association of Retired Persons (AARP), the National Committee to Preserve Social Security and Medicare, the Gray Panthers, and local senior citizens' groups. The importance of such organizations is seen in the fact that, as Turner (1988:52) explains, modern politics can often be conceptualized as a struggle between interest blocs and communities for political recognition of their needs and interests. Turner therefore suggests that modern capitalist societies are best understood as having a conflict between the principles of democratic politics (emphasizing equality and universal rights) and the organization of their economic systems (involving the production, exchange, and consumption of goods and services, about which there is considerable inequality). On one hand, people have political equality, but on the other hand, they lack social and economic equality.

This unresolved contradiction, in Turner's view, is a permanent feature of all modern societies and a major source of civil conflict. Ideologies of fairness are constantly challenged by the realities of inequalities, and they influence governments to try to resolve the situation through politics and the provision of welfare benefits. In the meantime, various groups, including those representing the aged, maneuver to protect their interests by influencing policymakers. Conflict theory provides a theoretical framework for analyzing interest group competition and the social policy that results from it.

SUMMARY

To date, it would appear that the most influential approach to theories of aging in social gerontology is structural-functionalism. Three of the five theoretical positions in social gerontology—disengagement theory, activity theory, and modernization theory—are all clearly grounded in a functionalist perspective. Each provides a macro-level view of the aging process in which older individuals are subject to norms requiring them either to disengage, to remain active, or to cope with reduced status because of modernization, while the larger society remains functional and relatively unaffected by large numbers of the elderly. Continuity theory has a micro orientation, but is limited to explaining personality adjustments in old age. The remaining major approach, age stratification theory, has also been identified as a functionalist approach in that it is essentially a macro theory of aging depicting the orderly flow of age cohorts through society (Estes, Wallace, and Binney 1989).

This does not mean that a functionalist perspective is the best theoretical approach in social gerontology; rather, functionalism was highly influential in sociology when social gerontology was first being developed in the 1950s. Other theoretical paradigms so far have provided little that is relevant in explaining aging. Particularly lacking is a broad micro-level approach such us that found in symbolic interaction. Symbolic interaction theory is especially oriented toward explaining the subjective meaning of social experiences and the manner in which reality is socially constructed between interacting individuals. But, in general, symbolic interactionists have conducted few studies in aging. Another theory that has potential is conflict theory, in explaining the situation of devalued older workers or how the elderly, as an interest group, compete for resources in society. To date, conflict theory has also been underutilized in social gerontology.

Of the functionalist approaches, disengagement theory and activity theory remain the most widely utilized theories at present in social gerontology. Disengagement theory views old age as a distinct phase of life decidedly different from middle age; it is a time when specific social and psychological forces come to bear on the person to make him or her aware of a reduced ability to function in society. Furthermore, disengagement theory suggests that disengagement of the elderly from society's important functions is beneficial not only for society, but also for the elderly person, who is freed from the stresses of the preretirement role. Although an overall decrease in social activity is generally observable in old age, disengagement theory does not account for the fact that many older people remain active (engaged) in some fashion and that such activity is significantly related to life satisfaction. So it is not at all clear that disengagement is inevitable, nor is it as personally satisfying an experience as the theory would suggest.

Activity theory, on the other hand, strongly supports the notion of a positive relationship between activity and life satisfaction. Yet its weakness lies in not explaining what happens to people who cannot be active or who do not believe that being active is the only way to keep happy in old age. The proposition that higher levels of activity are necessary for "successful" aging has not been conclusively demonstrated. And, of course, older people can finally reach a point where it is difficult or impossible to be active. Age stratification theory is highly promising. It describes the manner in which age classes develop their own class "consciousness" and relate to other age groups, and discusses how individual behavior is affected by large-scale (macro) processes in the aging experience. However, age stratification theory does not deal extensively with small-scale (micro) processes, nor does it fully account for differences within age cohorts, such as socioeconomic status and gender, which have an impact on the social experience of aging. Finally, there is modernization theory, which helps us to understand the status of the aged in modern society but, again, does not explain the effects of socioeconomic differences in aging. Moreover, there are cultural variations, as seen in Japan, where modernization theory does not adequately apply.

It is obvious that all of these theories in social gerontology are still in the formative stages. There are two major reasons for this situation. First, social gerontology is a relatively new field. As such it awaits the accumulation of an extensive body of research data that can come only with a considerable amount of work in the field. Second, research concerning the aging experience should include longitudinal or long-term studies of people as they age if social gerontology is going to be able to explain and perhaps to predict the changes in behavior that come with aging. Such research not only is expensive but, if done correctly, is going to take several years of data collection on aging cohorts before adequate theories can be formulated.

Chapter 5

PHYSICAL HEALTH OF THE AGED

The single most important determinant of the quality of an elderly person's life is health. Older people who are unhealthy lead relatively shorter and less satisfactory lives than older people who are healthy, feel good, and have the physical capability to pursue their chosen activities. Especially among the elderly, health matters affect all other areas of life, including social roles.

Moreover, positive feelings about one's health in old age go a long way toward determining whether or not an individual is happy. Although it might be thought that happiness declines with age more or less automatically because of a decrease in social activities and a failure to measure up to prevailing (youthful) standards of physical attractiveness, this does not appear to be the case. An analysis of national opinion polls in the United States found that happiness does not decline with age and perhaps never did (Witt et al. 1980). Popular opinion often maintained that being old meant being unhappy because no one really wanted to be old. When researchers asked older people themselves about old age, many confirmed this view. But what was misleading is that most of the studies conducted during the midtwentieth century did not go far enough in asking about various factors that might influence personal happiness in old age, such as health, finances, and social relationships.

The key difference turns out to be the *perception* of one's health (Witt et al. 1980). Although money, self-esteem, and other factors are important, what really seems to matter the most is how the elderly person perceives his or her health. Those elderly who believe themselves to be healthy for their age are clearly the happiest among older persons. This finding is true for recent studies as well as for those studies conducted in the 1940s and 1950s that correlated health with happiness. With increasing numbers of persons reaching old age in a healthy condition, it had appeared to some researchers that the aged population as a whole was happier than in the past. But, actually, the healthy aged were generally happy all along. The difference is that today there are significantly more of them, and this gave the false impression that being happy and old was something new.

PERCEIVED HEALTH STATUS

Because perceived health status is so important in determining the happiness of an elderly person, and because of research finding a high level of happiness among older people, it would appear that aged individuals in the United States tend to perceive their health in a positive fashion. But how can this be, if health deteriorates with age? Several studies have investigated this situation and found examples of both institutionalized and noninstitutionalized elderly rating their health status as very good (Cockerham, Sharp, and Wilcox 1983; Ferraro 1980; Fillenbaum 1979; Myles 1978). In fact, studies of the old-old have found them assessing their health even higher than do the young-old (Ferraro 1980; Linn and Linn 1980). An exception may be elderly African Americans, especially women, who tend to report more illness and disability, as well as more negative health status, than aged whites (Ferraro 1993).

The question thus arises as to whether or not such self-assessments are accurate measures of a person's health. Self-ratings of health have been criticized as subjective and unreliable. But John Ware (1986) points out that their subjectivity is their strength, because they reflect personal evaluations of health not captured by other measures. Ware states that there should be no doubt that self-perceptions of health are reliable measures. A number of studies have found that self-ratings of health among elderly adults are also valid measures of the respondents' objective health status and match up as well or better than physician evaluations (Ferraro 1980; Fillenbaum 1979; LaRue et al. 1979; Maddox and Douglass 1973; Mossey and Shapiro 1982). Moreover, research in Canada (Mossey and Shapiro 1982) and Israel (Kaplan, Barell, and Lusky 1988) has found that elderly persons who rate their health high have tended to live longer than those who rate their health less positively. Although research continues to imrove the methods for health self-assessments for the elderly (Johnson and Wolinsky 1993; Liang 1986; Wolinsky et al. 1983), the existing literature is clear that such ratings to date have been valid and reliable.

It may seem incongruent that, in spite of the fact that health declines with age, many older people tend to rate their health positively. But the fact remains that often older people perceive themselves as being in good health for their age. The reason for this appears to be that judgments concerning one's health by aged individuals are relative. Self-assessments of personal health by elderly persons are often based on how they compare themselves with peers of their own age and sex, and perhaps also on the expectations others have of their health. The tendency of aged persons to rate their health in this relative fashion is most likely rationalized in two ways.

First, simply surviving to old age in a condition reasonably free of serious illness or severe disability would be evidence of relatively good health. Only among the last few generations has survival to old age without severe health problems become fairly common. With increasing numbers living past age 65, many people in the older age categories are able to feel that their health has indeed been good. Eleanor Stoller (1984) suggests, for example, that older persons may expect a decline in their health as they age, but when the deterioration does not take place at the rate or to the extent they had anticipated, they may begin to assess their health above the rating they would assign to their age peers. Other research has found that health status and functional capacity are important in the self-esteem of the aged (Gubrium 1975; Hochschild 1973), leading Stoller (1984:267) to surmise that "perhaps as people become older, they tend to devalue the health of others as a way of increasing their own status." Nevertheless, it seems clear that the fact that they have survived to old age in a relatively healthy condition, when others have not, encourages them to feel that they can be positive about their health (Cockerham, Sharp, and Wilcox 1983; Stoller 1984).

Second, as John Myles (1978) reminds us, subjective responses to a health problem tend to be a function of how much of a person's life is disrupted by the condition. The extent of the potential disruption is determined by the level of physical and mental functioning required in a particular social environment. Elderly people are not usually required to maintain a highly active level of functioning and thus find it easier to perceive their health as good enough to meet their needs. As for the aged in institutions, who are likely to have the poorest objective levels of health, it should be kept in mind that institutions for the elderly are designed to minimize the effects of illness and disability. "If they are successful in this effort," states Myles (1978:518–519), "we should expect this to be reflected in their clients' subjective experience of illness." Therefore, as long as the institutional environment is able to buffer the effects of old age, including illness and disability, elderly individuals may be able to maintain the view that their health is adequate or even good for their surroundings. Being alive and able to function adequately apparently promotes the subjective impression that one's health in old age is relatively good.

At least this is the result of several studies conducted in Illinois (Cockerham, Sharp, and Wilcox 1983), northeastern New York (Stoller 1984), North Carolina (Maddox and Douglass 1973), and nationwide (Ferraro 1980; Wolinsky and Johnson 1992). One study conducted in central Wisconsin, however, produced different results (elderly respondents rated their health worse than middle-aged persons did) and concluded that "if elderly people do report more health optimism that younger individuals perhaps it is only when asked to compare themselves with their age peers" (Levkoff, Cleary, and Wetle 1987:118). This conclusion raises an important point. When younger people are asked to compare their health with that of others their age, the evaluation is likely to be "about the same"; elderly people, as discussed, appear more likely to rate their health higher than that of their peers. In old age, health differences between people become more obvious. Therefore, as Stoller (1984) explains, comparison with peers is of major importance in health self-assessments by the elderly, and it may be that such a comparison is a primary factor in influencing relatively high self-ratings. When asked to compare themselves with younger persons or with people generally, the aged may not rank their health as highly as they seem to do when comparing themselves with others in their age group.

Therefore, as David Mechanic and Ronald Angel (1987) suggest, the elderly appear to adjust their perceptions of their health as they modify their expectations with age. That is, as people become older, they change their definition of what it is to be healthy in order to fit their circumstances. If they have survived to old age in reasonably good condition and can function relatively well in their environment, health self-assessments tend to be very positive when the elderly compare themselves with their peers. Mechanic and Angel found in a study of low back pain, for example, that older people in a nationwide sample complained of less pain than expected in comparison with other age groups. Mechanic and Angel concluded:

> Subjective evaluations of health, we believe, are not absolute but on the contrary, are made in a context of self and other comparisons, and are always relative to some degree. As people age, they may attribute some of their discomforts to the aging process and are more likely to normalize bodily discomforts. Moreover, they may feel that they are doing relatively well compared to their reference groups and the physical demands of their life regimen. Indeed, there

may be less requirement for them to engage in the types of activities that exacerbate their discomforts.[1]

PHYSICAL HEALTH

Of course, the health of elderly people on the whole is not actually better than that of young adults. This is apparent when age differences in overall physical condition, stamina, hand and eye coordination, hearing and vision, and capacity for healing from disease and injury are considered. Although there are exceptions, older people generally cannot pursue a highly active physical lifestyle to the same extent as someone much younger. Rather, the health of many older people is quite good for their age. The health of other older people, however, may be poor. The fact remains that health does deteriorate with age, and this occurs later in some people than in others. But eventually everyone's health declines if one lives long enough. The key to a positive quality of life in old age appears to be that of maintaining one's health as long as possible and as close as possible to the time of one's death. In this section, we discuss the general situation of the aged in American society with respect to physical health.

Health Services Utilization

The two age groups using health services the most are the elderly and young children, but it is the elderly who have the poorest health and are hospitalized more often than other age groups. The general literature on health care utilization in the United States, including studies in Rhode Island (Kronenfeld 1978; Monteiro 1973), Los Angeles County (Galvin and Fan 1975), five New York and Pennsylvania counties (Wan and Soifer 1974), Cleveland (Coulton and Frost 1982), St. Louis (Wolinsky et al. 1983), and nationwide (Wolinsky, Mosely, and Coe 1986), substantiates the supposition that elderly people are more likely to visit a physician than are young adults. Studies of the utilization of health services by the aged indicate that such use is determined more by actual need for care than any other single factor (Coulton and Frost 1982; Wan 1982; Wolinsky et al. 1983). It is therefore not surprising that persons age 65 and older in the United States visited physicians an average of 10.9 times in 1993, much more than any other age group (National Center for Health Statistics 1995).

1. David Mechanic and Ronald J. Angel, "Some Factors Associated with the Report and Evaluation of Back Pain," *Journal of Health and Social Behavior* 28 (1987): 138.

Health Characteristics of the Aged

In the United States, as in other developed countries, there has been a reduction in infectious diseases and an increase in chronic health disorders. These chronic disorders—heart disease, cancer, hypertension, diabetes, and the like—are the most important problems of physical health facing older people today (Kart, Metress, and Metress 1988; Ory and Bond 1989). For example, Table 5–1 shows that the leading causes of death (in order) in the United States in 1900 were influenza and pneumonia, and tuberculosis. In 1993 these disorders had been replaced by heart disease, cancer, cerebrovascular disease or stroke, and pulmonary diseases as the major causes of death in an increasingly urban, industrialized, and aging society. Improvements in living conditions and medical technology had all but eliminated disorders such as tuberculosis, gastroenteritis, and diphtheria as major threats to life in 1993; but smoking, excessive consumption of calories and animal fats, stress reactions, and inadequate physical activity had helped promote other health problems, such as heart disease and other cardiovascular disorders, such as cerebrovascular diseases.

Although heart disease is America' s leading killer, since the mid-1960s there has been a decline in deaths from the disease for both men and women. About 308 of every 100,000 persons in the general population died from heart disease in 1950, compared with a rate of 145.3 persons per 100,000 in 1993. The decline in mortality from heart disease is but one example indicating improved health for older people.

The healthiest of the aged are those who live in community settings, rather than in institutions, such as nursing and old age homes. Only about 6 percent of all elderly are institutionalized; thus the overwhelming majority

TABLE 5–1 The Ten Leading Causes of Death in the United States, 1900 and 1993

1900	*1993*
Influenza and pneumonia	Heart disease
Tuberculosis	Cancer
Gastroenteritis	Cerebrovascular diseases
Heart disease	Pulmonary diseases
Cerebral hemorrhage	Accidents
Chronic nephritis	Influenza and pneumonia
Accidents	Diabetes
Cancer	AIDS
Diseases of early infancy	Suicide
Diphtheria	Homicide

(94 percent) live outside of an institutional environment, and their health is typical of the aged. The most prevalent health conditions for all persons age 65 and over by race, for the most recent year (1989) for which data were available, are listed in Table 5–2. Arthritis is the most prevalent health problem of older people with a rate of 483.0 cases per 1,000 persons 65 years of age and older. Moreover, arthritis increases with age; Table 5–2 shows a rate of 253.8 per 1,000 in the 45- to 64-year-old age group, 437.3 in the 65- to 74-year-old group, and 554.5 in the 75 and over group. Therefore, over half of the oldest people in American society have arthritis, whose effect on a person's ability to function varies from mild to severe. Table 5–2 also shows that blacks have 108 percent more arthritis than whites.

The second most prevalent health condition is hypertension, which is also greater among blacks (141 percent) than whites. Table 5–2 shows a rate of 380.6 cases per 1,000 persons age 65 and over, thereby indicating that more than one-third of the elderly have hypertension. Table 5–2 shows that the rate for hypertension increases from 229.1 per 1,000 for the 45- to 64-year-old group to 383.3 for the 65- to 74-year-old group, but then declines to 375.6 for those 75 and over. Most likely there is less hypertension in the oldest group because many of those afflicted at earlier ages did not survive. The next most prevalent health conditions for the aged are (in order) hearing

TABLE 5–2   Ten Most Prevalent Health Conditions for Persons Age 65 and over by U.S. Age Group and Race, 1989

| Condition | Age | | | | Race | | |
	65+	45 to 64	65 to 74	75+	White	Black	Black as % of white
Arthritis	483.0	253.8	437.3	554.5	483.2	522.6	108.0
Hypertension	380.6	229.1	383.8	375.6	367.4	517.7	141.0
Hearing impairment	286.5	127.7	239.4	360.3	297.4	174.5	59.0
Heart disease	278.9	118.9	231.6	353.0	286.5	220.5	77.0
Cataracts	156.8	16.1	107.4	234.3	160.7	139.8	87.0
Deformity or orthopedic impairment	155.2	155.5	141.4	177.0	156.2	150.8	97.0
Chronic sinusitis	153.4	173.5	151.8	155.8	157.1	125.2	80.0
Diabetes	88.2	58.2	89.7	85.7	80.2	165.9	207.0
Visual impairment	81.9	45.1	69.3	101.7	81.1	77.0	95.0
Varicose veins	78.1	57.8	72.6	86.6	80.3	64.0	80.0

In number per 1,000 persons.
Source: National Center for Health Statistics.

impairment, heart disease, cataracts, deformity or orthopedic (bone) impairment, chronic sinusitis (irritation of nasal passages), diabetes, visual impairment, and varicose veins. All of these conditions are more prevalent among whites than blacks, except for diabetes, which elderly blacks are twice (207 percent) as likely to have than their white counterparts. Of the ten most prevalent health conditions of the aged, only three (hypertension, heart disease, and diabetes) are fatal. The remainder cause discomfort and impair daily functioning.

The limitations on daily activities caused by chronic health conditions in 1993 affected some 38.9 percent of the elderly population (National Center for Health Statistics 1995). The most common limitation for both males and females is heavy housework, followed by meal preparation, light housework, and shopping. Although these impairments affect nearly 40 percent of the older population to varying degrees and are more of a problem for the oldest-old, the majority of over 60 percent of aged persons have no such limitations. The percentages of elderly males and females who cannot perform certain tasks at all is shown in Table 5–3. The data in Table 5–3 for 1991 indicate that, for both males (15.8 percent) and females (5.0 percent) age 65 and over, heavy housework is the activity they are least likely to be able to do. Next is meal preparation (12.4 percent of males and 1.2 percent of females). The older the person, however, the greater the likelihood of being unable to perform the activity, with the highest percentage (19.4 percent) reported by males age 75 and over for heavy housework.

Most elderly people do not suffer from a chronic health condition that prevents them from performing daily routines, however. The National Center for Health Statistics (1986, 1995) summarizes its findings by pointing out that

TABLE 5–3 Percentage of Elderly U.S. Males and Females Who Are Unable to Perform Certain Activities, 1991

Activity	Male			Female		
	65 years and over	65–74 years	75 years and over	65 years and over	65–74 years	75 years and over
Meal preparation	12.4	11.2	14.8	1.2	0.7	1.9
Shopping	2.8	2.2	4.0	1.2	0.6	2.1
Money management	2.3	2.0	2.8	1.5	1.0	2.1
Telephone use	1.1	0.9	1.5	0.3	0.2	0.5
Light housework	9.1	8.6	10.1	0.9	0.4	1.5
Heavy housework	15.8	14.0	19.4	5.0	3.2	7.6

Source: National Center for Health Statistics.

the health of older Americans is generally good, including those age 85 and older. As recently as 1993, over 60 percent of all elderly had not been confined to their bed for any number of days or had limitations on their activities, and 72 percent had reported their health as excellent or good. It should not be concluded that the health of the *total* elderly population is good; rather, the health of the majority of older people is relatively good but declines with age.

The most recent data compiled on nursing home residents by the National Center for Health Statistics (1987a) show that such residents typically are very old (45 percent are age 85 and over, and 39 percent are between the ages of 74 and 85); they also tend to be female (75 percent) and white (93 percent). Only some 6 percent of all nursing home residents are black, and 1 percent are either Asians, native Americans, or native Alaskans. Because of the preponderance of very old residents in nursing homes, many are in poor health and need assistance in performing basic activities of daily living, such as bathing (91 percent), dressing (78 percent), using the toilet or moving from a bed or chair (63 percent), and eating (40 percent). Loss of independence among nursing home residents is most likely to occur in bathing and least likely in eating. The trend in nursing homes is toward *greater* functional dependence for the residents, as compared with the past, because of the increasingly larger proportion of the old-old in such institutions.

Overall, however, most elderly people feel relatively good about their health status and feel that they are doing a good job of taking care of their health (National Center for Health Statistics 1986). A sense of control over one's health has been found to be significantly related to the number of physician visits in that those elderly persons with a strong sense of control tend to seek out doctors less often (Krause 1988) and to make healthier choices about their food, exercise, smoking, and alcohol consumption (Grembowski et al. 1993). Living with other people, who are able to help the aged deal with their daily activities, has likewise been found to reduce the need for health services (Cafferata 1987).

Overall, the health of older persons does appear to be relatively good. Greater numbers of people are living to reach old age. But greater numbers of elderly persons also means greater numbers with health problems and an increased demand in the future for health care delivery services to treat the problems of aging.

Stress and the Aged

Another important factor in considering the health status of an individual, not just those past the age of 65, is exposure to stress. Stress can be defined as a heightened mind-body reaction to stimuli inducing fear or anxiety in the individual. Usually stress occurs when people are faced with situations in which their usual modes of behavior are not adequate and the consequences of not adapting to the situation are perceived as serious. When an individual is subject to stress, the body responds primarily through the autonomic nervous system (which controls heart rate, blood pressure, and gastrointestinal functions) and the neuroendocrine system (which controls the secretion of hormones from the adrenal and pituitary glands, the parathyroids, and elsewhere). A number of studies have shown that an individual's inability to deal with stress and control stress-induced physiological changes in the body can promote heart disease, hypertension, ulcers, muscular pain, compulsive vomiting, asthma, migraine headaches, and other health problems (Cockerham 1995).

Of course, individuals who are highly stressed and develop serious health problems as a result are not as likely to live long lives. Stress, for example, is considered a major factor in early deaths from heart attacks among people who tend to be hard driving, overaggressive, and obsessed with meeting deadlines. However, stress is not absent from the lives of the elderly as they cope with the death of a spouse, retirement, loss of income and status, and the like. Research on elderly persons experiencing the loss of a spouse and other negative life events shows a decline in perceived health status (Fenwick and Barresi 1981; Weinberger et al. 1986). Yet Kenneth Ferraro (1989) points out that, even though aged women may suffer emotionally, they are more psychologically prepared to lose their spouse because widowhood is relatively common. But this does not mean that women escape the stress of the event; rather, it means they typically adjust more quickly. When it comes to experiencing grief over the death of a spouse, however, other research by Dale Lund and his associates (Lund, Caserta, and Dimond 1986) finds that there are more similarities than differences between elderly men and women in the bereavement process. Both are hit hard by the loss.

As for retirement, there is little evidence that this event has a negative health effect on the individual—again because it is an expected and normative transition for most people (Markides and Cooper 1987, 1989). This is not to say that the elderly are not affected by stress. Rather, it appears that older age groups respond much the same as younger groups. Social networks of family and friends significantly buffer and counterbalance the effects of stress on older individuals, as they do for younger persons, by providing social support in the form of love, affection, concern, and assistance (Cohen, Teresi, and Holmes 1985; George 1989; Krause 1986). Elderly people who lack this form of support fare worse in coping with stress (Matt and Dean 1993). Extensive research on health and stress among the elderly is just beginning, but both are important topics for future research because of the insight they provide into the effects of stress on people over the life course (Markides and Cooper 1989).

Health of the Elderly Poor and Minorities

To be poor is, by definition, to have less of everything in life, including health. Lower socioeconomic groups have the poorest health, and this is true throughout the world (Cockerham 1995). Persons living in poverty have greater exposure than more affluent individuals to physical (dust, dampness, extreme temperatures), chemical and biochemical (diet, pollution, smoking, alcohol and drug abuse), biological (bacteria, viruses), and psychological (stress) risk factors that produce ill health.

Those at the bottom of the socioeconomic scale, therefore, appear to be especially disadvantaged with regard to health. This disadvantage extends not only to communicable diseases associated with unhealthy living conditions, but also to chronic health problems like heart disease, which are prevalent in modern industrialized countries and which are strongly affected by how one lives. Lifestyle and social/environmental conditions, along with preventive health measures, primarily determine health status. A healthy lifestyle includes the use of good personal habits, such as eating properly, getting enough rest, exercising, and avoiding practices like smoking, abusing alcohol, and taking drugs. The type of lifestyle that promotes a healthy existence has been more typical of the upper and middle classes, who have the resources to support a healthy lifestyle, but there is evidence that participation in healthy lifestyles has begun to spread across class lines in the United States and Western Europe (Cockerham, Kunz, and Lueschen 1988; Lüschen et al. 1995). Nevertheless, crowded living conditions, poor diet, inferior housing, low levels of income and education, enhanced exposure to violence, alcoholism and problem drinking, and drug abuse all combine to decrease the life chances of the poor. This situation is reflected in the tendency of the poor generally (Cockerham et al. 1988; Cockerham 1995) and the aged poor in particular to have poorer health and rate their health worse than that of the more affluent (Grembowski et al. 1993; Mutran and Ferraro 1988).

According to James House and his colleagues (1994), socioeconomic differences in health are small in early adulthood, but increase with age until very late in life, when the oldest-old have essentially the same chances at being healthy. This nationwide study found that the interaction between age and socioeconomic status in predicting health can be substantially explained by the greater exposure of lower-class persons to health risks (resulting from greater stress and more unhealthy lifestyles and environment) during middle and early old age. As lower-class persons age, they are increasingly affected by conditions that promote poor health and are more likely to die before they reach the oldest ages.

Consequently, the poor are less likely to reach the oldest ages and, for those that do, surviving longer can be a constant struggle. In the United States, as noted in Chapter 2, 12.2 percent of the elderly lived below the poverty line in 1993. The greatest problem affecting the health of these persons is not access to health care. Americans age 65 and over are eligible for Medicare, the nation's publicly funded health insurance program, which pays for most medical services provided to older people. Rather, the central problem is living in an environment of poverty as an aged person and coping with the health disadvantages that such an environment promotes on a daily basis.

As for racial minority groups, Chapter 2 also disclosed that nonwhites generally have a lower life expectancy than whites. The remainder of this chapter examines the health of aged racial minority persons.

African Americans   Of all the American minorities, African Americans have the worst health profile and highest overall mortality rates. For example, although African Americans constitute 12 percent of the American population, they have 28 percent of the diagnosed hypertension (Hildreth and Saunders 1992). Hypertension is the leading cause of death from kidney failure and is a major contributor to death from end-stage renal disease, heart disease, and stroke. Black men who suffer from hypertension are 15.5 times more likely to die than white males 25 to 44 years of age. The ratio of black to white females dying from hypertension in the same age category is 17 to 1. Nearly 26 percent of all black females age 17 and older have hypertension. The end result is that black people have significantly more hypertension than whites and die from it at earlier ages. Blacks also rank at the top in major categories of mortality, such as heart disease, cancer, diabetes, and AIDS. This trend is substantiated in several studies, which report that African Americans have higher death rates from all causes and from many specific diseases than whites, native Americans, Hispanic Americans, and Asian Americans/Pacific Islanders (Harper 1992; Hildreth and Saunders 1992; National Center for Health Statistics 1995).

Direct comparisons between black and white mortality rates are shown in Table 5–4 on selected causes of death in the United States for 1993. Table 5–4 shows that, for all causes, the age-adjusted mortality rate for black males was 1,052.9 per 100,000 resident population, whereas the rate for white males was 627.5 per 100,000. The death rate for black females was 578.8 per 100,000 compared with 367.7 for white females. For heart disease, the death rate for black males was 287.9 per 100,000, as contrasted with 190.3 for white males; black females, in turn, had a mortality rate of 165.3 compared

TABLE 5–4   **U.S. Age-adjusted Mortality Rates for Selected Causes of Death, According to Sex and Race, 1993**

	Deaths per 100,000 resident population			
	White males	White females	Black males	Black females
All causes	627.5	367.7	1,052.2	578.8
Heart disease	190.3	99.2	267.9	165.3
Cerebrovascular diseases	26.8	22.7	51.9	39.9
Cancer	156.4	110.1	238.9	135.3
Pulmonary disease	28.2	17.8	26.6	12.2
Pneumonia and influenza	16.6	10.4	25.9	13.5
Liver disease and cirrhosis	10.8	4.6	16.1	6.6
Diabetes	12.2	10.0	26.3	26.9
Accidents	42.9	16.6	59.8	20.1
Suicide	19.7	4.6	12.9	2.1
Homicide	8.9	3.0	70.7	13.4
AIDS	19.0	1.9	70.0	17.3

Source: National Center for Health Statistics, *Health, United States, 1995* (Washington, D.C.: U.S. Government Printing Office, 1996).

with 99.2 for white females. For cancer, Table 5–4 shows the 1993 death rate for black males was 238.9 per 100,000 compared with 156.4 for white males; black females showed a rate of 135.3 compared with 110.1 for white females. The same general pattern (higher rates for blacks than whites) is also shown to be the case in Table 5–4 for deaths from cerebrovascular diseases (stroke), pneumonia and influenza, liver disease and cirrhosis, accidents, homicide, and AIDS. Besides heart disease and cancer, black males have especially high death rates from homicide and AIDS. Whites, on the other hand, show higher death rates in two categories: pulmonary (lung) disease and suicide.

Data like these clearly point to lessened life expectancy for blacks in comparison with whites. The black male, according to 1993 figures compiled by the U.S. National Center for Health Statistics (1996), with a life expectancy of 64.6 years, will typically live 8.2 years less than the white male, whose life expectancy is 73.1 years, and 14.5 years less than the white female, who has the highest life expectancy of all at 79.5 years. The black female, with a life expectancy in 1993 of 73.7 years, lives almost 6.0 years less on the average than the white female. Excess mortality for black adults in the United States appears to be largely attributable not only to risk factors such as smoking, cholesterol, high blood pressure, excess weight, alcohol intake, and diabetes, but also to the social, psychological, and physical environment associated with a low income (Otten et al. 1990). Given the socioeconomically disadvantaged position of many U.S. blacks, they may be less prepared to deal with potentially fatal diseases and are therefore more likely to die early from such afflictions (Cockerham 1995b, Hildreth and Saunders 1992; Markides 1989; Markides and Mindel 1987).

However, when it comes to the oldest-old, those age 85 and over, the remaining years of life expectancy for African Americans may be higher or equal to those of whites. National Center for Health Statistics (1986) data for 1984 show that black males had a life expectancy of 5.8 years at age 85, compared with 5.1 years for white males. Black females age 85 had 7.3 years, whereas white females of the same age had 6.5 years left on the average. More recent data for 1990 show black males with a life expectancy at age 85 of 5.0 years and white males with 5.2 years; among females, blacks had 6.3 years at age 85 and whites, 6.4 years. What is important is not that blacks have a slight advantage in life expectancy one year and whites have a narrow advantage in other years; rather, the difference between the races is not great at the oldest ages. According to Kyriakos Markides and Charles Mindel (1987) and others (Harper 1992; Manton 1980), the greater equality in life expectancy of blacks at age 85 is known as the *racial mortality crossover phenomenon*. Markides and Mindel explain that the racial mortality crossover may be misleading in that an advantage in life expectancy may be imputed to blacks. Instead, they point out that the existence of crossover actually signifies that a much greater proportion of blacks do not make it to advanced old age. A minority of blacks survive to very old age; most die much younger, and their deaths do not significantly reduce the life expectancy available to the relatively few blacks left alive at age 85. A much greater proportion of whites reach the oldest ages, and those who die early in old age reduce the average years of life expectancy computed for the longest-lived whites surviving well past age 85. Thus the average black person has more or equal years of life left statistically at age 85 because there are not as many blacks left to lower the computations for life expectancy.

Overall, it appears that blacks generally have poorer health than whites, but the differences are not great at the oldest ages (Ferraro 1988; Manton 1980; Markides 1989). That is, among old people, blacks and whites have about the same level of health, but there is a significantly smaller proportion of surviving blacks.

Hispanic Americans   Adverse differences in health are not limited to blacks: they also include Hispanic Americans. Health data on Hispanic Americans are limited because, until 1976, federal, state, and local agencies usually included Hispanic with non-Hispanic whites in the white category. Hispanics were also not included as a separate category on death certificates nationally until 1988. The existing information indicates, however, that Hispanics have higher mortality rates from diabetes, influenza, pneumonia, tuberculosis, and homicide, but lower rates of heart disease and cancer than non-Hispanic whites (Bassford 1995; Sorlie et al. 1993; Vega and Amaro 1994). Health problems such as influenza and tuberculosis among Hispanics are typically associated with poverty, and a large proportion of U.S. Hispanics have low incomes (Sorlie et al. 1993). Among Hispanics, Cuban Americans appear to have the best health and life expectancy and Puerto Ricans, the worst. Mexican Americans rank in the middle.

Among the elderly, Hispanics are more likely than non-Hispanic whites to have some type of physical impairment, and the onset of health problems generally appears to take place much earlier among Hispanics (Becerra and Shaw 1984). Some studies indicate that Hispanics have poorer health than non-Hispanics and somewhat better health than African Americans (Markides 1989; Markides and Mindel 1987), but there is not clear agreement about this situation (Sorlie et al. 1993; Vega and Amaro 1994). Similarly, whether or not Hispanics have a longer life span than non-Hispanics has yet to be determined. However, Hispanics are the racial minority group with the least likelihood of having health insurance. Over one-third (34.2 percent) of all Hispanic Americans under the age of 65 were not covered by health insurance in 1993. Nearly 40 percent of all Mexican Americans under age 65 lack health insurance, compared to 16.9 percent of Cuban Americans and 21 percent of Puerto Ricans. In contrast, some 16.2 percent of all whites under age 65 in 1993 did not have health insurance. Language barriers can also be an important problem for the Hispanic elderly in securing help from health care professionals and welfare agencies (Applewhite 1988).

Native Americans   Native Americans, consisting of American Indians and native Alaskans, have shown a dramatic improvement in their overall level of health in the last few years. Infant mortality rates dropped from 82.1 deaths per 1,000 live births in 1950 to 12.7 per 1,000 births in 1988, compared to 8.0 per 1,000 births for whites that same year. Life expectancy for native Americans was 60 years in 1950 but had climbed to 73.2 years by 1991 (69.1 years for males and 77.5 years for females). American Indians and native Alaskans have the lowest rates of cancer in the United States. Mortality rates from heart disease are also lower than in the general population, but heart disease is still a significant cause of death. However, American Indians have the highest mortality rates from diabetes in the United States, and the complications of diabetes take a further toll by increasing the probability of kidney disease, blindness, and heart disease.

American Indians also suffer more dysentery, strep throat, and hepatitis than do other Americans.

Other significant health problems include widespread ear infections (chronic otitis media) among children, which produce hearing problems, as well as extensive alcoholism, dietary deficiencies, and cirrhosis of the liver among adults. Alcoholism remains a major health problem for American Indians. More Indians also die from accidents, primarily automobile accidents, than any other racial group in American society, and the death rate from suicide is about 20 percent higher than that of the general population (Cockerham 1995b). Therefore, although native Americans have experienced a general improvement in overall health, significant problems remain. Considerably smaller proportions of Indians than whites survive to reach old age.

Asian Americans   In striking contrast to other racial minority groups, Asian Americans' health and longevity rank among the best in the country. Asian Americans have the highest levels of income, education, and employment of any racial/ethnic minority group in the United States, often exceeding levels achieved by whites. Consequently, it is not surprising that the lowest age-adjusted mortality rates in the United States are those of Asian Americans. Asians and Pacific Islanders in the United States showed an age-adjusted mortality rate in 1992 of 364.1 per 100,000 for males and 220.5 per 100,000 for females, which was the lowest at that time for any racial/ethnic group in the nation. Heart disease is the leading cause of death for Asians, but mortality from this disease is less than that for whites and other minorities. Asians have very low rates of death from infant mortality, homicide, suicide, and health problems associated with alcoholism. Overall, Asians and Pacific Islanders tend to be the healthiest racial group in American society.

Asians also have a tradition of strong family relationships and respect for the aged. It is more common in Asian families than in other U.S. families for elderly parents to live with their children. However, this is not to say that older Asian Americans do not have problems. Many older Asian Americans, especially those who live in inner-city "Chinatowns," speak little or no English, face cultural barriers in daily living and in securing health services, are in poor financial circumstances, have poor health, and live in isolation from the more affluent Asian community (Markides 1989; Markides and Mindel 1987).

HEALTH POLICY AND THE AGED

Health policy for the elderly is growing in importance as the number of the aged increases, the prevalence of chronic health problems in old age persists, and the costs of providing health care continue to rise. Prior to 1965, a nationwide financial barrier to health care existed for the aged. Unless they could pay for medical care themselves or had adequate private health insurance, older people, especially the poor, had to rely on the welfare policies of the various state governments and the charity of institutions and individual physicians.

However, in 1965, despite strong opposition from the American Medical Association, Congress passed legislation authorizing federally funded public health insurance for the elderly, known as Medicare. Opposition to this program from the medical profession had been based on the desire to (1) minimize the federal government's role in health care delivery and prevent the enactment of regulations reducing the prerogatives of physicians; (2) curtail any possible threat to the fee-for-service system in which physicians set the fees and patients or their insurance companies pay them; and (3) offset the possibility that a public health insurance program for the aged might be turned into a national health insurance scheme for the entire nation, thereby significantly reducing the autonomy and perhaps the income of physicians. The elderly, on the other hand, had been almost priced out of the private health insurance market because they were hospitalized more often than the rest of the population and had to pay high premiums on reduced incomes. Clearly there was a need for protection of the aged against the high costs of health care, especially hospitalization.

As it turned out, Medicare, along with its companion program for the poor (Medicaid), did not place physicians under the supervision of the federal government or change the structure of health care delivery services. In fact, Medicare became a financial boon to organized medicine and to hospitals, as billions of dollars have been channeled into health care over the years. Moreover, Medicare has made two significant contributions to health care delivery in the United States. First, although it may not have met all the needs of the elderly for health care, it has provided needed services for many of the aged where these services were not previously available. Overall, the financial barrier to health care has been significantly reduced for older people, and the benefits have improved the quality of life and longevity of many elderly Americans. Second, Medicare has helped establish the precedent of the federal government's involvement in the administration of health care. Such involvement is now an important and substantial reality, and whatever happens in the future, the organization and scope of health services in the United States is now dependent on federal government decisions.

Medicare currently provides hospital insurance (part A) and supplemental medical insurance (part B) for people 65 years of age or older, regardless of financial resources; disabled persons under age 65 who receive cash benefits from Social Security or railroad retirement programs; and certain victims of chronic kidney disease. Hospital insurance benefits in 1996 include (1) inpatient hospital services for up to 90 days for an episode of an illness, with the first 60 days covered completely and the next 30 days covered at a cost to the patient in 1996 of $184 a day; (2) a lifetime reserve of 60 additional days of hospital care after the initial 90 days have been used; (3) care in a nursing home for up to 100 days after hospitalization; and (4) up to 100 home health visits after hospitalization.

Supplementary Medicare insurance benefits include (1) physicians' and surgeons' services, certain nonroutine services of podiatrists, limited services of chiropractors, and the services of independently practicing physical therapists; (2) certain medical and health services, such as diagnostic services, diagnostic X-ray tests, laboratory tests, and other services, including ambulance services, some medical supplies, appliances, and equipment; (3) outpatient hospital services; (4) home health services (with no requirement of prior hospitalization) for up to 100 visits in one calendar year; and (5) outpatient physical and speech therapy services provided by approved therapists.

There are specified deductible and coinsurance amounts for which the beneficiary is responsible. The deductible in 1996 on the hospital insurance (part A) was $736 and on the medical insurance (part B) was $100, with a 20 percent coinsurance amount also required for most part B services. The hospital insurance was financed primarily through Social Security payroll deductions, whereas the medical insurance plan, whose participation is voluntary, was financed by premiums paid by the enrollees and from federal funds. The medical insurance premium in 1996 was $42.50 a month.

One change that was approved in Congress was the passage in 1989 of the Physician Payment Reform Act. This legislation, which took effect in 1992, changed the way medical doctors are paid. The law stipulates the amounts to be paid for physician services, with increases over current allowances being given to physicians in family practice (38 percent) and in internal medicine (17 percent), whereas doctors in specialties such as ophthalmology, radiology, pathology, general surgery, and others will be paid lower percentages than in the past. Ten percent bonuses are paid to doctors who practice in rural and inner-city areas. The law also limits how much a physician can charge a Medicare patient above the scheduled amount. This measure is intended not only to reduce costs, but to provide greater emphasis on primary and preventive care by increasing the amounts paid to doctors working in those areas.

The Medicare program is under the overall direction of the Secretary of Health and Human Services and is supervised by the Bureau of Health Insurance of the Social Security Administration. Most of the day-to-day operations of Medicare are performed by commercial insurance companies and Blue Cross/Blue Shield plans that review claims and make payments. Requests for payment are usually submitted by the provider of services and signed by the beneficiary; reimbursement is made on the basis of reasonable charges as determined by the private insurance companies who issue the payments. In 1993, a total of $150 billion in Medicare benefits were paid under coverage that extends to about 36.3 million people.

A continuing controversy about Medicare is how to pay for it. In 1967 the federal government spent $4.5 billion on Medicare; by 1980, the cost reached $35.7 billion and went over $150 billion in 1993. Congress has favored Medicare beneficiaries themselves paying for extra costs in the form of monthly deductions from Social Security checks and an annual surcharge based on income. Many of the elderly, in turn, feel that the cost of the additional benefits should be absorbed by the general population.

One far-reaching cost-cutting measure passed by Congress in 1983 was the establishment of Diagnostic Related Groups (DRGs), a fixed schedule of fees for care rendered to Medicare patients by hospitals. Hospitals make money if they keep costs below what Medicare pays, and they can lose money if their costs exceed the rate. This situation requires hospitals to be both cost conscious and more efficient when it comes to treating patients covered by Medicare.

Besides the rising cost of the Medicare program, there is a gap in coverage for long-term treatment in nursing homes or in the patient's home. Only some 29 percent of elderly requiring long-term care lived in institutions in 1988. The remainder lived at home and were assisted by family members and other informal sources, such as neighbors or friends, who provide the majority of care for the noninstitutionalized. In-home care for the aged from formal health care providers tends to be used primarily by those elderly who are better educated, have financial resources, and have the worse mental or physical health (McAuley and Arling 1984). In 1993, Medicare paid 5.8 percent of its budget for nursing home care. In effect, Medicare provides little support for nursing home residents. Some elderly persons receive public insurance benefits for nursing home care under Medicaid, the federal government's health insurance program for the poor administered by the various states, but in order to qualify for this coverage, a person's financial assets must be low. After exempting the value of one's house, automobile, and personal property, the person's assets usually cannot exceed $2,000. For elderly people with savings who are facing long-term care in a nursing home, this means they must eliminate nearly all of their savings before they can qualify for Medicaid. Once on Medicaid, all income except a small personal allowance must go to nursing home costs, with Medicaid paying the remainder. Financing the costs of long-term care in institutions for the elderly is clearly going to be a major policy issue in the United States in coming years.

On balance, however, when it comes to provision of hospital and medical care on a national basis for the aged, Medicare, despite its problems, has been a success. Many elderly people have been able to overcome the financial barrier for health care that blocked both their access and their ability to pay in the past. Future legislation is likely to expand benefits and address the problem of long-term care in either in-home or institutional settings.

SUMMARY

This chapter has focused on the health of the elderly in the United States and has found that the general level of health is good. Elderly people tend to rate their health very positively, especially when they compare themselves to their peers, because they have survived to old age and are able to function in their environment. Of course, elderly people are usually not in as good a physical condition as younger adults, and the health of some aged persons is poor. But overall, a majority of older people have been able to maintain a good state of health.

Older people are hospitalized more often than any other age group in U.S. society. However, a majority (94 percent) live outside of institutions like nursing and old age homes, and most (72 percent) not only rate their health as good or better than average, but have not been confined to a bed for a single day in the past year (60 percent) or had any limitations on their activities. A majority likewise claim that they do a good job taking care of their health.

Health problems nonetheless exist because health seriously declines for all older people at some point. Heart disease is the most significant life-threatening physical illness for the aged. Some particular difficulties experienced by the aged are caused by stress associated with loss of a spouse or close friends through death. Of all the elderly, black Americans tend to have the poorest health, whereas Asian Americans, on balance, have the best. Compared with older non-Hispanic whites, the health of elderly African Americans and native Americans is clearly worse, and that of Hispanics is not likely to be better.

The principal policy measure for enhancing the health of the aged is the federally funded health insurance program Medicare. Medicare is expensive and surrounded by controversy with respect to increasing costs, and gaps do exist in the program—such as relatively few benefits for long-term care like that given in nursing homes. But, in general, Medicare has been a success and has played a key role in improving the health of the aged in America.

Chapter 6

MENTAL HEALTH OF THE AGED

The significant increase in numbers and percentages of elderly persons has profound consequences for the mental health care delivery system. Trends toward greater longevity signify an increased demand for mental health services by the aged. This does not mean that elderly persons will have more mental disorder in the future than will younger persons. Rather, it means that, with more elderly persons in the general population, there will also be an increase in the number of elderly patients needing mental health services. In this chapter we examine the psychological effects of aging, with a focus on disabling mental disorders—especially dementia.

THE PSYCHOLOGICAL EFFECTS OF AGING

Normal aging has an effect on basic cognitive processes, including information processing and attention. It is generally believed that aged persons experience an inevitable decline in cognition. As British psychologist Graham Stokes (1992:54) explains, there is no doubt that one fundamental and pervasive change occurring with age is a slowing of thought and behavior. Slowness of thought, however, does not mean that people cannot think well; rather, it just takes them longer to process information. Major contributing factors to this situation are declines in vision and hearing, which affect the reception of information by the older person. Yet the basic cause of cognitive slowing in older individuals appears to be the aging of the central nervous system as part of the overall process of biological aging. When aged persons perform tasks with which they are experienced, they are more proficient and faster, but cognitive slowness is most apparent when the elderly person is faced with relatively unfamiliar and demanding activities (Birren, Sloane, and Cohen 1992; Stokes 1992).

Another cognitive function affected by age is attention, or the motivation to focus on the task at hand. Older people are more easily distracted and subject to fatigue, but, again, it is not that they are unable to perform tasks; rather, they require much more time to complete the work. Stokes (1992:60) states that "overall, it would appear that attention is age-sensitive only when the tasks are demanding in terms of speed, sustained effort, and memory." Cognitive slowing is undoubtedly a major psychological effect of the aging process. However, as Stokes reminds us, delays in information processing in the nervous system in the elderly are not necessarily great (fractions of a second), and aged persons have the advantage of drawing on experience, previous learning, and logic to compensate for reduced cognitive efficiency. Consequently, most aged persons are able to function adequately in most situations, especially if it is something with which they are familiar (Birren, Sloane, and Cohen 1992; Stokes 1992).

Two other areas of psychological functioning that appear to be affected by aging are learning and memory. Studies consistently find that, the older a person is, the longer it takes to learn something new (Cunningham and Brookbank 1988). Thus learning performance tends to decline with age, although the decline is not significant until after age 70. It is commonly believed that all aspects of memory—encoding (processing information), retention, and recall—also decline with advancing age (Atchley 1994). Short-term memory, or the recall of recent events, seems to be particularly affected by aging. Yet some aged persons suffer little or no memory loss and maintain a high capacity for recall, even when they are quite old. In sum, the aging process does affect the nervous system in ways that slow cognitive functioning and degrade information processing, attention, learning, and memory. But these natural declines can be offset by experience and familiarity with one's roles, tasks, and environment.

As for intelligence, the elderly tend to do less well on one-time intelligence tests that put a premium on speed of response, but perform well when tested several times over a long period. However, to date, the exact effects of aging on intelligence are unknown. It cannot be demonstrated that people generally become less intelligent just because they get old, but some older people do show the decline in cognitive functioning discussed in this section.

For the elderly in general, education appears more important than age in explaining individual differences in intellectual ability.

THE PREVALENCE OF MENTAL DISORDER IN OLD AGE

Unfortunately, the aging process for some people is accompanied by a severe loss of mental abilities and the onset of mental illness. For example, in 1992, some 16 percent of all residents in American mental hospitals were age 65 and over. The largest percentage (52 percent) of these elderly persons were in state and county mental hospitals, where chronically ill or incurable patients are most likely to be found. Others (23 percent) were in general hospital psychiatric units, veterans' hospitals (13 percent), and multiservice mental health organizations (1 percent), where patients do not typically remain on a long-term basis. The remainder (11 percent) were in private mental hospitals.

Table 6–1 shows the distribution of residents in state and county mental hospitals for 1992 by type of mental disorder and age. For all age groups, other than those 18 years and under, schizophrenia accounted for the most patients. *Schizophrenia* is a disturbance in mood, thinking, and behavior manifested by distortions of reality involving delusions (disturbance in thought) and hallucinations (disturbance in perception). Schizophrenia accounted for the largest percentage (38.1 percent) of patients age 65 and over, but the proportion was much less than that of persons in the 25–44 and 45–64 age groups, whose percentages were 56.7 and 54.2 percent, respectively. Persons age 65 and over are shown in Table 6–1 to have the highest percentage (27.5 percent) of patients with dementia, which is related to aging and characterized by loss of memory. Another 11.1 percent of state and county mental patients age 65 and older have mood disorders, which include depression.

However, data on mental hospital patients do not represent the true prevalence of mental disorder in a population, because they do not include outpatients or untreated cases that fail to come to the attention of mental health reporting agencies. Hospital admission rates may also be affected by the availability of facilities, thereby limiting the number of patients who can be admitted. Estimates of the true prevalence of mental disorder provide a more complete view of mental health problems in a community, because they include both treated and untreated cases. Such data are obtained for treated cases from hospital and physician records and for untreated cases by community surveys that include measures of mental health and psychological well-being. Community surveys, however, are not precise measures of the prevalence of mental disorder, because they seldom involve a full psychiatric

TABLE 6–1 Resident Patients in U.S. State and County Mental Hospitals, by Mental Disorder and Age, 1992

Major Diagnosis	Number	Under 18	18–24	25–44	45–64	65 and over	All Ages
Mental retardation	2,575	2.0	6.0	3.5	2.9	1.2	3.1
Alcohol-related	2,077	0.9	2.8	2.3	3.0	3.2	2.5
Substance-related	1,491	2.1	4.1	2.5	0.6	0.3	1.8
Dementia	7,418	2.4	5.1	4.6	9.0	27.5	8.9
Mood disorders	9,892	20.2	12.3	10.0	13.3	11.1	11.9
Schizophrenia	40,417	9.7	36.2	56.7	54.2	38.1	48.5
Other psychotic	3,612	4.5	7.2	4.6	3.7	3.2	4.3
Anxiety/Somato./Dissoc.	292	1.2	0.6	0.3	0.3	0.3	0.4
Personality disorders	1,227	2.3	4.3	1.6	0.8	0.3	1.5
Preadult disorders	2,121	27.1	1.8	0.6	0.5	0.3	2.5
Other nonpsychotic	3,063	19.8	6.8	2.6	1.5	1.0	3.7
Social	246	0.7	0.7	0.3	0.2	0.1	0.3
No mental disorder	440	1.0	0.7	0.5	0.4	0.3	0.5
Deferred/undiagnosed	8,449	6.1	11.4	9.9	9.6	13.1	10.1
Totals	83,320	100.0	100.0	100.0	100.0	100.0	100.0

Source: National Institute for Mental Health, 1994.

examination of the respondent and instead rely on psychological tests to esti-mate mental status. Nonetheless, it has been found that such surveys do pro-duce consistent findings and provide a reasonable approximation of the types and extent of mental disorder in a population (Cockerham 1996).

When it comes to estimates of the true prevalence of mental disorder among the elderly, 15 percent of all aged persons are estimated to be in need of mental health services. Whereas schizophrenia is the diagnosis assigned to the largest proportion of elderly mental hospital patients, mood disorders—especially depression—are the most common form of mental disorder among aged persons generally (Cockerham 1996; Mirowsky and Ross 1992).

Mood Disorders

The basic feature of *mood disorders* is a fundamental disturbance in mood. The term *mood* in this context refers to a condition of prolonged emotion consisting of either depression or elation. Mood disorders are the most preva-lent type of severe mental disorder in the United States generally, with at least 2.5 percent of the population expected to suffer from a mood disorder at some time in their lives. When all forms of mental disorder are considered, mood disorders, as noted, rank at the top for the aged; however, adults at any age can be severely depressed, and the elderly do not necessarily have more mood disorders than younger age groups (Stokes 1992). About one in five adults is significantly affected by a severe depression over the life course, with women having a higher prevalence than men.

The two major forms of mood disorders are depressive disorders and bipolar disorders. *Bipolar disorders*, consisting of a combination of manic and depressive episodes, with depression being the more prominent, usually occur before age 30 and are not typically found in aged persons. Depressive disorders, however, afflict many older people. According to the American Psychiatric Association's *Diagnostic and Statistical Manual of Mental Dis-orders*, fourth edition (DSM-IV), published in 1994, the essential feature of a depressive disorder is a period of at least two weeks during which a person experiences either a depressed mood or loss of interest or pleasure in nearly all activities. The individual must experience at least four additional symp-toms, including changes in appetite or weight, sleep, or psychomotor activ-ity; decreased energy; feelings of worthlessness or guilt; difficulty thinking, concentrating, or making decisions; or recurrent thoughts of death or suicide ideas, plans, or attempts. In a major depressive episode, DSM-IV points out that the individual typically describes his or her mood as depressed, sad, hopeless, discouraged, or "down in the dumps."

The high prevalence of depressive disorders among the aged is related to the fact that a sense of loss is particularly common among older people (Matt and Dean 1993). The elderly are confronted with multiple and simultaneous losses, such as death of a spouse, relatives, or friends; declines in physical health; and changes in status. Many aged persons may cope satisfactorily with feelings of loss, but it is natural for feelings of depression to be generated in such circumstances, and some may experience extreme sadness and grief. Losses in late life can cause older people to expend large amounts of emotional and physical energy in grieving and resolving grief; therefore, it is not surprising that depressive disorders are the primary mental health affliction of the old.

Suicide

Suicide, which is often related to depression, is also an important problem for the aged. Between 1981 and 1986, suicide rates among older Americans increased from 17.1 per 100,000 to 21.3 per 100,000—an increase of 25 percent. This was a surprising development, because no other Western nation was experiencing such a trend. It suggested that the quality of life for older Americans was not especially appealing, but the exact reason for the rise in suicides was never determined. Some suggestions are that the quality of life available to people living physically longer lives may not be especially appealing for many of them. Longevity may produce greater concerns about becoming senile or contracting some other incurable health problem, such as cancer or heart disease, in which the individual is relatively helpless and the financial cost is great. There is also a growing awareness among researchers of "rational suicide" by the elderly, in which the person is not psychologically distressed but simply decides that his or her life is no longer worth living.

Since 1986, however, suicide rates have declined somewhat and stood at 19.8 per 100,000 persons age 65 and older during 1990 through 1992. Despite the slight decrease, the elderly, especially non-Hispanic white males, are more likely to take their own lives than any other age group. For 1990 through 1992, the suicide rate for non-Hispanic white males age 65 and over was 43.1 per 100,000; the rates for other aged males were 22.6 for Hispanics, 17.8 for Asians and Pacific Islanders, and 15.1 for blacks. For older females, Asians and Pacific Islanders had the highest suicide rate, at 8.3 per 100,000, followed by 6.6 for non-Hispanic whites, 2.8 for Hispanics, and 2.4 for blacks. Suicide rates for elderly native Americans were negligible but are the highest in the nation for males age 15 to 24 years (42.5 per 100,000).

The pattern of suicides in the United States is typical of developed countries generally, in that men have a greater risk of suicide than women, with the risk highest for men in old age and highest for women in middle age. Great Britain, for example, has the same general pattern as the United States, with higher suicide rates in the older age groups mainly accounted for by higher rates of male suicides (Pilgrim and Rogers 1993). The reason men are more likely than women to take their own lives and why suicide rates increase with older age among men but not women is not known (Posner 1995). But the fact remains that the highest suicide rates in economically advanced countries are found among elderly males. Elsewhere, in developing countries, research by Chris Girard (1993) suggests a different age pattern for suicide. In third world nations, suicide peaks in early adulthood, and rates for young women may equal or exceed those of young men.

Dementia

The mental disorder most often associated with aging is senility, or dementia. Women are significantly more likely than men to have dementia, but this is largely due to the greater numbers of women surviving to old age. Dementia can be caused by vascular complications, AIDS, head injury, and substance abuse, but its major form is *Alzheimer's disease*, which is the deterioration of previously acquired intellectual abilities to the extent that usual social behavior is severely affected. The most prominent symptom is loss of memory, although there may also be impairment in judgment and control of impulses. Another symptom may be personality change in which the older individual begins to act markedly different from his or her typical self. The person may become unusually compulsive, cantankerous, uncooperative, paranoid, or perhaps withdrawn from others.

Although dementia is a particularly terrible affliction of old age, it is not a normal feature of the aging experience. DSM-IV states that only some 3 percent of the aged population have severe cognitive impairment caused by dementia. An additional 5 to 10 percent may be mildly or moderately impaired. The age of onset for Alzheimer's disease is the late sixties or early seventies. However, the chance of developing the disease rises significantly with increasing age, particularly after age 75. Among persons age 85 and over—the fastest-growing segment of the population—15 percent or more are severely afflicted. The prevalence of dementia in a society as a whole depends on the proportion of the population that survives to old age (Stokes 1992). Given the growth in numbers of aged persons worldwide, dementia is likely to afflict increasingly larger numbers of people. This means that dementia will significantly increase in the future, not only in North America and Europe, but also in Africa, Asia, and Latin America. Current evidence from China, India, and Nigeria shows rising life expectancy has been accompanied by increased dementia; in fact, in India, the prevalence and types of dementia may have already reached the point at which they are not especially different from the West (Desjarlais et al. 1995; Levkoff, MacArthur, and Bucknall 1995).

What makes dementia especially feared is that the disease involves a distinct loss of self, and there is no medical cure at present (only 15 percent of dementia patients have treatable conditions). Thus the majority of victims suffer a significant loss of their mental life and personal history. As one patient suffering from dementia of the Alzheimer's type explained:

> Alzheimer's disease is worse than death. It leaves bone and flesh intact while it erases judgment and memory. I could live with death. Death is a part of the cycle of life. It's like spring, the end of winter. But this disease—it's unnatural. It's the end of hope.[1]

Although dementia is a particularly dreadful affliction of old age, it is not a normal feature of the aging process. The majority of aged individuals do not experience the disorder. The notion that, if a person lives long enough, he or she will become senile is clearly a myth (Butler 1985; Stokes 1992). As discussed, only a small percentage of all elderly become victims of Alzheimer's disease, and for those that do, the goal of treatment is to preserve whatever ability they have to function.

In summary, it should be kept in mind that most older people (over 80 percent) do not suffer from any mental disorder and lead lives that are not constrained by such afflictions. The vast majority of older persons also live in the community, not in institutions, so that they are able to pursue the social activities common to their age group. Old age, for most, means a time of memories and reflection, as one's mental abilities recall experiences and, it is hoped, satisfactions from the past; it means a time to look forward to enjoying the years that are left in a mentally and physically healthy condition. Although future trends in longevity point toward greater numbers of mentally disordered elderly, they also point toward significantly greater numbers of mentally healthy aged.

SUMMARY

As people age, their cognitive functions tend to be slowed. Consequently, information processing, attention, learning, and memory abilities decline somewhat in old age. Declines in vision and hearing can contribute to this

---

1. Donna Cohen and Carl Eisdorfer, *The Loss of Self* (New York: W. W. Norton, 1986), 60.

situation. However, slowness of thought does not mean that older people are less intelligent; rather, it can take longer for them to process information. Moreover, the degree of cognitive slowing can be slight, and older people are able to function normally in most circumstances that do not demand speed, sustained effort, and memory. Experience and familiarity with their environment also helps to compensate for cognitive slowing and assists the aged in maintaining effective levels of functioning.

Mood disorders, specifically depressive disorders, are the most common form of mental illness among the aged, as they are among the population generally. The high prevalence of mood disorders among older people is related to the sense of loss (deaths of friends and loved ones, loss of status) that is common in old age. Suicide is also a particular problem for the elderly, especially for non-Hispanic white males, who have the highest suicide rates of any age group in American society. Dementia, which includes Alzheimer's disease as the major form, is the mental disorder most often associated with aging. Dementia affects women more than men, and its most prominent symptom is loss of memory. Dementia is not a normal feature of aging and causes severe cognitive impairment in only 3 percent of the aged population. An additional 5 to 10 percent have mild or moderate impairment. As people age, the potential for dementia increases, and some 15 percent of all elderly over the age of 85 are severely afflicted.

Chapter 7

THE AGED SELF

The focus of this chapter is on the perception of aging and its effects on the self-concept of the older person. How do aged persons view themselves? Are they different because they are old? Or are they essentially the same people they always were—just older? This chapter explores this aspect of the aging process by initially reviewing the literature in sociology on the concept of self and then extending the discussion to account for the self-images of the elderly in contemporary society.

THE SELF

The self is the image that the individual has of his or her self "as a physical, social, and spiritual or moral being" (Gecas 1982:3). The best-developed analysis of the concept of self in sociology is found in symbolic interaction theory, which is explicitly focused on the study of micro-level social relationships. The contributions of George Herbert Mead, Charles Horton Cooley, and Erving Goffman provide the foundation for this approach and are reviewed in this section. A discussion of the self-concept in old age follows.

Mead

Symbolic interaction theory, as introduced in Chapter 4, has its origin in the work of George Herbert Mead (1863–1931) in social psychology at the University of Chicago in the early twentieth century. Mead advocated, in *Mind, Self, and Society* (1934), that the concept of "self" refers to an individual's awareness of being a distinct entity in society. In other words, the self is the awareness that one is a particular individual, distinct and different from other people, but nonetheless part of the same society. Mead explained, however, that a sense of self is not present at birth; rather, it arises in the process of social experience, as people relate to other individuals and the wider society. In this way individuals gain an understanding of themselves and their place as particular persons in the larger social order.

A child is born into a family of significant others who are significant because they provide that child with a specific social identity. This identity includes not only a name and an appraisal of physical and intellectual characteristics, but also knowledge concerning the social history of a particular family and group, with all that means in terms of social status, worldview, and cultural background. People become social objects to themselves as they experience how they are viewed by other people and the social group, community, or society as a whole to which they belong. Thus individuals gain a sense of who they are through interacting with other people and experiencing the manner in which others respond to them socially and they, in turn, respond to others. They may not necessarily be passive in this exchange when it comes to asserting their sense of who they are, but definitions by others are a central component in formulating one's own concept of self.

Yet Mead points out that, in order for the self to develop in its fullest sense, it is necessary not only to take on the attitudes of other individuals directed toward the self as a social object, but also to acquire the attitudes of the group and society in which the person holds membership. To accomplish this, the individual has to learn to take the role of others; that is, to develop the capability to comprehend a situation from the standpoint of other people.

Mead illustrates the process by which this happens in his discussion of play, the game, and the generalized other. When children play at being mothers, fathers, astronauts, and the like, they are in essence acting out what they perceive to be the roles of those kinds of people. Thus, through play, they learn that certain roles represent specific types of behavior. When children become older, they begin to play in organized games that have formal rules that apply to everyone. In order to play a game correctly, the child must understand his or her role in relation to the roles of the other players. When playing baseball, for example, a player must know how the other players are supposed to play their positions if he or she is going to play according to the rules and be part of the team. When members of a team come to know and understand one another's roles, they can anticipate one another's play and capitalize on this familiarity to react collectively to situations that develop during the game.

Insofar as the child is able to understand the roles of others and allow the actions and attitudes of these others to influence his or her role with reference to common goals, the child is well on the way to developing a distinct sense of self and becoming a socialized member of society. Realization about specific roles and attitudes is followed by recognition of the more widespread roles and attitudes. Peter Berger and Thomas Luckmann describe this development as follows:

> Primary socialization creates in the child's consciousness a progressive abstraction from the roles and attitudes of specific others to roles and attitudes in *general*. For example, in the internalization of norms there is a progression from "Mummy is angry with me *now*" to "Mummy is angry with me *whenever* I spill soup." As additional significant others (father, grandmother, older sister, and so on) support the mother's negative attitude toward soup-spilling, the generality of the norm is subjectively extended. The decisive step comes when the child recognizes that *everybody* is against soup-spilling, and the norm is generalized to "*One* does not spill soup"—"one" being himself as part of a generality that includes, in principle, *all* of society insofar as it is significant to the child.[1]

At this point, the child can identify not only with significant others (specific people), but also with a generalized other (defined as the attitudes of a society, community, or group as a whole). The generalized other is not a person at all; rather, it is a conscious awareness of the society that exists outside of the individual. Mead states that it is in the form of the generalized other that a group or society influences behavior by entering as a determining factor into the individual's thinking. Thus Mead claims that the self reaches its fullest development by becoming a reflection of the general social system or group to which the person belongs.

Mead makes a further distinction about the self by describing what he surmises are the self's two basic components: (1) the "I" (the unsocialized self) and (2) the "me" (the socialized self). The "me" is that part of the self that is conscious of the norms, values, and traditions of society; it governs the "I" in such a manner that the self reflects the influence of the generalized other. At times, however, the "I," which is that part of the self that is selfish,

---

1. Peter L. Berger and Thomas Luckmann, *The Social Construction of Reality* (New York: Anchor, 1967), 132–133.

impulsive, and oriented toward self-fulfillment, takes over and directs behavior toward purely individual ends. Consequently, the self may embrace behavior that conforms to social expectations and collective interests, or it may pursue its own self-interest even if it is at the expense of the group. Nevertheless, as Herbert Blumer (1969) explains, in asserting that the human being has a self, Mead is pointing out that people are able to perceive themselves as social objects, to communicate with themselves, and to act toward themselves and others on the basis of their own self-direction.

Cooley

Charles Horton Cooley (1864–1929), Mead's contemporary at the University of Michigan, further illustrates the development of the self with his theory of the "looking-glass self." Cooley (1964) likewise maintained that self-concepts are the result of social interaction in which people see themselves reflected in the meanings and evaluations that other people attach to them as social objects. Cooley compares the reflection of self that people see in others to a reflection in a mirror, or looking glass:

> Each to each a looking glass
> Reflects the other that doth pass.

What Cooley is describing is a form of self-consciousness in which the individual becomes aware of his or her self in relation to others by imagining what he or she looks like to others. Cooley's looking-glass self-concept has three basic components: (1) people see themselves in their imagination as they think they appear to the other person; (2) they see in their imagination the other person's judgment of their appearance; and (3) as a result of what they see in their imagination about how they are viewed by the other person, they experience some sort of self-feeling, such as pride, satisfaction, or humiliation. Consequently, an individual's perception of self as a social being is strongly related to the reactions of other people. The second element in the theory of the looking-glass self—the imagined judgment by others—is, in Cooley's view, quite essential to the formulation of an individual's concept of self. The way people *think* they appear to others is a major basis for their self-image.

Goffman

Erving Goffman (1922–1982), who was on the faculty of the University of California at Berkeley and the University of Pennsylvania, is noted for the dramaturgical, or "life as theater," approach in sociology. The symbolic interaction orientation is obvious in Goffman's (1959, 1967) belief that, in order for social interaction to be viable, people need information about other people in social situations. Such information is communicated through (1) a person's appearance, (2) a person's experience with other similar individuals, (3) the social setting, and (4) most important, the information a person communicates about himself or herself through words, gestures, and actions. This fourth category of information is decisive because it is subject to control by the individual and represents the impression the person is trying to project—the impression others may come to accept. This information is significant because it helps to define a situation by enabling others to know in advance what a person expects of them and what they may expect of him or her. Goffman calls this process *impression management.*

Goffman says that people live in worlds of social encounters in which they act out a line of behavior, a pattern of verbal and nonverbal acts by which individuals express their view of a situation and their evaluation of the participants, particularly themselves. The positive social value that individuals claim for themselves by the line that others assume they have taken during a particular encounter is termed a "face." This face is an image of self projected to other people who may share that face. One's face is one's most personal possession and is the center of security and pleasure, but Goffman is quick to point out that a person's face is only on loan to him or her from society and can be withdrawn if the person conducts himself or herself in a manner others deem as being unworthy. A person may be in the "wrong face" when information about that person's social worth cannot be integrated into his or her line of behavior, or a person may be "out of face" when he or she participates in an encounter without the line of behavior of the type that participants in that particular situation would be expected to take.

Goffman further explains that the maintenance of face is a condition of interaction, not its objective. This is so because one's face is a constant factor taken for granted in interaction. When people engage in "face-work," they are taking action to make their activities consistent with the face they are projecting. This is important because every member of a social group is expected to have some knowledge of face-work and some experience in its use, such as the exercise of social skills like tact. Goffman sees almost all acts involving other people as being influenced by considerations of face; for example, a person is given a chance to quit a job rather than be fired. A person must be aware of the interpretations that others have placed on his or her behavior and the interpretations that he or she should place on their behavior. Therefore, Goffman's view of the self is that it has two distinct roles in social interactions: first, the self as an image of a person formed from the flow of events in an encounter; and second, the self as a kind of player in a ritual game who copes judgmentally with a situation.

Goffman claims that the self is a sacred object. This is because the self represents *who* we are. For someone to challenge the integrity of that self as a social object is an embarrassing situation. Each self is special; it is always with us; and in social relationships, that very special self we have tried to nourish and protect for a lifetime is put on display. Goffman has said that role-specific behavior is based not on the functional requirements of a particular role, but on the *appearance* of having discharged a role's requirements. Thus stress could be induced when people perceive their chosen face or performance in a given situation to be inconsistent with the concept of self they try to maintain for themselves and others in that situation. Otherwise, people might not be so willing to take such great care that they act out lines of behavior considered appropriate to their situation.

What the work of Goffman, Cooley, and Mead signifies for an understanding of the concept of self is that people have an image in their mind about who they are in relation to other people in terms of their appearance, social standing, role relationships, personal qualities, and other attributes. They acquire this sense of self through interactions with others in which they display their self-image and test its validity. Their self-concept thus becomes the basis on which they see themselves and present themselves to others. In a very real sense, people are social objects interacting with other people in social situations in which their behavior is guided by their sense of self. Self-concepts are extremely important to each person; they influence a person's course of action and are important in understanding and predicting behavior. We will now discuss what aging does to one's self-concept.

AWARENESS OF AGING

In analyzing how older age affects the self-concept of adults, a brief review of the manner in which old age begins to present itself to the individual is in order. As Lynn White (1988) explains, although growing older may have positive and pleasurable aspects, it is unarguable that aging is associated with declines in physical condition and appearance. Old age is also associated with a loss of more youthful social roles.

Physical Losses and Denial

People who are aging typically experience reduced energy, weight gain, higher fat-to-body-weight ratios, thinner hair, increasingly loose skin, and worsening teeth, hearing, and vision. And, as White (1988) and others (Korthase and Trenholme 1982; Stokes 1992) point out, such changes are generally regarded as reductions in attractiveness. "The evidence," states

White (1988:488), "seems to make it clear that aging is associated not simply with changes but with *declines* in performance and attractiveness." Aging is most apparent in one's appearance. The skin becomes dryer, wrinkles, and begins to sag; hair thins or falls out; and excess weight, beginning especially in middle age, may appear. All of these conditions go against prevailing standards of attractiveness in Western society, where pleasing, youthful looks and a physically fit body are the norm for beauty, and beauty, in turn, is a form of status.

Murray Webster and James Driskell (1983), for instance, found in their research that not only is it considered better to be beautiful than ugly, but people who possess a high state of attractiveness are considered more competent as well. Even though no direct relationship between doing things well and beauty may exist, more attractive people were simply *assumed* by the Webster and Driskell sample of college students to have more ability. In other words, because they looked good, they were thought to be able to cope better in most situations. Because normative standards of beauty may be equated with status, failure to measure up promotes lower status, although clothing, cosmetics, hairstyle, and a strong or interesting personality can help otherwise plain people become attractive. But when it comes to beauty per se, old people are able to sense that they are at a distinct disadvantage. As Malcolm Cowley (1980:7), in his book on what it is like to be 80 years old, comments, sometimes when old people look at themselves in the mirror, they ask themselves, "Is this really me?"

Declines in sensory acuity, such as hearing and vision, although perhaps not always as obvious as the loss of physical attractiveness, nevertheless may influence an older person's sense of self. Hearing changes in old age include a decreased ability to hear higher-frequency sounds and pitches, discriminate between sounds, and determine where sound emanates from. There may also be a decreased sensitivity to touch, smell, and taste. Older people, for example, may have difficulty detecting sweet and salty tastes because of decreased numbers of taste buds; hence, they may use large amounts of sugar or salt to compensate for the loss. Visual changes include a decrease in pupil size (which decreases the amount of light entering the eye), reduced night vision, decreased sensitivity to subtle changes in colors (especially greens and blues), increased sensitivity to glare, and a decrease in the ability to discriminate fine visual detail, perceive depth, and have good peripheral vision. Cowley describes the effects on an 80-year-old person as follows:

> We don't have to read books in order to learn that one's eighties are a time of gradually narrowing horizons. Partly the narrowing is literal and physical, being due to a loss of peripheral vision: "Incipient cataracts," the oculist says.

Trees on a not-so-distant hillside are no longer oaks or maples, but merely a blur. It is harder to distinguish faces in a crowd—and voices, too, especially if several persons are speaking at once. Would you like to see or hear by drawing closer? Your steps are less assured, your sense of balance is faulty; soon you hesitate to venture beyond your own street or your home acres. Travel becomes more difficult and you think twice about taking out the car.[2]

Other changes in old age, as discussed in Chapter 6, involve the central nervous system. These include a slowing of psychomotor responses, reaction times, and performance of complex tasks. Short-term and recent memory loss takes place in many older people; learning performance and attention also tend to decline with age.

Another important area of change involves sexuality. Older men take longer to become sexually aroused and ejaculate; the latency period between intercourse takes longer, perhaps several days; and erections may be less firm. Older women, in turn, experience less vaginal lubrication and a reduction in breast and vaginal engorgement and nipple erection during sexual stimulation. However, the elderly do not lose the ability to have sexual intercourse. The best single predictor of an ongoing sex life when old is the pattern of one's sex life when young (Barash 1983; Masters, Johnson, and Kolodny 1992). As Helen Singer Kaplan (1974) explains, elderly men remain potentially responsive to sexual stimulation, especially if active sexuality has been maintained over the years. Kaplan further points out:

> As far as the purely sexual functions are concerned, some men compensate for their age-related decline in sexuality by seeking out and creating intensely stimulating erotic situations, fantasies and partners. They may avail themselves of sexual techniques that rely heavily on intense physical stimulation of genitals and of erogenous areas. Other men, by contrast, cease having sexual intercourse in their fifties and sixties. This abstinence is, of course, not purely a function of the physical effects of age, but rather a psychological avoidance of the painful feelings of frustration, anxiety, or depression that may be elicited by confrontation with their declining performance. Impotence is a frequent complaint in this age group.[3]

As for older women, Kaplan indicates that following a peak period of sexual responsiveness in their late thirties and early forties, women move into the menopausal years of the fifties. At this point there is an abrupt cessation of ovarian functioning and drastic decline in the secretion of estrogen and progesterone. In some women, these endocrine changes produce irri-

---

2. Malcolm Cowley, *The View from 80* (New York: Viking Press, 1980), 54.
3. Helen Singer Kaplan, *The New Sex Therapy* (New York: Quadrangle, 1974), 109.

tability, depression, and emotional instability. Other women are not emotionally affected by menopause. Sexual responsiveness at this time, as in the earlier ages in women, varies among individuals. After menopause, Kaplan summarizes female sexuality for women in their sixties as follows:

> A woman who has regular sexual opportunity tends to maintain her sexual responsiveness; without such opportunity, sexuality declines markedly. Apart from the effect of opportunity, a slow gradual physical decline in sexual drive seems to occur in women as in men. After 65, a women tends to be less preoccupied with sex than she was at 40, but still may seek out and certainly can respond to sexual opportunities.[4]

Thus people can maintain and enjoy an active sex life in old age. Old age nonetheless means a change—a decline—in sexual responsiveness at some point for both men and women. Moreover, as David Barash (1983) points out, regardless of how the elderly feel about sex, the young seem to be uncomfortable about sexuality in the elderly. Sexually active aged men may be depicted as lewd and reprehensible ("a dirty old man") by younger adults, and sexuality in old women is traditionally regarded, according to Barash's analysis, as laughable. Negative stereotypes such as these, combined with evidence of a declining capacity for sex, might well contribute to a devaluation of self in a youth- and sex-oriented culture.

White (1988) studied awareness of physical aging among men and women ages 20 to 60 in a national sample of over 1,500 persons. These persons were initially interviewed in 1980 and were then asked in 1983 whether, in the last three years, either they or their spouse had experienced a change for the worse in eyesight, hearing, teeth, energy, hair, and skin. White found, as expected, that the perception of physical aging increases with age. However, women were generally no more sensitive than men to signs of physical aging. Rather, there were more similarities than differences in the ways that men and women perceived themselves as becoming old. This finding led White to conclude that both sexes become aware of aging in much the same way and to reject the notion that women are more sensitive to aging than men.

White also found that people tend to maintain relatively youthful images of themselves for as long as they can; that is, they tend to deny the physical evidence of aging for as long as possible. White's (1988:500) findings supported earlier research by Zena Blau (1956) "that awareness of aging is a change in self-concept that is avoided as long as positive responses from our social environment make such avoidance possible."

4. Ibid., 112.

Although White's sample did not include persons over the age of 65, her findings regarding the tendency to deny signs of aging in one's appearance are consistent with the results of other studies that included samples of the elderly. This research depicts older Americans as tending to reject the idea for as long as possible that they are old (Bultena and Powers 1978; Drevenstedt 1976; Rosow 1974).

For example, Gordon Bultena and Edward Powers (1978) studied 611 people in Iowa in 1960 and returned in 1970 to restudy 235 of the original respondents. Most of the remainder had either died or moved away. The median age of people in the restudy group was 76, and more than one-fourth were over age 80. Bultena and Powers found that a majority rejected the idea that they were old. Instead, many defined themselves as middle-aged; a few said they were simply elderly. Irving Rosow (1974) likewise found that older people often refuse to acknowledge that they are old; the older they are, the later they claimed that "old age" begins. Or, as one senior citizen put it, "To me old age is always fifteen years older than I am" (Rosow 1974:11).

In sum, old age is a time of physical decline and loss of youthful body. Resistance to the idea of a less attractive physical self appears to underline, as suggested by White (1988), tendencies among the elderly to deny old age for as long as possible. Signs of physical aging present a clear threat to the self-image of many of the elderly.

Social Losses

Rosow (1974) explains that old age is also the only stage of life that has systematic social losses rather than gains. When one is elderly, the major tasks in life, such as having a career and starting a family, are finished. Thus an older person's responsibilities decline, whereas dependence on others because of reduced income or physical and mental infirmities may increase. Roles for the elderly include those of being (1) retired, (2) widowed, (3) an aged dependent, or (4) chronically ill. As Harold Cox (1996) reminds us, these roles are not highly valued, nor do they bring high status. Moreover, there is not a specific role meant for the elderly in developed countries that confers enhanced status in the wider society as a result of age alone. Also, in U.S. society people are not typically socialized to experience decline. Thus Rosow argues that the elderly are not prepared by society for the inevitable social losses that old age brings, nor are they taught how to lead a dignified life within the limitations of advanced age. "With no incentives or compelling pressures from the culture to embrace their age," states Rosow (1974: 148), "and no meaningful norms by which to live, they simply are not socialized to an aged role."

However, Robert Atchley (1994) observes that Rosow's argument about society's not socializing the elderly for participation in a particular role of "old person" is not an entirely accurate description of role relationships among the aged. Atchley points out that elderly persons usually have few required contacts with the general community. Instead, they associate on a daily basis primarily with people they know and who know them. Typically, they continue to function in their usual roles in the family and in their networks of friends; they are just older. Therefore, Atchley makes the important point that most roles older people perform are roles they have experienced for a long time.

Furthermore, the role of retirement for the elderly may be enjoyable and provide greater freedom to pursue one's personal interests. In fact, the elderly have greater freedom of choice and a wider range of choices about how to spend their time than any other age group in the United States (Keith et al. 1994; MacNeil and Teague 1987). Therefore, although the aged may not generally fill roles of great power and influence because of their age, old age does have its compensations, and the effect of role loss in the wider community can mean a greater preoccupation with one's self and private activities.

SOCIETY'S VIEW OF THE AGED

Many past studies, as will be discussed, suggest that society's general view of the aged, at least in the Western world, tends to be negative. According to Rosow (1974), the position of the elderly has several consequences; namely, that they are devalued, are negatively stereotyped, are excluded from social opportunities, lose roles, confront severe ambiguity in later life because they have no specific role, and struggle to preserve self-esteem through youthful self-images. The crux of the problem, indicates Rosow, is not that the elderly do not have role models, but that such models are primarily youthful. Rosow explains:

> The elderly judge themselves according to standards of youthfulness. This implies norms of minimal change, or preserving roles, activity, health, energy, beauty, vitality, and élan. The best life is presumably that which changes least from middle age. This minimal change increases their chances of retaining social position, participation, prestige, and other advantages of middle age.[5]

5. Irving Rosow, *Socialization to Old Age* (Berkeley: University of California Press, 1974), 146.

Because the aged generally do not perform vitally important functions for a society that emphasizes youth, aged persons typically reach the point in their lives when their importance wanes. As Rosow points out, the most youthful and well-preserved aged are the most admired among the general public. When older people look less well-preserved, their social worth is likely to decline. "Older people's youthful self-conceptions," states Rosow (1974: 147), "contrast sharply with younger persons' treatment of them." In other words, the elderly may regard themselves as middle-aged, but younger persons may see them as old. Eventually, flattering self-images of youthfulness by older people are challenged. Rosow asks that, if the elderly view themselves as middle-aged, whereas others see them as old, what is the social reality of the situation? He answers this by claiming that the standards that govern are those of youth. Therefore, if older people are perceived and treated as elderly by younger people, their social position becomes established.

Cowley (1980) explains that, although many older people like to think of themselves as still young, messages from the social environment are louder, in most cases, than those from within the person. "We start growing old in other people's eyes," states Cowley (1980:5), "then slowly we come to share their judgment." Cowley provides an example of this situation by relating his feelings when he almost had a collision with another automobile and the driver of the other car jumped out and started to yell at him until he got a good look at him. The angry motorist then said, "Why, you're an old man!" and got back in his car and drove away. Then a young woman offered him her seat on a bus. Although the offer was meant to be kind, Cowley found it devastating. Cowley states:

> "Can't I even stand up?" I thought as I thanked her and declined the seat. But the same thing happened twice the following year, and the second time I gratefully accepted the offer, though with a sense of having diminished myself. . . . All the same it was a relief to sit down and relax.[6]

Humor can also be an important indicator of social attitudes, because it often reflects widely held social stereotypes. Erdman Palmore (1971) studied attitudes toward aging as suggested by humor. Some 264 jokes were singled out and analyzed to indicate prevalent societal attitudes. Over half of the jokes reflected a negative view of aging, the most disparaging being those whose principal subject matter was physical ability, appearance, age concealment, mental abilities, and being an "old maid." The majority of jokes about being a male "old timer" and still having sexual ability were either positive or ambiva-

6. Cowley, *The View from 80*, 5–6.

lent. Jokes dealing with old men generally tended to be much more positive than those dealing with old women; in fact, most of the age-concealment jokes referred to women. This study suggested that (1) the popular culture generally devalues old age, and (2) a double standard may exist in which aging women are viewed more negatively than aging men.

The so-called double standard in aging may be related to sex-role stereotypes in American society that equate female beauty and sexuality with youth. With few exceptions, aged women are not depicted in the popular culture as "beautiful," but aged men may be more likely to be considered "handsome" or "distinguished." Instances of older men marrying young women, for example, tend to be more common than older women marrying young men.

The groups in society that appear to hold the most negative views of old people are young and middle-aged adults. By contrast, past studies involving children find little evidence of devaluation of old age. In a review of children's literature, Mildred Seltzer and Robert Atchley (1971) found little evidence of negativity toward aging. Elizabeth Thomas and Kaoru Yamamoto (1975) found a rather positive attitude toward the aged in a study of children and adolescents. There was general agreement that older people were "good" and "wise," and the qualities of being "pleasant," "happy," and "exciting" were seen to decrease with age but were nonetheless present in old age. Only on the qualities of being "active" and having "power" were the elderly rated negatively. Thomas and Yamamoto suggest that, rather than developing negative attitudes toward aging in childhood, what apparently happens is that people acquire negative stereotypes of aging as they themselves begin to feel threatened by old age.

The above discussion, however, pertains to conditions in Western society. In Asia, the elderly typically occupy a position of respect and honor largely because of the lingering influence of Confucianism and the tradition of ancestor worship. In the Confucian system of social relations, a clearly defined order of superiority-subordination guided behavior. This system subordinated the young to the old, females to males, and subjects to rulers. Although the Confucian system was overturned in China and North Korea by communism, and in South Korea and Japan through rapid industrialization and capitalism, the cultural traditions it fostered persist. In China today, the old are not left to live alone but are expected to remain in the family setting and serve in an honored role. To be old is to be accorded greater respect in Chinese society, for age is equated with wisdom (Fairbank 1989). Japan has a national holiday, Respect for the Elders Day, which honors the aged; the sixty-first birthday is also a time to be honored by the family. The young are taught to be respectful to the old, and seats are reserved on buses and trains for aged citizens. In many Asian countries, approximately three-fourths of the elderly population live with their children (Hermalin 1995; Martin 1988). Although the reality of actual living conditions for many of the elderly in Asia may be less than ideal, their social role is equated with much higher status than in the West.

The stereotypes of old age in the United States have, in the past, emphasized characteristics like economic insecurity, poor health, loneliness, rigid attitudes, and failing physical and mental powers. Despite the fact that the majority of the elderly have not been poor, lonely, in bad health, senile, or mentally ill (Atchley 1994; Neugarten 1970, 1971) negative stereotypes have tended to persist (Larson 1978; Stokes 1992; Ward 1979). Keeping in mind that the current generation of the elderly in the United States is better educated and more economically affluent than past generations, there are signs that negative stereotypes are beginning to change. Robert Binstock (1983) has found that the stereotypical views of elderly people have changed from the 1970s' characterization of them as poor, frail, politically powerless, and victimized by mandatory retirement and a youth-oriented society. In the 1980s, Binstock observed that a view of the elderly emerged that depicted them as relatively affluent, politically powerful, and receiving more than their fair share of the federal budget.

Binstock's findings identify a potential change in social perceptions of older people. As America passes through the 1990s into the twenty-first century, the image of the aged may well be different from and exceedingly more positive than what most of the past literature suggests. This changing perspective is likely to be influenced by the significantly larger population of elderly persons, their more prominent role in influencing national politics, and their greater economic resources. An adjustment for the better thus appears to be coming in society's view of the aged.

This development is consistent with modernization theory. As discussed in Chapter 4, modernization theory holds that the status of the elderly will improve in mature modern states as these societies come to terms with their aged populations (Cowgill 1986). As noted, this is especially likely to be the case as the aged accumulate political power and economic influence by virtue of their large numbers and proportions in developed societies. Modernization theory is an important perspective on aging for understanding the aged self, because it explains how and why developed societies have formulated negative norms and values concerning old people and their social roles. In societies oriented toward achievement, activity, and productivity, the aged typically do not fill important positions or contribute strongly to mainstream economic activities. Occupying not only a less desirable, but also an actually devalued, social position relegates the aged to a marginal position in such societies. Consequently, the view of self in old age is operationalized in a less than positive social environment. However, modernization theory suggests that this environment is going to change with a maturing of the process of modernity. This means that the general social context in which elderly people find themselves in the future is likely to be increasingly supportive of positive views of the aged.

The Aged's View of Themselves

A review of the research literature shows that a few older studies (Mason 1954; Rosow 1967) found low feelings of self-worth and well-being among the aged. However, the bulk of the research indicates that the elderly have a generally positive impression of themselves. For example, Caroline Preston (1967) compared the attitudes of retired and nonretired older people and found no significant differences between the two groups in terms of life satisfaction. She suggested that the aged felt more positive about themselves than had previously been assumed. Other research (Riley and Foner 1968) suggests that negative orientations toward the self tend to decrease with age.

Bernice Neugarten (1971) in turn argued that a major problem with many past studies had been to try to generalize that most old are either unhappy or happy. These generalizations failed to take into account considerable variance among individuals in their coping with the aging experience. Neugarten pointed out that the aged in American society are not a homogeneous group. She demonstrated this in a 15-year longitudinal study at the University of Chicago on the adaptational patterns of about 2,000 people aged 70 to 79. Three principal areas of life among the aged were examined: personality, life satisfaction, and extent of social-role activity. As a result of their data, they were able to construct four major types of personalities common to the aged: (1) integrated, (2) defended, (3) passive-dependent, and (4) disintegrated.

The majority of these respondents were classified as having an *integrated* personality; that is, they were characterized as being high in life satisfaction, mature, and open to new experiences, and as having good cognitive abilities and a view of themselves as competent. The integrated personality consisted of three subtypes, each of which was based on the person's role activity. One subtype, termed the *reorganizers,* included those who engaged in a wide variety of activities, such as business and community affairs. The second subtype was classified as the *focused*; these were people who remained active, but only in a few select roles. The other subtype was the *disengaged,* people with well-integrated personalities who experienced satisfaction with their lives but demonstrated low activity. Members of this latter group had high self-esteem and appeared to be complex, self-directed individuals, yet they had voluntarily withdrawn from role commitments to be content with the "rocking chair" approach to old age.

The second major personality category was the *defended.* These were hard-driving, ambitious, achievement-oriented individuals who were very defensive about aging. The defended personality consisted of two major subtypes. First was the *holding-on* group, which continued to work hard and maintain relatively high levels of activity as a means of obtaining satisfaction from life. Next were those defended personalities described as *constricted.* Constricted individuals combated aging by trying very hard to maintain their health through diet and general activities, while also being oriented toward maintaining youthful physical appearance.

The third major personality was identified as *passive-dependent.* There were two subtypes common to this group. *Succorance-seeking* individuals had strong needs to be dependent and have other people respond to them. They were somewhat active and seemed to adjust to aging in a positive manner, as long as they had some other person or persons to depend on for assistance and support. The second subtype, of whom only a small number were found, was the *apathetic.* The primary characteristic of this person was passivity. These people had little interaction with others, engaged in few activities, and seemed to have little interest in what went on around them.

The fourth major personality type was the *disintegrated.* Very few people qualified for this category. The disintegrated personality consisted of people who demonstrated gross psychological disorganization and who were generally able to maintain themselves outside an institution only because of family arrangements or the tolerance of other people in their social network.

Although recognizing that other personality types common to patterns of aging may exist, Neugarten suggested two important conclusions about aging in American society. First, she pointed out that older people deal with aging in a number of ways. She was impressed by the fact that variation rather than similarity seems to be the rule among the aged, and she suggested that such variation may become even more pronounced in the future. This was so because, at the time of her study, most data on the aged were derived from people who tended to be poor, foreign born, and poorly educated. As Americans who have enjoyed the financial affluence and higher standards of education characteristic of the mid-twentieth century become old, she believed these people would have even greater freedom in selecting their lifestyles. And, second, she suggested that people age in accordance with the behavior that is generally typical of lifelong patterns of responses. In other words, people do not change their basic personality just because they grow old.

However, two variables that have been found to have a significant impact on the self-perceptions of older individuals are health and socio-economic status. Regardless of one's personality, a particularly significant variable affecting an individual's adjustment to old age is his or her level of health. As discussed in Chapter 5, one's health in old age is the single most important factor in determining the quality of life that is available. Aged persons in good health are invariably found to have a better quality of life and a more satisfying lifestyle, as well as a more optimistic outlook on life in general, than do those in poor health (Haug and Folmar 1986; Maddox 1962; Palmore 1981; Posner 1995).

For example, Preston (1968) studied older people who were about to retire. She found that those who reported more chronic health disorders and more incapacity due to illness showed a greater tendency to think of themselves as being "old" than those who did not report such health problems. In another study, Arthur Schwartz and Robert Kleemeier (1965) examined two groups of elderly people and two groups of young people who were categorized by age and state of health (sick or well). They noted that, among those who were sick, illness tended to have a greater effect on the self-perceptions of the aged than the young, but the relationship was due to the combined effects of illness and age, not just to age alone. Palmore (1981), in a series of longitudinal studies carried out at Duke University between 1955 and 1976 among a sample of aged persons living in North Carolina, found that high satisfaction with life contributed, in turn, to better health in that those who felt positive about life had a better mental outlook and were more prone to be physically and socially active.

The second variable that needs to be mentioned is socioeconomic status. As Arlie Russell Hochschild (1973) has observed, the assumption that old age is the great leveler because it affects the rich and poor alike is not necessarily true. It is much better to be old and rich than to be old and poor. The upper social classes tend to have a longer life expectancy than the lower classes. In effect, what Hochschild is saying is that, the shorter a person's life expectancy, the poorer that person's health and morale. Therefore, lower-class people may begin to "feel" old at progressively earlier ages than upper-class people. For instance, Caroline Preston and Karen Gudiken (1966) found that indigent older people expressed significantly more negative than positive feelings about themselves when they compared themselves with "others my age." Negative self-reporting among the indigent aged appeared to be a manifestation of depression. George Maddox (1962) also noted that social class position is related to optimism and pessimism about health. Older people of high social status were much more likely than other people to be optimistic about their health. Older people of low social status tended to be pessimistic about their health, even when they were medically assessed to be in good health. In sum, as Palmore (1981) found, persons with higher socioeconomic status have, on the whole, better physical and mental health, higher intelligence, greater happiness, and more social activities in old age.

Besides the effect of poverty on the health status and general outlook of the aged, the aged poor are more likely to be socially isolated. Rosow (1967) found that middle-class older people in Cleveland tended to have more good friends in old age than working-class older people had. Hochschild summarizes this situation as follows:

> Removed from the economy, the old have been cast out of the social networks that revolve around work. Lacking work, they are pushed down the social ladder. Being poor, they have fewer social ties. Poverty reinforces isolation. To eliminate enforced isolation, we have to eliminate poverty, for the two go together.[7]

However, to summarize the literature on the self-image of the aged held by the elderly, the overall situation seems to be that older people feel quite good about themselves. But health and socioeconomic status influence such perceptions, either positively or negatively, depending on one's level of health or income and lifestyle. On balance, most elderly people seem to define themselves in a positive manner and do so regardless of negative views of the aged prevalent in the wider society.

Personality Change in Old Age

As reported in the preceding section, Neugarten (1971) found that people do not change their basic personality as they age. This is an important finding and speaks directly to the issue of whether or not self-concepts differ in old age. According to continuity theory, discussed earlier in Chapter 4, the personality tends to remain stable over time. Continuity theorists, like Neugarten (1964), point out that, if changes in personality do occur, they tend to be minor. There may be some personality change in old age as people adapt to new situations, but the change is not likely to be great or out of character with the individual's past approach to life. As a person grows to maturity and passes on to the stages of later maturity and old age, he or she will have developed a stable set of values, attitudes, norms, and habits which have become an integral part of his or her personality. Therefore, if the personality undergoes change in old age, that change tends to be consistent with past

---

7. Arlie Russell Hochschild, *The Unexpected Community* (Englewood Cliffs, NJ: Prentice-Hall, 1973), 140.

traits and predispositions—unless the individual has never developed a stable personality.

Neugarten (1964) indicates that the *only* internal dimension of the personality that seems to change with age is introversion. Older people tend to turn their interests and attention more inward on themselves and less on external factors. This turning inward is not a withdrawal from the external world; rather, it appears to be just a greater emphasis on an inner life aimed at gaining greater self-understanding and self-acceptance. In old age, perhaps the person focuses more on placing his or her life in personal perspective.

The position that there is a large amount of continuity in the central features of one's personality appears correct; that is, one's basic personality is not likely to change greatly in old age from what it was as a younger adult (Atchley 1994; Stokes 1992). If a person had a positive self-image when young, he or she is likely to have a positive self-image when old. As Graham Stokes (1992) explains, psychological defenses such as denial tend to reduce threats to the older person's self-concept and maintain consistency in self-definition. This does not mean that concepts of self are not subjected to minor adjustments in order for new experiences and perceptions to be accommodated. Therefore, as Stokes (1992:97) observes, "despite the buffeting people are subjected to in later life as they experience a decline in personal competence and an erosion of their support network, self-definition is remarkably resilient to negative re-appraisal."

THE AGED SELF

The sociology literature on the concept of self, reviewed at the beginning of this chapter, discussed the work of Mead, Cooley, and Goffman. Mead (1934), described how the self is formed as a result of social experience and illustrated the evolution of the self with the example of play, the game, and the generalized other. Mead emphasized the importance of being able to take the role of others and recognize the existence of external norms, values, and attitudes that function as a generalized other in the person's thinking. Cooley (1964), with his concept of the looking-glass self, like Mead, emphasized the role of other people in influencing the individual's perception of self. People tend to incorporate into their self-image the image of themselves that they see reflected in others. This process would suggest that the elderly might tend to have a negative self-concept because of a declining physical condition, the loss of valued roles, or the prevalence of youthful norms.

Yet it should be noted that Mead's focus is on the self that emerges during childhood and adolescence as part of primary socialization. Cooley's insight also has particular relevance to the time in life when one's sense of self is being formed. In old age, the self is mature and rests on a lifetime of noting the responses of others. At this point, one's self-concept is likely to be entrenched, and feedback from significant others should be less important than when young.

The self that Goffman (1959, 1967) describes, however, is particularly relevant for the old as well as for the young. One of Goffman's central themes is that the self is a sacred object to individuals because it represents who and what we are. Thus people take particular care to nurture and protect their self-image by employing "face-work" during social interactions and letting conditions of "face" (both theirs and others') guide their behavior. Although this situation promotes the idea that the self is not a possession of the person, but rather is a product of the interaction between the person as an actor and his or her audience, Goffman points out in his essay on role distance (1961) that there is a distinctly personal side to people. It is the personal or sacred aspect of human conduct, states Goffman (1961:152), that "has to do with 'personal' matters and 'personal' relationships—with what an individual is 'really' like underneath it all when he relaxes and breaks through to those in his presence." In the profane and worldly part of one's behavior, Goffman sees the self as a player in a ritual game of social interaction, coping judgmentally with situations. People expose themselves to others and, as Goffman (1967:31) puts it, sometimes "lead themselves into duels," in which they take their shots from other people as they place their self-concept at risk in the game of life.

It would seem that the elderly likewise participate in the game of "life as theater," because aging also usually requires the older individual to defend a positive self-image. As Atchley (1994) explains, falling back on their past successes, discounting messages that do not fit their self-concept, and refusing to apply general beliefs about aging to themselves are all ways older people defend themselves against ageism. Atchley's basic point, as noted earlier, is that most people maintain a sense of themselves that reflects a positive level of esteem, and this level of esteem, based on past life experience, is not likely simply to disappear by virtue of old age alone. People who lose self-esteem in later life, notes Atchley, are those (1) whose physical condition has severely deteriorated, (2) who have become too dependent or whose life has become too restricted, or (3) who have lost control over their living situation so that they are essentially defenseless. As shown in numerous studies, most people have the resources to maintain a positive self-concept in old age (Atchley 1994). In fact, self-esteem often increases with age.

British author J. B. Priestley has suggested that in old age there is often a sharp break between how one feels and how one looks, as if the older person is forced by society to adopt a false identity—that of an elderly person—even if they do not feel old. British sociologists Mike Featherstone and Mike Hepworth (1990) refer to this process as the "mask of aging," in which the aged person's appearance conceals an essentially youthful identity. They cite Priestley's work to illustrate their point:

> It is as though [states Priestley], walking down Shaftesbury Avenue as a fairly young man, I was suddenly kidnapped, rushed into a theater and made to do the grey hair, the wrinkles and the other attributes of age, then wheeled on stage. Behind the appearance of age I am the same person, with the same thoughts, as when I was younger.[8]

Other research in Britain likewise finds that many old people do not think of themselves as elderly—despite the fact that they have physically aged. For example, one 80-year-old woman reported that "I don't feel my age. It's just my legs that feel old, not me head. I don't feel nearly eighty" (Thompson, Itzin, and Abendstern 1991:112). British sociologist Jane Pilcher (1995) points out that older people often do not use their appearance and the functional ability of their aged body to determine their own subjective age. "To this extent," observes Pilcher (1995:104), "signs of old age can be understood as a mask or disguise, which acts to influence younger people's attitudes and behaviour toward old people and conceal the individuality of old people themselves."

Two excellent studies that aptly describe the aged self are those of Sharon Kaufman (1987) and Walter Gove, Suzanne Ortega, and Carolyn Briggs Style (1989). In her book *The Ageless Self,* Kaufman reports on the results of her two-year study of some 60 urban, white, middle-class Americans between the ages of 70 and 97 living in California. Although her data may not be representative of all elderly people—namely, the poor and racial minorities—her findings are nonetheless highly suggestive of how the self may generally cope with aging. Kaufman's central theme is that the self is indeed ageless. The old people in her study expressed a personal identity that had maintained continuity over the life span, regardless of the physical and social changes that came with old age. In other words, they defined themselves as being essentially the same person they were when younger; they had only gotten older. For example, one woman, age 92, was asked whether she felt differently about herself than when she was younger. The woman replied:

---

8. Mike Featherstone and Mike Hepworth, "Images of Ageing," in *Ageing in Society*, ed. J. Bond and P. Coleman (London: Sage, 1990), 253.

No, not too differently from the way I felt before. Except that I tire more readily. But the fact is, one isn't a different person, though perhaps some personality traits do become more pronounced.

I always think of myself as younger, though not at any specific age, just at some time in the past. Whenever I'm walking downtown, and see my reflection in a store window, I'm shocked by how old it is. I never think of myself that way.[9]

Responses from other elderly persons reflected the same perspective. From a man, age 78:

Psychologically, I don't think I'm any different than I was when I was a young man. I haven't got the fire and ambition that I had in those days, but outside of that, I don't think I'm radically different.[10]

From another man, age 92:

No. I have the same attitude now, toward life and living, as I did 30 years ago. That's why this idea of not being able to walk along with other people—I'm more slowed down—it hurts my ego. Because inside, that's not really me.[11]

Another man, age 81:

I can see that there are certain traits in me that have carried through from youth to now. A conservative attitude, a wish to conform to the law, to pressures. And, I've always been cheerful. I still am. I mean I don't wake up with a gloomy or grumpy attitude. And I do like to be busy; I have always been friendly. I still feel that way.[12]

A woman, age 84:

I feel the same now as I did then, oh yes. The only way I know I'm getting old is to look in the mirror. But I've only *felt* old a few times—when I'm really sick.[13]

Consequently, Kaufman advances the notion that old people maintain a sense of continuity with their past lives that helps them cope with changes that occur with advanced age. They stay the same (in their mind), but their

9. Sharon R. Kaufman, *The Ageless Self* (Madison: University of Wisconsin Press, 1987), 9.

10. Ibid.

11. Ibid., 11.

12. Ibid.

13. Ibid., 13.

body becomes old. The factors that figured most prominently in influencing the lives of the elderly people in Kaufman's study over the life course included socioeconomic status in childhood (many had originally come from poor families; others began life in relatively affluent circumstances), family ties, level of education, geographic mobility (where they had lived), and work (their occupation or profession). These factors, along with their own personal values and goals, gave them a sense of who they were—regardless of the fact that they were now old. Kaufman concluded:

> All research participants made it clear to me that *aging* per se is not a substantive issue in their own lives. They do not, now that they are over 70, conceive of themselves in a context of *aging* and act accordingly. Rather, they deal with specific problems, changes, and disabilities as they arise, just as they have been doing throughout their lives, and they interpret these changes and problems in light of already established themes. It appears that the concept of aging is too abstract, too impersonal to be an integral part of identity. This is not to say that my informants ignore or deny limitations which arise in that process. Nor does it mean that the changes experienced in old age have no psychological effects. But while dealing with the physical and mental manifestations of old age, old people also maintain an ageless sense of self that transcends change by providing continuity and meaning.[14]

Successful adaptation to old age, in Kaufman's view, involves older individuals' connecting meaningful past experiences with current circumstances. Thus being old does not mean adopting a new self-concept; instead, older people take their sense of self and personality with them to the last stage of life and adapt to the situation as best they can. Kaufman's message is that the elderly do not perceive meaning in aging itself; rather, they perceive meaning in being themselves in old age.

The Gove, Ortega, and Briggs Style (1989) study consisted of a national survey of nearly 2,250 adults, 18 years of age and older. Gove and his colleagues determined that, as people age, their self-concepts are not qualitatively different from those of younger persons, except that they may feel somewhat more positive about themselves, have fewer negative attitudes, and be somewhat better integrated individuals. Moreover, both males and females appear to experience their sense of aging in similar ways. As in the Kaufman study, the general impression of Gove and his associates was that as people age they become increasingly comfortable with themselves and their situation. "There is no evidence," states Gove and colleagues (1989: 1138), "that old age is associated with a poor evaluation of one's self and one's life."

14. Ibid., 161.

A major contribution of Gove and colleagues' research was to reject a role theory of aging. Briefly stated, the role theory of aging maintains that the degree to which people have a meaningful existence over the life course is dependent on their social roles. Young adulthood is a time of role acquisition; then in late middle age a person moves into a position of role transition, followed in old age by role loss. Because a person's self-esteem is associated with his or her roles, that person's sense of self would be more positive at younger adult ages and then decline with age because of role loss.

However, because Gove and his associates found that one's sense of self did not decline in old age, a role theory of aging did not provide an adequate explanation of the self-concepts of the aged. Instead, Gove and associates suggest that there is an adult psychological maturation process in old age, in which the aged person moves from an absorption with self, characteristic of younger and middle-aged people, toward an acceptance of one's being. Gove and associates note that their findings are consistent with Erik Erikson's (1963) concept of the last stage of life, known as ego integrity. In the stage of ego integrity, there is an acceptance of one's fate and a sense of continuity with earlier stages of one's life. The person looks inward and attempts to gain a sense of meaning and integrity at the end of life. Cowley, in the conclusion to his book *The View from 80,* captures this feeling very well:

> There are tangible aids to remembering, notably letters, old snapshots, day-books, and mementos, if we have saved them. Old tunes ring through our heads and some of them bring back pictures; this one was "our" song, Doris said, and you see the look on her face when she hummed the words. What became of Doris after she married somebody else and moved to California? And Mr. Wagner, the boss who used to dance the gazotsky at office parties? Characters crowd in on us, each making a contribution, and gradually our world takes shape. We tell stories about it, perhaps only to ourselves, and then arrange the stories in sequence: this must have been our second act and this was the third. All these efforts, if continued, might lead to an absolutely candid book of memoirs; old persons have nothing to lose by telling the truth. For others it might lead to nothing more than notebook jottings and advice to the young that might or might not be remembered. No matter: it is a fascinating pursuit in itself, and our efforts will not have been wasted if they help us to possess our own identities as an artist possesses his work. At least we can say to the world of the future, or to ourselves if nobody else will listen, "I really *was*"—or even, with greater self-confidence, "I was and am *this.*"[15]

15. Cowley, *The View from 80,* 73–74.

SUMMARY

At the beginning of this chapter, the following was asked: How do aged persons view themselves? Are they different because they are old? Or are they essentially the same person they always were—just older? The answer would appear to be that the self is ageless; in other words, the elderly have essentially the same self-concept they had when younger. Their physical bodies will have changed with age, and perhaps certain adjustments in their sense of self may have been made to accommodate the fact that they have become old; but overall it appears that they remain in their mind the same person they were when younger. In effect, the continuity of their lives from childhood into old age provides them with a full sense of who and what they are.

This chapter began with a review of the concept of self in sociology and social psychology as expressed by Mead, Cooley, and Goffman. Mead explains how the self is formed during childhood as a result of social interaction with significant others and develops through play and games to a realization of the generalized other. The generalized other refers not to a person but to the attitudes, norms, and values of an organized group, community, or society as a whole. Cooley is known for his theory of the looking-glass self, which helps us to understand that individuals see themselves reflected in other people, which plays an important role in the formation of their own self-concept. Goffman, through his notion of face-work, explains the manner in which people nourish, display, and protect their sense of self. Goffman, representing the "life as theater" approach, explains that people put their sense of self at risk as they confront social situations.

The problem that the elderly face in relation to their self-concept is that old age is a time of physical and social decline and perhaps loss. Moreover, younger people and society itself have in the past not generally held the aged in high regard. The elderly, in contrast, have tended to have a positive view of themselves, and the evidence generally suggests that personality does not change in old age, nor do old people change their self-concept radically from what it was when they were young. In fact, older people, as they come to terms with their life and develop a feeling of continuity with their life experiences, appear to feel somewhat more positive about themselves than do younger people.

From the standpoint of social theory, the symbolic interaction perspective—as represented by Mead, Cooley, and Goffman—provides a particularly useful approach for analyzing the self-concept in general, and in old age in particular. Symbolic interaction theory explains the origin of self in childhood in relation to significant others and its development through the life course through social experiences with other people. It allows us to see that, when a person reaches old age, he or she has typically constructed a sense of self formulated over time and in response to the views of others and the wider society.

Two other theories focusing more directly on aging—continuity theory and modernization theory—further our understanding of the aged self. Continuity theory explains the manner in which the basic personality of the individual in old age is continued. That is, the elderly person's overall personality is generally consistent with what it was in younger adulthood (Neugarten 1964). Modernization theory, in turn, helps to explain why modern societies have generally devalued the aged, but notes that stereotypes of old people are becoming more positive in advanced stages of modernization (Cowgill 1986). The fact that people tend to maintain a positive self-concept in old age and the trend toward more positive images of old people in the most developed societies suggest that a social environment more supportive of the aged self is evolving.

Chapter 8

AGEISM, GENDER, AND RACIAL MINORITY STATUS

Thus far in this book we have reviewed the situation of the aged and found a general improvement over conditions in the midtwentieth century and earlier. This is not to say that the elderly do not have problems as a group or that life for many older people is not unpleasant. However, we see that, as the twenty-first century approaches, there is an increasingly larger population of people over the age of 65; and, especially in developed countries like the United States, overall living conditions for the aged are improving. The current generation of older people in the United States is more numerous, better educated, and more affluent than in the past, and this trend will continue. Furthermore, the overall health of the aged in the United States is relatively good, and their sense of self is typically not impaired just because they have become old. For that matter, studies cited in the last chapter indicate that there is a tendency in late life to feel even more positive about one's self.

However, the aged in society face some special problems that are caused not by themselves, but by society at large. A particular problem is that of *ageism*, or prejudice against the aged, in which old people may be discriminated against simply because they have become old. Gender and racial minority status can also produce differences in the aging experience, in that older women and minorities have to cope with more negative situations than do aged men and members of the white majority. In this chapter, we review these issues.

AGEISM

A negative influence in the daily lives of old people is ageism, a form of prejudice against people because they are old. *Prejudice* is a term describing an unfavorable attitude toward a category of people which is based on traits believed to be negative. Often prejudice exists in the form of a prejudgment, in that people have a negative attitude toward an individual or specific group in society before having any personal knowledge about them. If people are prejudiced and keep their prejudices to themselves, then little actual harm is likely to be done to the person or persons against whom the prejudice is directed. However, if those prejudices are operationalized in the form of *discrimination*, which means *acting* on one's prejudices, people will not be treated fairly or equally.

Discrimination can be either positive (providing special advantages) or negative (subjecting others to disadvantages). When it comes to being old, typically there have been more disadvantages than advantages. The U.S. elderly have been subject to discrimination in employment and in treatment from public agencies with respect to job training and vocational rehabilitation (Atchley 1994; Chudacoff 1989; Graebner 1980; Quadagno 1988a; Skocpol 1995). Ageism has been documented in modern Canada (Novak 1993) and Europe (Hugman 1994; Pilcher 1995) as well. For example, in Great Britain, Jane Pilcher (1995) and others (Arber and Ginn 1991) have found age discrimination to be reinforced by British culture and social institutions—particularly in the labor market. Preferences for younger people are the basis for discrimination against the aged.

Ageism, or age prejudice, can therefore be described as a dislike of old people that is based on the belief that old age causes the elderly to be unattractive, unintelligent, asexual, unemployable, and senile (Comfort 1976). Although one-fourth or less of the U.S. population has been found to express negatively prejudicial attitudes against the aged (McTavish 1971), Robert Atchley (1994) estimates that most Americans have at least a mild degree of prejudice against aging and old people.

Ageism causes the elderly to be stigmatized. According to Erving Goffman (1963:3), a *stigma* can be defined as "an attribute that is deeply discrediting." Goffman, a symbolic interaction theorist, explains that the term *stigma* apparently originated with the ancient Greeks, who used it to refer to marks on the body. These marks were intended to represent something unusual or morally bad about the persons having them. Usually, the marks were brands cut or burned into the body to identify the bearer as a criminal, slave, or traitor. Thus any citizen encountering the stigmatized person was entitled to treat him or her badly or, once aware of the mark, was expected to avoid contact altogether with that person. In contemporary society, Goffman explains, there are three main sources of stigma: (1) abominations of the body, such as various types of physical deformities; (2) blemishes of individual character—that is, perceived mental disorder or weakness, homosexuality, dishonesty, criminality, drug and alcohol addiction, political radicalism, and so forth; and (3) the stigma of race, religion, and nationality. The person with such attributes is therefore someone who is different from most other people, but different in a negative (supposedly less human) way. "On this assumption," stated Goffman (1963:5), "we exercise varieties of discrimination, through which we effectively, if often unthinkingly, reduce [a person's] life chances."

The old are stigmatized largely in regard to "an abomination of the body"; that is, they have lost their youthful looks and lack physical attractiveness. And they may also suffer "blemishes of individual character" in that they may be perceived as senile, slow, stupid, or some other personal trait that is associated with the fact that they are old. The question thus arises as to how old people became stigmatized in society, and the answer appears to lie in two general areas: (1) fear of aging and (2) social values in relation to aging.

Fear of Aging

Becoming old is something that most people probably wish to avoid, because it signifies loss of physical attractiveness, a decline in health, and the nearness of death. Even some of the elderly themselves may be fearful of continued aging because of what it signifies (Klemmack and Roff 1984; Stokes 1992). This negative image of old age, as Bernice Neugarten (1971) pointed out, is responsible for the fear of aging and the rejection of the thought of becoming old. Young people do not wish to be old or reminded of the fact that old age is inevitable, so they avoid the elderly and devalue them. In effect, they are denying that they, too, will someday be old. In disliking aging, the tendency for some is also to dislike those persons in general who are experiencing it and to consider them inferior because of it.

Aging and Social Values

Russell Ward (1979) explains that any stigma attached to the elderly must also be seen in relation to what is valued in society and presumed lost by becoming old. What the aged principally lose are their former role as a productive and active contributor to society and their self-image as physically attractive. Developed societies tend to remove the aged from the mainstream of social activity through planned retirement. This event takes place at a time of life when the aged person is usually no longer responsible for child rearing, financial support for children, and other tasks central to family maintenance. Although there is a positive side to this situation, in that the aged person gains the freedom to pursue his or her own interests and pleasures without work and family responsibility, it nevertheless is true that the elderly enter a status—retirement—that is not particularly important in achievement-oriented societies. In essence, the elderly go to the sidelines, and younger people assume the active social roles that contribute to and are valued by the larger social system.

In the United States, the normative expectation is that people will be active, achievement oriented, productive, and able to plan for the future. Aged persons generally do not meet these expectations because these are norms for young adults. The United States is a youth-oriented society, a situation that can easily be verified by examining the range of consumer goods and advertising that emphasizes youthfulness—even for elderly people. For example, cosmetic companies in the 1990s are grappling with how to approach the increasingly larger population of older consumers. The trend has been to emphasize the youthful looks and beauty that an older woman can maintain if she fights against looking old by using cosmetics.

Regardless, to be old is to enter a stage of life that is socially devalued, because it indicates that the person no longer participates in adult roles on the same level as before. Looking at the situation from Goffman's (1959) perspective of "life as theater," the old would no longer be serious players in social interaction. They would be on the sidelines. This problem is compounded by the lessened physical appeal assigned to the old by a youth-oriented society.

In order to show how this situation came about in the United States, David Fischer (1978) examined the impact of modernization on the elderly. His thesis is consistent with the modernization theory of aging, which holds that the processes that cause societies to change from a rural and agrarian system to an urban and industrial society change the roles of the elderly and reduce the status and esteem they are accorded (Cowgill 1986). Fischer, a social historian, began his analysis with the colonial period. Less than 2 percent of the population in the American colonies was age 75 or over. Because mortality rates were high and old age relatively rare, the elderly were regarded by most people as special. Elders, especially among the Puritans in New England, were placed in charge of churches and held the most important positions in town councils. The old were not just esteemed out of affection or deference to age, but, Fischer found, they were almost venerated along religious lines. They were seen as good, wise, and experienced in a manner consistent with biblical norms. There was no concept of retirement because of age, so the elderly leaders of the church and the community usually continued in office until they died.

However, not all of the elderly were regarded with esteem. Upper-class old people were held in high esteem. But the aged among the lower class, in stark contrast, were scorned because they were old (but not considered wise) and particularly because they were poor. Nonetheless, the general view of the aged in colonial times was one of authority and respect. This position was reinforced among the affluent because the control of land was usually maintained by the oldest male in the family, thus ensuring that younger family members accorded him the respect due his position as manager of the family's economy. Thus, from about 1607 to 1770, the predominant attitude toward the aged was one of respect.

Fischer explained that this situation resulted in a cult of old age in which the aged person of affluence was revered. But this cult of old age was significantly weakened and eventually replaced in the eighteenth and nineteenth centuries by a cult of youth. Between 1770 and 1820, a transition in attitudes, influenced by revolutionary values, spread which was far more supportive of youth as the ideal. At this time, wealth replaced age as a qualification for leadership; fashions in clothing became more youth-oriented; and derogatory terms were coined, like *gaffer, codger, fuddy-duddy*, and *geezer*, which made fun of old people. After 1820 until the midtwentieth century, youth became increasingly emphasized at the expense of age. With the establishment of mass education for the young—along with retirement programs, residential separation, and diminished income for the aged—older people were pushed into a lower status. The country turned to youthful heroes for inspiration: Daniel Boone, Andrew Jackson, the defenders of the Alamo, George Armstrong Custer, Teddy Roosevelt, Charles Lindbergh, and the like. In politics, youth was often considered an asset if political and social change was an important issue. Old people, in turn, were increasingly considered a social problem, requiring welfare in order to establish adequate pension and health benefits.

Carole Haber (1983) notes that the rejection of the old was not the result of any sudden aversion to old age, but evolved over time as aging became associated with poverty. Dependence in old age, a lack of material goods, and poor earning power for old people in general resulted in the notion that poverty was the elderly's usual state. Even though there were powerful and responsible elderly men and women, they were clearly a minority, and being old came to mean also being poor and relatively useless. Howard Chudacoff (1989), in turn, identifies late nineteenth-century industrialization as the period when discrimination against the aged began in earnest in the United States. By the early twentieth century, the belief that old people could not keep up with modern manufacturing and business methods became especially strong. The result was the spread of ageism in the workplace and the wider society.

Thus modernization and poverty, as well as decreased physical attractiveness, have undermined the position of the aged in a society emphasizing achievement and youth. Yet the story is not over. The elderly at the end of the twentieth century are in the best position they have been in as a group since the colonial period. Today they have large numbers, greater wealth, and more political power than they have ever had, and, as they occupy a more dominant role in national affairs and consumerism in the twenty-first century, attitudes may become exceedingly more positive. Signs of this trend are already appearing, as seen in the findings of Robert Binstock (1983) and others (Bell 1992; Kite, Deaux, and Miele 1991), indicating that the stereotype of the elderly is changing in the United States from that of being poor and victimized by society to one of being relatively well off and politically powerful, and taking up too much of the federal budget.

As the aged gain increasingly greater benefits as a result of their political influence (22 percent of all voters in the 1988 presidential election were age 60 or over), lead interesting and active lives, and become a major focus for the marketing of goods and services, ageism is likely to diminish in U.S. society. Although modernization theory maintains that the elderly lose status and esteem when societies urbanize and industrialize, it also predicts, as previously noted, that—when modern societies come to terms with having large aged populations—more positive cultural and institutional adaptations for the elderly will take place (Cowgill 1986). Social historians in the twenty-first century are likely to see a marked improvement in both the status of the aged in Western societies and attitudes toward them.

GENDER

Whether or not ageism affects women more than men is not known, although this may be the case. Certainly, men are devalued in old age, but the situation may be more acute for women. The major problem that women face in relation to society's reaction toward them as an old person is a loss of attractiveness. Society's standards of female beauty and physical appeal are more or less exclusively youthful. Therefore, women may be more aware of the aging process than are men because the physical signs of aging produce graver social consequences for them (Levy 1988). Denial of aging has therefore been considered more of a female trait, because older men have often been considered more attractive than older women, especially if they are wealthy or powerful (Drevenstedt 1976). When it comes to physical appearance, a double standard seems to exist in the popular culture, in that elderly men may be thought of as "handsome" or "distinguished," but elderly women are not as likely to be considered "beautiful." As discussed in Chapter 7, this tendency toward a double standard rests in the fact that U.S. sexual stereotyping equate female beauty with youth more than it does male handsomeness. Marriages among couples of widely varying ages typically consist of older men marrying much younger women, rather than the other way around. As a result, women have been characterized as clinging to a youthful self-image longer than men. What is suggested by this situation is that aging is more threatening to women than to men because it has more negative implications. But this situation may become less true of future elderly cohorts as more positive views about the aged in general become more prevalent in advanced societies.

Lynn White (1988) has suggested, however, that both men and women become aware of aging in much the same way. White found that men tend to report more decline in their hearing and greater hair loss than women, whereas women tend to report greater declines in eyesight and energy as well as in the quality of their skin and figure. But women do tend to have worse uncorrected vision than men and to be more obese, whereas hair loss is invariably a male rather than a female condition, and men tend to have greater hearing loss (Verbrugge 1982). White (1988) suggests, accordingly, that male-female differences in awareness of aging are largely the result of real differences in the aging process and that, when all signs of aging are considered, there is really not much difference between the sexes in recognizing the onset of old age.

When the effects of aging on people are considered on the basis of gender, it seems most likely that there is indeed little or no difference in awareness of the actual process among men and women. Gray hair, dry skin, wrinkles, and loss of energy—along with the fact of chronological age—provide indisputable evidence of aging. The impact of that process, however, may be somewhat greater on women when it comes to social consequences and connotations of beauty and sexuality. But the struggle against the inevitable change in one's looks most likely peaks in late middle age rather than old age. Once women are aged, there may be little or no difference about the effects of aging on their appearance in comparison with old men. It is only a minority of elderly men who retain physical attractiveness in late life; for the great majority of aged people, men and women, there are more important matters than looks. In fact, old age may be the time of life when looks matter the least.

Gender differences in the aging experience are most likely to occur in relation to changes in work and parental roles that take place in late middle age. Ken Smith and Phyllis Moen (1988) studied role changes in midlife among women and found that events at this time have particular significance for later life. *Midlife* is the period when the last child usually leaves home, thereby typically providing the woman with a sense of loss and mild depression, but also lessened responsibility and greater freedom to pursue personal interests. Generally, the departure of the last child from the home—the so-called empty nest transition—is anticipated and does not significantly disrupt the lives of women experiencing it (George 1989). Some women may join the labor force at this time or continue to be employed without child care duties in the home. Employment outside the home for women ages 55 to 64 has, in fact, risen since the 1950s because of the expansion of employment opportunities in the post–World War II economy (DeViney and O'Rand 1988). Others may participate in enhanced social activities or travel. This time in late middle age can be a preretirement period in which one begins to prepare for older age.

A second major event identified by Smith and Moen (1988), which occurs frequently among women in midlife, is marital dissolution through either divorce or death of their husbands. Smith and Moen note that divorce is increasingly less common as couples age together, but older wives are especially likely to lose their husbands through death. The average age at which people experience loss of a spouse through death is age 56 (Lopata 1973), and most widowed women spend approximately twenty years of their life in that status (Ferraro 1989). Becoming a widow in late middle age signifies the beginning of the transition into old age, with reduced chances for financial well-being. Whereas the empty nest transition tends to increase financial well-being by ending the expenses of raising children, marital dissolution through death or divorce tends to decrease it. Therefore, to a large extent, a married woman's financial situation at the beginning of old age is strongly influenced by events during late middle age. Smith and Moen (1988) note that those women who remain married in the middle years have greater economic well-being in later life.

Another area of research concerning differences between older men and women pertains to retirement from a job. Women historically have had less access than men to pension plans, and they tend to receive smaller pensions than men when they are entitled to them. Jill Quadagno (1988b) suggests that the reasons for this include the fact that many women do not work long enough at a particular job to accumulate seniority and that often women have been employed in jobs that do not provide pensions, have few fringe benefits, and offer little job security. Typically, these are small businesses that rely on temporary labor or firms whose policy is not to provide pensions to their employees because of the cost. Long-term workers in such businesses are thus disadvantaged, but they work at these places because they need the job. Other research suggests that the responsibilities of women for child care reduce the chances of many women's being competitive in obtaining and retaining better-paying jobs; this also leads to lower pensions (O'Neill 1985).

In a study of patterns of retirement in some 93 countries, including the United States, Fred Pampel and Sookja Park (1986) found that the majority of women worldwide withdraw from the labor force during old age. The rates of withdrawal are greater than for men and take place even in countries where formal retirement is rare and pension systems are weak. The level of a nation's industrial development (high or low) and the status of women (high or low) both contribute to the position of women in the labor force and their situation in old age. Highly industrialized societies had better pension plans for both men and women, and the quality of these helped influence the time of retirement for both sexes. But the study also found that the positive effects of industrial development on female retirement were constrained by sexual inequality (which existed in all societies) and large family size (high fertility disrupted careers and labor force participation, leading to lower retirement benefits). Overall, pension benefits for women are less than those for men, and this appears to be the case in both developed and especially in developing countries.

Women also live longer than men, on the average, and some researchers have characterized very old age as primarily a female experience (Longino 1988). Longevity has mixed benefits, however, as women are more likely to be widowed and experience poverty in old age. Moreover, women tend to have smaller Social Security benefits and less retirement income from pension plans. As Judith Levy (1988) suggests, these lesser benefits likely reflect the long-term and cumulative effects of women's disadvantaged work histories, wage differentials, and segregation into lower-prestige jobs at earlier ages. Consequently, elderly men and women, particularly at the oldest ages, tend to have different living arrangements and relationships. Levy states:

> Because men tend to marry younger women who eventually outlive them, men age 85 and older are far more likely to remain married in old age. They are also more likely, in view of women's longevity rates, to have a spouse to care for them should they become infirm or disabled. Should their spouses die, the comparatively larger proportion of single eligible females permits men more opportunities for remarriage. Perhaps for these reasons, men are more likely to experience old age while living in their own homes; women are far more likely

to experience the last phase of the life course residing in an institution or with relatives.[1]

In sum, women are much more likely to be disadvantaged in old age than men.

MINORITY GROUPS

An unanswered question regarding racial minority groups in U.S. society is whether they are placed in a situation of "double jeopardy" as a result of old age; that is, does being both old *and* a member of a minority group place a person in particularly adverse circumstances? Some have suggested that it does not, because aging is so powerful an experience that all old people face similar problems despite their race (Kent 1971). In other words, what distinguishes an elderly white, black, Hispanic, Asian, or native American from other people is the fact that first and foremost he or she is old. If race is a negative factor in his or her life, then it is due more to the association of race with poverty than to race per se. Aged persons living in poverty are among the most disadvantaged groups in society, regardless of their race.

It appears that old age has the attributes of a master status in that it overrides the significance of other statuses. The situation for elderly whites and racial minority persons, if poor, is much the same; the situation for elderly whites and minority persons, if affluent, is also much the same. Therefore, what most determines quality of life in old age is socioeconomic status and health, not race. These conditions favor whites in the United States but are not exclusive to them.

Although some earlier studies (Dowd and Bengston 1978) support the double jeopardy hypothesis, there is not a great deal of current evidence showing that aged members of minority groups suffer more than their white counterparts at the same socioeconomic level. The damage to a person's life caused by racism most likely happens at earlier ages. Old age appears to bring more similarities than differences for persons sharing the same socioeconomic status. The problem for minorities is that fewer of them are financially affluent, and life is thus harder for them in old age because of their greater poverty over the life course.

1. Judith A. Levy, "Intersections of Gender and Aging," *Sociological Quarterly* 29 (1988): 484.

African Americans

African Americans constitute 8 percent of all persons over the age of 65 in the United States. Elderly blacks do not have worse health generally than older whites (Ferraro 1988), nor do they lose more income when they retire (Pampel 1981). However, this does not mean the situation for older blacks is especially good. Proportionately fewer blacks than whites, as noted in Chapter 5, live long enough to reach old age. Blacks in general also have lower incomes than whites. Although levels of income decline more for whites than for blacks in old age, blacks have less income to begin with. Thus the relative advantage remains with whites.

In addition, blacks are more likely than whites to retire because of poor health, be unemployed in old age, or find it necessary to continue working when old in order to support themselves (Markides and Mindel 1987). Blacks are also more likely than whites not to live with a spouse in old age (Gibson 1986). Furthermore, most elderly blacks living in poverty are women, and their financial situation tends to be worse than that of men because of a history of especially low incomes. All of this would suggest that many elderly blacks are disadvantaged because they are also poor. The 1993 median income for black families headed by persons age 65 and over was $17,782, compared with $25,965 for elderly white families. Thus the median income of elderly black families is about one-third less than that of aged white families. Blacks are also more likely to have fewer financial resources from earlier periods of employment to use in old age than whites because of either unemployment or low-paying jobs.

According to William Julius Wilson (1987), the African-American population in the United States as a whole has been in a disadvantaged position, initially as a result of slavery (until 1865) and later because of massive undereducation, which lasted well into the twentieth century. As the United States moved from an agricultural/early industrial stage in the nineteenth century to a late and postindustrial period in the midtwentieth century, blacks were generally not as competitive in the labor market as whites for skilled positions. A majority of white immigrants to the United States were able to secure levels of education and income that provided them with a good standard of living; blacks, on the other hand, were handicapped by racial discrimination and lower levels of education and income. A majority lived outside the political, social, and economic mainstream of society.

Yet significant numbers of blacks were able to take advantage of increased opportunities following the civil rights gains of the 1960s. Many

African Americans have seen a great improvement in their life situation and have achieved social, economic, and political success. For the poorest African Americans, however, life chances appear to be deteriorating further (Farley 1984; Pinkney 1984; Wilson 1987). For example, the gap between blacks and whites in underemployment and unemployment in the nation's large cities has widened substantially since the 1970s, with young, poorly educated blacks having the most difficulty securing jobs (Farley 1984; Lichter 1988; Massey and Eggers 1990; Pinkney 1984).

Wilson (1987) points out that the social conditions facing low-income urban African Americans have worsened to the extent that rates of unemployment, out-of-wedlock births, households headed by females, dependence on welfare, and violent crime have increased to their highest levels ever. Wilson blames this development not so much on racism as on the increasing isolation of lower-class blacks in a changing economy. Wilson notes that both middle-class black professionals and working-class blacks have moved out of ghetto neighborhoods in the inner city in search of safer neighborhoods and better schools for their children. Left behind is a high concentration of the most disadvantaged segments of the black population—a black underclass—whose social and economic isolation has become more pronounced than ever before. At the same time, the U.S. economy has been changing from a manufacturing to a service and information-oriented base. This situation has produced extraordinary rates of joblessness for those persons, many of them low-income blacks, who lack the education and job skills to adapt to these economic changes. The inner-city black poor, therefore, rank among the most disadvantaged groups in American society; they may, in fact, have the poorest life chances of anyone. Elderly blacks living in inner-city poverty obviously share the disadvantages common to the urban black underclass as a whole.

However, Rose Gibson (1986) suggests that, for many blacks, the retirement years are the happiest and most secure of their lives. Gibson provides two possible reasons for this situation. First, declining physical health in old age, combined with the more strenuous and distasteful jobs at the bottom of the occupational hierarchy, which many blacks hold, makes work more punishing. Second, many blacks in retirement can look forward to a steady and reliable income from Social Security. For those blacks living in poverty, a steady income may have been infrequent at earlier ages.

Gibson also refers to elderly blacks as "psychological survivors," pointing out that, even though they lack adequate financial security, education, and often the company of a spouse, they seem to be able to sustain themselves psychologically as they age. She observes, for example, that suicide rates among the elderly are much lower for blacks than for whites and that older black women, who are the most likely to be poor, have lower suicide rates than either elderly black males or whites in general. Gibson suggests that religion is a particularly strong factor in the lives of the African-American elderly by providing strength through prayer and a sense of belonging. "I suspect," states Gibson (1986:368), "that it is the communal as well as the intrinsic aspects of prayer that are helpful to older blacks; 'getting together to get things done.' " Other research on the function of religion in the lives of older blacks supports Gibson's claim. Neal Krause and Thanh Van Tran (1989) found in a nationwide sample of elderly blacks that the effects of stressful life events and negative feelings of self-worth were offset or counterbalanced by religious involvement. Robert Taylor and Linda Chatters (1986) found that informal support from church members in time of need was second only to support from family members among elderly blacks. Church members were a greater source of informal help than friends and were the preeminent source of aid during illness.

Gibson (1986) also notes the use of informal support networks in dealing with problems. Gibson found that older blacks draw from a more varied pool of informal helpers—family, church members, friends, acquaintances— than whites and are more versatile in utilizing these helpers in old age. Whites, in contrast, were more likely to seek help just from their spouses in old age or from specific family members if spouses were not available. Other research finds that black elderly parents tend to both give and receive help from family members more than do elderly white parents (Mutran 1985). Blacks thus appear to be involved with a larger informal support system in late life than whites.

In sum, Gibson concludes that not all aspects of old age have negative connotations for blacks. For elderly blacks in general, Gibson suggests that certain psychological factors may be very important in sustaining their longevity and life satisfaction. These factors include a positive outlook on life, effective ways of dealing with stress, and the use of informal networks of social support in obtaining help in time of need. Gibson is particularly impressed with the strengths in late life of black women, who are experiencing the most rapid increase in population of any racial/ethnic group in American society 80 years of age and older. The increase in numbers of elderly black women, combined with the high proportion (about 45 percent) of black families with only a female head of household, may mean, in Gibson's view, that the adults in many black families in the future will consist of several generations of women. Consequently, an important role for the older African-American woman appears to be that of serving as a surrogate parent to her grandchildren in families without the father present, whose absence is due to unemployment, divorce, separation, or death.

Hispanic Americans

Most Hispanics living in America either are descendants of people residing in territory that was annexed by the United States following the war with Mexico in 1845, or they or their relatives entered as legal or illegal immigrants sometime thereafter in a pattern of northward migration that continues today. Many of these persons were unskilled laborers who worked in agriculture in the American Southwest during a period of rapid industrialization and urbanization. As a result, the Hispanic population, the majority of whom are Mexican Americans, have tended to have relatively low-paying and less prestigious jobs. Many Hispanics today, however, live and work in urban areas. For example, about 80 percent of all Mexican Americans live in cities (Gelfand 1982). But, as a group, they remain economically and socially disadvantaged relative to non-Hispanic whites (Markides and Mindel 1987).

An important fact about Hispanics is that they will become the largest minority group in American society in the twenty-first century. Approximately 400,000 Hispanics a year enter the United States, either legally or illegally, as immigrants—considerably more than any other ethnic group from elsewhere in the world. Current migration patterns, combined with a high fertility rate (the fertility rate of Hispanic Americans is about 50 percent higher than that of non-Hispanics) is resulting in a large population gain. From a population of 9.1 million in 1970, the number of Hispanics had increased to 14.6 million by 1980 and to 22 million in 1990. By 2010, Hispanic Americans will exceed 35 million and, if this trend continues, which is likely, Hispanics will replace African Americans as the nation's largest minority group. By 2050, U.S. Census Bureau projections show that non-Hispanic whites will comprise 52.8 percent of the American population, followed by Hispanics 24.5 percent, African Americans 13.6 percent, Asian Americans 8.2 percent, and native Americans 0.9 percent.

As Fernando Torres-Gil (1986) points out, the United States is already the fifth largest Spanish-speaking country in the world, after Mexico, Spain, Argentina, and Colombia. If Puerto Rico is included, the United States ranks ahead of Colombia. According to Torres-Gil (1986:326), the presence of rapidly increasing numbers of Spanish-speaking persons in the United States "forces us to acknowledge a reality that we have too long ignored: the Western hemisphere is composed primarily of Spanish-speaking persons with a Latino heritage." And people with this heritage are becoming an increasingly significant segment of the American population.

Hispanics are a highly diverse group in the United States. In the mid-1990s, the Hispanic population in the United States was composed not only of Mexican Americans (over half of all Hispanics), but also of significant numbers of Puerto Ricans, Cubans, and persons from Central and South America, the Caribbean, and elsewhere. Within this population, Puerto Ricans generally have the highest unemployment rates and lowest incomes and levels of education. Cubans, in contrast, have the highest incomes and education, along with the lowest unemployment rates. Mexican Americans generally fall between these two groups with respect to income, education, and jobs—but have less health insurance coverage than any other racial/ethnic group in American society.

When it comes to aging, however, Hispanics represent a young group within an aging society. Over one-third of all Hispanic Americans were under the age of 25 in 1994, in comparison to over 20 percent of the general population. Hispanics constitute only about 3 percent of the population age 65 and over in the United States. However, Hispanics are aging, too, and the number of Hispanics reaching old age each year is increasing. In time, Hispanics will constitute a much larger proportion of the elderly population than they do now. As a relatively young population group increasing rapidly in a society that is growing older, Hispanic Americans will face a unique situation. "No other American population group," states Torres-Gil (1986:328), "has had to evolve, assimilate, and attempt to achieve full participation in American social, economic, educational, and political life while the country was being increasingly affected and redirected by its aging population." There are more questions than answers about how the twin processes of Latinization and aging will affect the future of the United States.

This situation is further complicated by the lessened assimilation of Hispanic groups into an Anglo culture. Hispanic Americans live in closer proximity than do other immigrant groups to their original homelands and thus are better able to maintain cultural and family ties. Although many Hispanics have assimilated, others have maintained their language, culture, customs, and ethnic solidarity. Today, Hispanics appear to be the least assimilated minority group in American society. Another problem is poverty. Hispanics are twice as likely as non-Hispanics to be poor (Torres-Gil 1986), and some have claimed that this is true for the elderly as well (Locayo 1984). Figures for 1993 show that the median income for Hispanic families headed by persons age 65 or over was $20,459, compared with $25,965 for non-Hispanic white families with aged persons as the head. Consequently, when it comes to median income, elderly Hispanic families in general have about one-third less income than elderly non-Hispanic white families. Data on income for Hispanics, however, is somewhat skewed, because Cubans tend to receive relatively high incomes, whereas Mexican Americans and Puerto Ricans receive considerably less. Moreover, many Hispanics are likely to have had significantly less earnings than non-Hispanic whites over their life span, so they, like blacks, have accumulated fewer financial resources to draw on in old age. Poverty, therefore, is a fact of life for a considerable portion of the Mexican-American and Puerto Rican population as a whole and for the elderly within that population.

Little is known about the retirement experience of Hispanic Americans. The existing research, however, suggests that retirement is not a distinct event (Markides and Mindel 1987). Rather, the aged Hispanic works at a job as long as he or she is able. Withdrawal from the labor force thus tends to be gradual. Many Hispanic workers are forced out of the labor market before retirement age because of deteriorating health (Becerra and Shaw 1984). Furthermore, because of irregular employment, especially among Hispanic migrant workers, elderly Hispanics tend to draw lower Social Security benefits than Anglos and are less likely to receive retirement incomes from private pensions.

A positive factor for elderly Hispanics is the Hispanic family and neighborhood. Hispanic families tend to be large and feature an extended network of relatives who are available to provide social support. Although some sources suggest that the level of support rendered to its elderly by the Hispanic family has eroded, Hispanics are more likely than Anglos to live near large numbers of family members, and a sense of responsibility toward aged family members remains a tradition (Becerra and Shaw 1984; Locayo 1984). Neighbors and friends in predominantly Hispanic neighborhoods are also an important source of help, friendship, and social interaction for older Hispanics. In fact, older Hispanics tend to draw on friends for assistance and social interaction in old age more than do elderly Anglos. As Rosina Becerra and David Shaw (1984) explain, despite the poor physical environment found in Hispanic enclaves or barrios, studies of life satisfaction among aged residents show a very high proportion satisfied with their lives in these communities. The reasons for this satisfaction appear to be found largely in the context of barrio life, which provides social and cultural familiarity and the presence of established networks of friends and relatives. In addition, older Hispanics are more likely than their Anglo counterparts to live in households with relatives. Despite adverse living conditions, such as poor housing and high crime rates, many elderly Hispanics prefer the barrio as a place to live because of its generally supportive nature.

Hispanic Americans represent an important ethnic group in American society, whose increasing size and cultural distinctiveness only partially explain its potential impact on the larger social system. Particularly important is the fact that Hispanics constitute a young population group in an aging society. As the wider society will be faced with adjusting to increased Latinization when Hispanics become the nation's largest minority group in the twenty-first century, Hispanics will have to cope with being young in an aged social structure. This social structure will undoubtedly place great emphasis on securing advantages for old people. Hispanics, on the other hand, will be interested in securing greater political and economic gains for Hispanics. Thus there is a very real potential for conflict in which majority-minority group relations between Anglos and Hispanics will be affected by both ethnic and age differences. Yet, as Torres-Gil (1986:344) reminds us, Hispanics are aging, too, and they have a stake in ensuring that *all* elderly are treated fairly.

Native Americans

As the original settlers of North America, native Americans, or American Indians, suffered a series of military defeats and dislocations at the hands of whites from the seventeenth until the late nineteenth century. In the aftermath of the Indian wars, most American Indians lived on reservations in relatively isolated sections of the country and worked in predominantly agricultural occupations. In the midtwentieth century, significant proportions of Indians began to migrate to cities, so that today about half of the Indian population lives in urban areas. A majority, however, have relatively low-paying and less-prestigious jobs.

American Indians and native Alaskans constitute less than 1 percent of all persons 65 years of age and older. The exact number of older people among native American populations has been difficult to determine, but 1990 census data placed the number at that time at 171,763. This makes them the smallest major racial/ethnic group among the aged. About 30 percent of the aged Indian population lives on reservations, and perhaps another 25 percent lives in rural areas. Some social services are available to aged Indians on reservations, but Indians living elsewhere suffer disadvantages similar to those of poor blacks (Atchley 1994); that is, they are severely disadvantaged in terms of education, income, jobs, and housing.

In many traditional Indian tribal cultures, there was no concept of retirement. Older people remained active as long as they were able; once they were senile or no longer physically fit, they were abandoned, killed themselves by starvation or exposure to extremes of weather, had a member of their tribe or family kill them, or were allowed to die of old age. Yet despite the trend toward a quick death once productivity was impossible, elderly Indians generally enjoyed high esteem because of their age and experience. Very often they (especially males) served in tribal positions of leadership. Today, the prestige associated with old age has persisted among Indians, and old people are often highly regarded in Indian communities. The concept of retirement has also become more accepted; and, because of high rates of unemployment among Indians generally, it is not uncommon for elderly Indians to help support younger family members with their old age benefits (Edwards 1983). Overall, aged Indians join older blacks and Hispanics in being in a disadvantaged position relative to non-Hispanic whites.

Asian Americans

Most Asian Americans of Chinese and Japanese descent are relatives of persons who migrated to the United States during the nineteenth and (for the Japanese) early twentieth centuries primarily as agricultural workers. The majority settled in Hawaii and California. The Chinese came first, beginning in the 1840s and continuing until 1879 when Congress passed a Chinese Exclusion Act. With renewals, this act prohibited Chinese immigration until its repeal in 1943, when China was a World War II ally of the United States. Japanese immigration took place largely between 1870 and 1924 until their immigration was likewise halted. Intense competition with whites in the labor market on the West Coast, reinforced by strong feelings of racism, led to the ban. Filipinos came in large numbers in the 1930s and had fewer immigration problems because the Philippines was a possession of the United States between 1899 and 1934; a second wave of Filipino immigration took place in the 1970s. The majority of migrants from China, Japan, and the Philippines came as unskilled laborers who were attracted to greater economic opportunities. Many eventually entered service occupations and started small businesses, whereas others remained in agriculture.

Immigration from other parts of Asia has been more recent. Some Koreans immigrated to the United States at the turn of the century, but this immigration was cut off in 1905 when the Japanese established military control over their country. Migration from South Korea has taken place largely since 1965, and Koreans are currently America's fastest-growing Asian minority group. The most recent migration has involved South Vietnamese and Cambodian refugees who entered the United States in the 1970s in the aftermath of the Vietnam War. In the 1990s, Chinese and Filipinos constituted the largest groups of Asians in the United States, followed by the Japanese. In total numbers (about 3 million), Asians are a distant third behind African Americans and Hispanics as an American minority group.

As noted, the first Asians who settled in North America in relatively large numbers were from China and Japan. Initially, almost all of the Chinese and Japanese migrants were men, but eventually families migrated as well, or the men arranged for brides to be sent to them from their homeland. Despite severe prejudice and discrimination, both the Chinese and the Japanese have shown remarkable economic and social mobility, especially in the period following World War II. They reached the point at which a high proportion have now surpassed whites in levels of education and occupational prestige. The Japanese, however, became somewhat more integrated than the Chinese into the American social and economic system. Many Chinese retreated into "Chinatowns" in large cities and entered service occupations such as the restaurant and laundry business. Of all the Asian minority groups, the Japanese have the highest incomes (Kitano 1991).

Asian Americans constitute 1 percent or less of all elderly persons in U.S. society. Their situation has been described by Morrison Wong (1984). Wong points out that approximately half of all elderly Asian Americans live in California. Most of the remainder live in either Hawaii or New York. By ethnic group, about 50 percent of all aged Japanese live in California, and another 40 percent live in Hawaii; Chinese and Filipinos are only slightly more dispersed, with significant proportions (about 15 percent) also living in New York. The great majority of elderly Asian Americans is thus concentrated in three states, and almost all of them also live in urban areas. In terms of education, income, and socioeconomic status generally, elderly Asians as a group rank below aged whites. The socioeconomic gains of Asian Americans are largely an achievement of younger and middle-aged persons, for older Asians tended to have low-paying and less-prestigious jobs. As Wong (1984:205) explains, a majority of aged Asians "were involved in jobs in the periphery—jobs that are characterized as low in status and pay and offering little chance of advancement." This is especially true of elderly Chinese, because about one-third live below the poverty line. Large numbers of Chinese elderly are single men, and a majority tend to live in low-income housing in "Chinatowns" in major cities. However, Japanese and Filipino elderly show a fairly low proportion—about 8 and 4 percent, respectively—living in poverty.

In traditional Asian culture, old age is esteemed, and elderly parents often live with their children. To a certain extent, such traditions are eroding in modern Asia (Martin 1988) and have eroded to a greater degree among Asians in the United States. As Toshi Kii (1984) explains, the majority of Asian elderly are immigrants who broke away from the traditional work and family organization when they were young and entered a new environment. In addition, there is a considerable sexual imbalance, especially among Chinese elderly, with the greater proportion being males who never married or who left their wives in China because of immigration restrictions. The children of Asian Americans have also obtained greater economic freedom from their parents and have had greater opportunities for upward social mobility through education and careers in more prestigious occupations. Consequently, the traditional Asian family structure, featuring a close-knit extended family, has tended to break down. Nevertheless, the proportion of elderly Asians living with their families is still somewhat higher (ranging from 23 percent for Filipinos to 16 percent for Japanese) than the national average of about 12 percent (Kii 1984). Like Hispanics, many Asian elderly—especially Chinese and, to a lesser extent, Japanese—have settled in ethnic enclaves in large cities, where they have found informal support systems among others who share their language and socioeconomic experiences. Kii summarizes the situation of aged Asian Americans by noting:

> Despite the general understanding that Asian Americans are more familistic in terms of caring for their elderly, the history of their immigration has forced many contemporary elderly to live outside of the normal family structure. Their occupational careers have not prepared them for comfortable retirement. Indeed, poverty is more rampant among them than among the elderly in the general population. Ethnic communities appear to be important lifelines for many of the Asian American elderly simply because of the language barriers they face and because of the discrimination and prejudice they have encountered in the wider society.[2]

SUMMARY

This chapter has discussed various ways in which society influences the aged. A very negative influence from the wider society is ageism, a form of prejudice against the elderly simply because they are old. Ageism stigmatizes older people and causes them to be socially devalued by young adults in particular and the larger society in general. The reasons for these developments stem from a widespread fear of aging and from social values in contemporary society that are youth oriented. Such values may be changing, however, as larger numbers of elderly persons with higher levels of education and income influence the direction of society in the twenty-first century.

Old age is a more difficult period for older women than for men because of the greater likelihood of experiencing poverty and the loss of one's spouse through divorce or—most likely—through death. Moreover, retirement benefits are generally not as much for women as for men because of a history of lower-paying jobs for women, lessened seniority on the job

2. Toshi Kii, "Asians," in *Handbook on the Aged in the United States*, ed. Erdmore Palmore (Westport, CT: Greenwood, 1984), 206.

due to absences for childbearing, child care, and other family responsibilities, and jobs that do not provide pensions. Sexual inequality in work and retirement has been found to exist throughout the world (Pampel and Park 1986).

As for racial minority groups, the common denominator for elderly blacks, Hispanics, native Americans, and Asians is that they are more likely than non-Hispanic whites also to be poor. Poverty, rather than race, is typically the greatest problem for minorities in old age. Aged minorities are not necessarily in double jeopardy (suffering from both race and age discrimination), because age tends to bring more similarities than differences—regardless of race—for persons sharing the same socioeconomic status. The problem for minorities is that fewer of them are financially affluent, and life is thus harder for them in old age because of their greater poverty. The damage caused by racial discrimination to a person's life and economic well-being is something that usually happens at earlier ages rather than late life.

Hispanics represent the fastest-growing minority in U.S. society and will overtake blacks as the largest minority in the twenty-first century. Yet Hispanics as a whole tend to be younger than the general population, which may present some special difficulties in an aging society. That is, in the next century, the United States will be experiencing both greater Latinization and greater aging at the same time. Obviously, this situation will require major social and cultural adjustments. But Hispanics are aging as well, and the quality of life of aged Hispanics, as well as aged blacks, American Indians, and Asians, will be important social issues in years to come, as the aging of society forces adjustments to the nature of social life in the United States.

The aged in society currently have significant problems with respect to their position as old people and the manner in which old age shapes situations involving ageism, gender differences, and minority group experiences. The problems of the aged, however, appear to be ones caused largely by society, rather than by the aged themselves. As the age structure of society changes toward increased numbers of elderly, the direction of change featuring a decline in ageism is positive and appears to be happening. But inequities in the quality of life available to elderly women and racial minorities persist.

Chapter 9

WORK AND RETIREMENT

A person's occupation or profession represents one of the most important features of that person's social identity. One's job is clearly a major factor in determining self-esteem, satisfaction with life, and socioeconomic status. Yet old age represents the time of life in modern society when a person begins to end his or her working career and enter a new phase of social existence— retirement—which is a role typically identified with old people. Although it is becoming increasingly common for persons to retire in late middle age, retirement remains *the* normative social expectation for the lifestyle typical of the aged in Western society. This situation is especially true for males, but is also becoming the case for employed females (Pampel and Park 1986). To make the transition from a valued work role to a role of secondary importance to society, that of retirement, marks one of the most important status passages in an individual's life course. Consequently, the situation of the aged in relation to work and retirement is central to understanding the social processes that influence the later stages of life.

WORK

Until the early twentieth century, older persons tended to remain in the American labor force because of the demand for workers to support the nation's industrialization. Retirement was not common. Employed persons worked as long as their health permitted. Labor unions emerged in the late nineteenth century and, in negotiation with management for improved worker benefits, began obtaining job security and old age pensions for older workers. However, in some cases, increased security was gained along with mandatory retirement rules. That is, senior workers were not to be the first to be laid off or fired in an economic recession and were to be given a pension at retirement, but they were also required to retire at a certain age (usually age 65) whether they wanted to or not. Job security and mandatory retirement were initially considered to be a form of protection for older workers; yet, during the surge of industrial development in the early twentieth century, mandatory retirement also became a means to get rid of aged employees and bring in younger people.

According to William Graebner (1980), discrimination against older workers became particularly acute in the late nineteenth and early twentieth centuries, despite efforts by labor unions to protect them. A capitalist economy that was highly competitive and committed to high productivity in the pursuit of short-term profit preferred youth. Many employers felt that aged workers could not maintain productivity in enterprises requiring speed and the ability to keep up with machines. For example, in the printing business, Graebner (1980:22) found that "between 1895 and 1915, older workers were phased out for younger men with better eyesight, more speed, and more endurance." Age limits on hiring became commonplace in American industry, and some companies simply fired workers when they became old. Graebner comments on the situation for machinists:

> Aging machinists faced the same problems as their counterparts in printing and arrived at similar conclusions. Faced with the competition of younger men and liable to dismissal at the first sign of age, machinists who had not yet reached middle age felt compelled to deceive their employers by dyeing their hair. As employers demanded more from their workers and increased the speed of their tools, older machinists who could not keep pace were replaced by boys.[1]

A few businesses favored older workers because of their dependability and experience; but most, faced with constantly improving technology, felt that, in a rapidly changing business world, adaptability was an essential quality that was not characteristic of most older workers. This situation was compounded by workers' demands for shorter working hours, so a way had to be

---

1. William Graebner, *A History of Retirement* (New Haven: Yale University Press, 1980), 24.

found to combine shorter hours with high productivity. Younger workers had the energy to turn out more goods in shorter time than older workers. Hence, young workers were in demand, although a certain number of older workers were usually maintained because of their experience, dependability, and loyalty to the company.

Retirement thus became a means to restructure the age components of the workforce, and it had the advantage of being impersonal and egalitarian. Retirement "allowed," states Graebner (1980:53), "the powerful turn-of-the-century impulse toward efficiency to coexist with a system of labor-management relations that was still permeated with personal and human relationships." Just firing older workers outright was a policy that most public and private employers would have found difficult to carry out (although some did) because of the opposition of labor unions, politicians, and the general public. It was not good for business to have a reputation for age discrimination and disloyalty to long-time employees. Retirement was an acceptable method to replace older workers with younger ones and thereby reduce unemployment and fuel the national economy. The effect on the aged worker, however, was nonetheless negative, because it devalued his or her potential and forced retirement regardless of the individual's ability, talents, experience, or desires.

Malcolm Morrison (1986) explains that many of the negative stereotypes about older workers actually developed during 1920–1940—before retirement became fully institutionalized in the United States. At this time, prevailing management techniques, cloaked in the aura of "scientific methods" and featuring an assembly-line approach to manufacturing, mandated increases in the speed of work regardless of the consequences for the workers. Morrison describes the outcome as follows:

> Management's concentration on speed was based on the theory that a worker's lifetime individual capacity was relatively fixed, and that it declined over time until it was exhausted. The intense speed required for industrial work was thought to increase stress, which, it was assumed, would result in an absolute decline of productive capacity with age. With an increasing immigrant labor supply, union demands for reduced weekly hours, and the advent of automation, this "wear-and-tear" theory gained wide credence and was used to justify both the dismissal of older workers as well as the imposition of age limitations in hiring.[2]

Although there was never much objective support for beliefs about the relationship between age and declining capacities, these views have persisted

---

2. Malcolm H. Morrison, "Work and Retirement in the Aging Society," *Daedalus* 115 (1986): 276.

over time and have hardened with the addition of negative assumptions about skills obsolescence, reduced learning capacity, resistance to change, and slower decision making with aging. Despite considerable scientific evidence that, for most tasks, age is not related to reduced performance and that individual variations preclude any valid generalizations about age and performance, the belief persists that age results in declining productive capacities. This belief has proven extraordinarily difficult to change.

During the economic depression of the 1930s, the aged possibly suffered more than any other group, for older workers had the highest unemployment rates; also, many elderly people lost their life savings when the stock market crashed and the economy slumped (Achenbaum 1983). As the plight of the elderly became increasingly clear, Congress passed the Social Security Act of 1935, which provided monthly payments to persons age 65 and over. This landmark decision was a major step in establishing a welfare system in the United States and marked a fundamental change in government policy toward the aged.

However, this was not the first time the United States had established a government-sponsored pension system that supported the elderly. In 1862, during the Civil War, Congress authorized a pension for Union soldiers and sailors who were disabled as a result of injuries or disease incurred during military service. Amounts were based on military rank and degree of disability. Widows, orphans, and other dependents of Union personnel who died from causes associated with wartime service were also allocated pensions at rates their relatives would have received. Only one dependent relative per family received benefits, although extra amounts for children were added to payments to widows in 1873.

In 1890 the Dependent Pension Act ended the link between pensions and war wounds. Pensions were authorized for all veterans who had served honorably for at least 90 days, regardless of whether or not they had been in combat—if they became too disabled to perform manual labor at some point in their lives. As Theda Skocpol (1994:94) explains, "in practice, old age alone soon became a sufficient disability, and in 1906 the law was amended to state this explicitly." Consequently, the Civil War pension system ultimately evolved into an old age pension program for elderly Union veterans. By 1910, Skocpol finds, some 28 percent of all American males age 65 and older (562,615 men) were receiving federal benefits averaging $189 annually. Skocpol concludes:

> Civil War pensions became one of the politically most successful social policies ever devised and sustained in the United States. Expanded very significantly right at the beginning of the country's modern national history—during

an era that most historians claim was dominated by limited government and rugged individualism—these pensions signaled the potential for honorable, crossclass, and crossracial social provision to flourish in American democracy. Civil War pensions at their height were America's first system of federal social security for the disabled and the elderly. This pioneering effort was not to be sustained beyond the lifetimes of the generation that fought to save the Union. But, politically speaking, it was an harbinger of things to come in American democracy.[3]

What followed in 1935 was a nationwide social security program whose benefits were eventually expanded for all elderly. The federal government for the first time assumed a broad responsibility for all elderly— not just Union veterans of the Civil War—whose well-being had historically been left to individuals, families, employers, and private groups. In accomplishing this shift, the federal government mediated between various interest groups, including labor unions, large business corporations, and various agencies within the government (Quadagno 1984, 1988a; Skocpol 1994).

Thus the federal government assumed a major responsibility for the welfare of aged persons, and the aged, conversely, became legally entitled to benefits from the state; that is, older persons were given the *right* of financial support from the government. Although there is evidence to suggest that the Social Security Act was designed to get older workers out of the marketplace in order to improve job opportunities for younger workers who could be hired at lower wages (Graebner 1980; Quadagno 1984, 1988a), the intent of the legislation was also to provide income security in old age in the form of a basic subsistence payment (Achenbaum 1983; Morrison 1986). Elderly workers were left to decide for themselves if they wanted to be employed, but a limit on their job earnings was imposed if they wanted to draw full Social Security benefits. The reason for this measure was to ensure that such benefits were not simply a supplement to income from employment, but were compensation for job earnings lost because of retirement.

Successive amendments to the Social Security Act since 1935 have extended coverage to disabled persons and widows and their dependent children, while generally liberalizing eligibility requirements. For those elderly who desired to keep working, the Age Discrimination in Employment Act of 1967 provided protection from denial of employment on the basis of age for all workers age 40 and over. The act was amended in 1978 to abolish manda-

3. Theda Skocpol, *Social Policy in the United States* (Princeton, NJ: Princeton University Press, 1994), 71.

tory retirement in the federal civil service and raise the mandatory retirement age from 65 to 70 in most other occupational groups. A subsequent amendment in 1986 eliminated mandatory retirement altogether in almost all jobs. This law thus ended forced retirement at age 70 and allows Americans to retire at older ages than previously. It is now legally possible for most elderly people to remain employed, regardless of their age, for as long as they have the ability and desire to work.

Because of this legislation, many experts expected an increase in the number of workers remaining in the labor force past age 65, but this has not happened. The decline in aged workers is shown in Table 9–1, which presents the age and sex distribution of persons in the U.S. labor force from 1960 to 1994. For the age group 65 and over, Table 9–1 shows that the percentage declined from 4.6 percent of all workers in 1960 to 2.9 percent in 1994. For men age 65 and over, the percentage dropped from 4.9 in 1960 to 3.1 in 1994; the figures for women for the same period show a drop from 3.9 percent to 2.8. Therefore, even though the elderly have the right to continue to work if they so desire, there has been a decline since 1960 in the proportion of the labor force made up of older persons. The reasons for this trend are threefold: (1) labor market problems for older workers (not having skills that are in demand, plant closings, corporate layoffs, relocation of businesses, difficulty finding work after becoming unemployed); (2) declining health; and (3) opportunities for retirement (Atchley 1994).

The U.S. Department of Labor also projects that the number of employed older workers is going to continue to decline between 1994 and 2000. For males, age 65 years and older, the 2.2 million workers in 1994 will shrink to 1.4 million in 2000; for females, the 1.7 million figure for 1994 will become 1 million in 2000. On the whole, it appears that, if current trends continue, fewer aged workers will be represented in the labor force at the beginning of the twenty-first century.

The great majority of persons who leave the labor force after age 62 do so because they want to retire, but declining levels of health also make it more difficult for them to work. Research on retirement concludes that the majority of persons who retire for reasons other than health had the option to remain in the labor force but declined to do so (National Center for Health Statistics 1987b). Rather, they had reached the time of life when, for them, retirement was preferable to continued employment.

Unlike past periods of American history, the twentieth century has seen elderly workers gain the right to remain in the workplace. The Social Security Act and its various amendments provide them and their dependents with financial support as a basic right. In 1965, during the adminis-

TABLE 9-1, U.S. Civilian Labor Force, Percentage Distribution by Sex and Age, 1960–1994

Year and Sex	Civilian Labor Force (thousands)	Percentage Distribution						
		16–19 Years	20–24 Years	25–34 Years	35–44 Years	45–54 Years	55–64 Years	65 Years and Over
Total: 1960	69,628	7.0	9.6	20.7	23.4	21.3	13.5	4.6
1970	82,771	8.8	12.8	20.6	19.9	20.5	13.6	3.9
1980	106,940	8.8	14.9	27.3	19.1	15.8	11.2	2.9
1985	115,461	6.8	13.6	29.1	22.6	15.0	10.4	2.5
1990	124,787	5.9	11.1	28.7	25.5	16.4	9.5	2.8
1994	131,056	5.7	10.8	26.2	28.9	18.6	8.9	2.9
Male: 1960	46,388	6.0	8.9	22.1	23.6	20.6	13.8	4.9
1970	51,228	7.8	11.2	22.1	20.4	20.3	13.9	4.2
1980	61,453	8.1	14.0	27.6	19.3	16.1	11.8	3.1
1985	64,411	6.4	12.9	29.2	22.5	15.3	11.0	2.7
1990	68,234	5.7	10.7	29.0	25.3	16.4	9.9	3.0
1994	70,817	5.5	10.6	26.6	26.8	18.3	9.1	3.1
Female: 1960	23,240	8.8	11.1	17.8	22.8	22.7	12.8	3.9
1970	31,543	10.3	15.5	18.1	18.9	20.7	13.2	3.3
1980	45,487	9.6	16.1	26.9	19.0	15.4	10.4	2.6
1985	51,050	7.4	14.6	28.9	22.7	14.6	9.7	2.3
1990	56,554	6.3	11.6	28.3	25.8	16.5	9.0	2.7
1994	60,239	6.0	10.9	25.7	27.0	18.9	8.8	2.8

Source: U.S. Department of Labor, 1995.

tration of President Lyndon Johnson, two other important measures were passed by Congress on behalf of the elderly. One measure, Medicare, provides financial support for medical treatment in old age, and the other, the Older Americans Act, authorized funds for a number of programs (such as area agencies on aging and senior citizens' centers) to improve the quality of life of elderly Americans. Consequently, by the late twentieth century, the aged had emerged as a bona fide interest group that had a role in establishing national priorities. Their impact on the government since the 1930s, states W. Andrew Achenbaum (1985:47), "depended not on whether they were given a chance to present their case, but on how well they competed against others in claiming an ever-growing share of the federal budget."

When it comes to participation in the labor force, older workers not only can decide for themselves when they will retire, but now have legal safeguards against discrimination on the basis of age. The trend currently appears to be one of encouraging the elderly to remain employed for a longer period of time. The cost of retirement benefits can be as high as 20 percent of the budgets of government agencies and private business corporations, and these costs are likely to increase as the proportion of older people in the general population increases. The cost benefit of retiring older workers on a pension and hiring younger workers at lower wages to take their place is disappearing. Furthermore, many companies are finding advantages to keeping older employees. "Prejudices against the elderly worker," states Achenbaum (1985:155–156), "are becoming harder to justify in the face of mounting evidence that older workers' skill, loyalty, and reliability typically outweigh the decrements of age."

The aging of the population also means that there will be a smaller pool of younger persons in the labor force, so older workers may find themselves in greater demand. The number of males ages 20 to 24 in the labor force is expected to decline from 7.5 million in 1994 to 7.2 million in 2000, and the number of males ages 25 to 34 will decline from 18.9 million to 17.2 million during the same period. For females ages 20 to 24, the decline will be from 6.6 million to 6.4. million. For ages 25 to 34, there were 15.5 million women in the labor force in 1994, which will drop to 14.9 million in 2000. Losses in numbers of younger workers will be greater for males than females, but the overall pattern is toward fewer younger workers. There may be greater need for older workers in the twenty-first century, not only because of their experience and reliability, but also because they are needed to fill the thinning ranks of younger employees. This situation forecasts greater participation by the elderly in job training (or retraining) programs and second careers.

RETIREMENT

Retirement constitutes a major status passage brought on by the aging process in an individual's life course. According to Barney Glaser and Anselm Strauss (1971:2), a *status passage* entails movement through a social structure in which people either gain or lose status, privileges, power, and prestige. There may be changed identity and sense of self, as well as a possible change in behavior. Although a person has a certain status associated with his or her socioeconomic position, there comes a time when that person must vacate the position. As Glaser and Strauss pointed out, a temporal dimension is implicit in all kinds of status; no one is able to assume a position or status forever. In any status passage, a person begins with a certain status and ends with a different one. Marriage (or divorce), promotion (or demotion) at work, initiation into a fraternity or sorority, graduation from school, or completion of specialized training are all forms of status passage.

The transition from work to retirement is such a status passage, in that the person moves from being employed and an active member of a particular organization to being retired and no longer active in the organization. At the end, one's status has changed and become markedly lower than previously, because the individual is no longer a day-to-day participant, nor can he or she exercise his or her former status, authority, and influence. The status passages associated with aging (childhood to adulthood, adulthood to old age, work to retirement) are inevitable and irreversible; everyone goes through them, and no one has any choice in the matter because becoming old is universal.

Until the twentieth century, the United States did not have an explicit social policy regarding quality of life available to the aged after they retired. Old people were expected to get by as best they could and look to their families, religious organizations, labor unions, benevolent societies and charities, or local community if they needed support. Some private companies, especially railroads, began pensions in the late 1800s; later, a few states started pension funds for teachers, and, in large cities, retirement plans were initiated for policemen and firemen (Achenbaum 1985). Veterans of military service also received a pension from the federal government. Other programs providing old age support came under the jurisdiction of various states and counties and were subject to considerable variation in administration and financing (Quadagno 1984, 1988a). In these programs, the aged were placed in the same category as the poor and were subjected to similar administrative requirements. In a very real sense, being old came to mean being poor.

By the early 1930s, only 15 percent of all nonfarm workers and 20 percent of all labor union members had some type of pension plan (Achenbaum

1985). The federal government also had a retirement system for its employees, which went into effect in 1920. Few states provided any type of old age pension, although some 18 states had plans for old age relief. By 1935, only Wisconsin had unemployment benefits. Thus the majority of Americans simply had nothing in old age other than their own resources or what they could draw on from their family and whatever help was available in the community. There was no national pension plan, even though the majority of Western European countries had established government-sponsored retirement plans and national health insurance programs between 1883 and 1914.

The Social Security Act brought the United States into the ranks of the welfare states with respect to old age benefits, but not with regard to health care. The United States remains the only major industrialized country in the world without some form of national health insurance for the majority of its citizens. But, with the passage of the Social Security Act in 1935, a national policy for aging emerged in which the provision of assistance to old people has become a major priority. The passage of Medicare, 30 years later in 1965, provided funds to help pay for the majority of costs for medical care for the aged. Thus the elderly are prime beneficiaries of the American welfare state.

The Social Security Act is the most important event leading toward the establishment of a nationwide retirement system for the elderly in the United States. This act set the age for entitlement to old age benefits at age 65. An amendment to the act passed in 1983 raised the minimum age of retirement for the receipt of full Social Security benefits from age 65 to age 66, beginning in the year 2000, followed by an increase to age 67 by 2022 (Clair, Karp, and Yoels 1993). The latter measure was intended to encourage older people to continue working and to hold down the amount of federal funds spent on Social Security payments as the proportion of younger workers making contributions declines in the twenty-first century. By 2035, there will be only 1.9 workers per retiree (compared with 3.4 workers in 1995).

Table 9–2 shows that the number of beneficiaries, the amount of payments, and the average monthly benefits of the Social Security program increased significantly between 1970 and 1993. In 1970, Table 9–2 indicates, over 26 million retired workers, survivors of retired workers, and disabled workers received Social Security benefits; by 1993, the number of beneficiaries had reached over 42 million. Benefit payments, as shown in Table 9–2, rose from almost $32 billion in 1970 to over $302 billion in 1993. For the same period, average monthly payments to retired workers rose from $118 to $674, to disabled workers from $131 to $642, and for widows and widowers from $102 to $630. Social Security benefits are financed by taxes. In 1937, employees paid only 1 percent in Social Security taxes on only their first

TABLE 9–2 Number of Social Security Beneficiaries in Current-Payment Status and Average Monthly Benefit, 1970–1993

Year	Number of Beneficiaries (thousands)				Benefit Payments (millions of dollars)				Average Monthly Benefits (dollars)		
	Total	Retired Workers	Survivors	Disabled Workers	Total	Retired Workers	Survivors	Disabled Workers	Retired Workers	Disabled Workers	Widows and Widowers
1970	26,229	17,093	6,470	2,665	31,863	21,076	7,721	3,067	118	131	102
1975	32,086	20,323	7,411	4,353	66,923	42,645	15,864	8,414	207	226	194
1980	35,585	23,309	7,598	4,678	120,472	78,025	27,010	15,437	341	371	311
1985	37,058	25,989	7,162	3,907	186,195	128,536	38,824	18,836	479	484	433
1990	39,832	28,369	7,197	4,266	247,796	172,042	50,951	24,803	603	587	557
1991	40,592	28,824	7,255	4,513	268,098	185,545	54,891	27,662	629	609	584
1992	41,497	29,296	7,297	4,903	285,980	196,688	58,203	31,089	653	626	608
1993	42,238	29,633	7,341	5,264	302,402	206,365	61,440	34,598	674	642	630

Source: Social Security Administration, 1994.

$1,000 in earnings; in 1995, employees paid 7.65 percent on their first $61,200 of earnings.

The Social Security program has had a major impact on establishing the social expectation that retirement is normal in old age. A majority (over 75 percent) of retired persons have income in addition to Social Security—from savings, investments, and government or private pension plans—but establishment of Social Security has done the most to link the onset of old age benefits with a retired status in the public mind. In other words, people expect that elderly persons are retired and that retired persons, in turn, are elderly. Thus old age and retirement operate in tandem to produce a role in society—that of being retired—which is more or less exclusively that of the aged. Some people retire relatively young, in their midfifties, for example. But early retirement has not reached such large proportions that it has changed the normative expectation that retirement is associated with old age. This situation is borne out by the fact that some 89 percent of all persons in the United States age 65 and over are retired. People are considered retired when they do not work full time on a year-round basis and when they draw most of their income from a retirement pension.

Currently, there is a "'push-pull" effect with respect to retirement in the United States and other developed countries. The "push" toward retirement comes primarily from economic growth and the need for a young and recently trained labor force; the "pull" comes from government policies and private pension plans developed to make retirement more attractive financially and to induce older workers to leave the labor force voluntarily (Pampel and Weiss 1983).

The growth in the number of retired workers over age 65, particularly males, has also produced a need and demand for better private and public (government and military) pension benefits (Pampel and Williamson 1985). These enhanced benefits, in turn, made it attractive for males under the age of 65 to retire as well. As Stanley DeViney and Angela O'Rand (1988:536) explain, "Policies that were earlier a response to the retirement of one age group (over 65) later became a factor in the retirement of another, younger age group." For men, this expectation is being realized in the United States at increasingly earlier ages (55 to 64).

The retirement role is of particular interest to social scientists because it tends to be age specific (a role for the elderly) and represents a major status passage from previous adult roles (namely, loss of one's former work role or career). Consequently, retirement represents a major change in an individual's life and requires an adjustment to new circumstances. The fact that retirement means the person leaves his or her former professional or occupational role—through which that person obtained a considerable degree of self-identity and status—and assumes a role of lesser importance to the wider society has suggested that this may be a time of stress and sensed personal loss. At the very least, it means a turning point in an individual's life experiences and the necessity to modify one's past lifestyle. In the next four sections we review the problem of stress, the manner in which people typically experience retirement, differences among people who retire, and family relations.

Is Retirement Stressful?

On retiring, the individual departs from his or her usual environment of employment, in which the roles, functions, and personal relationships associated with work typically are well established. If the person has an important position or at least a position that is meaningful or even habitual for that individual, there can be discomfort and a distinct sense of loss at giving up one's occupational role. In fact, for some people, that role is their central role in life; that is, it is the role that provides them with their master status, which is the principal source of their social identity and position in the social system. Yet, although some may be reluctant to retire from their job because of the cost in terms of lost income, status, and self-identity, others may look forward to the experience as a time to relax and pursue their own schedule and interests. Achenbaum (1983) points out that, on the basis of his review of relevant studies, many older workers do not consider it a "privilege" to continue working past retirement age. Achenbaum (1983:157) states: "Except for a minority of cases, older people wish to be occupied and enjoy a satisfying personal life, but they do not want to continue working."

Consequently, retirement may not have intense negative ramifications for the individual, because, as research shows, people typically have time to anticipate the experience and plan for it prior to its actual beginning (Mutran and Reitzes 1981). Other research shows that retirement does not affect one's health adversely and is not a direct cause of premature death (Ekerdt et al. 1983; McGoldrick 1989; Palmore 1981; Streib and Schneider 1971). People sometimes do die shortly after they retire, but it usually appears to be the result of a preexisting health condition rather than the effect of retirement per se (Parker 1982; McGoldrick 1989). Some studies, including those of a sample of retired men from an oil refinery in Texas (Owen and Belzung 1967) and a group of men in Great Britain from several different occupations who retired early (McGoldrick and Cooper 1989), report improved physical health to be a benefit of retirement. Among persons who retired because of ill health, retirement resulted in a reduction in the level of demands placed on them, which, in turn, was perceived by the respondents as a positive health measure (Ekerdt, Bossé, and LoCastro 1983). In sum, there does not seem to be a negative relationship between health and retirement.

In an extensive review of the literature on stress and retirement, with a focus on early retirement, Anne McGoldrick (1989) determined that retirement cannot be assumed to be a stressful life event for most people. Apparently only a minority view retirement negatively, and this seems especially so if it results in a significant loss of income. Otherwise, it appears that most people reach the point in their lives when retirement is desired. Research investigating retirement planning among males, for example, shows that most accurately predict their time of retirement and therefore are able to plan for it (Ekerdt, Vinick, and Bossé 1989). Thus retirement was not an event that was not anticipated. Other studies have found no serious adverse consequences resulting from retirement for men (Fillenbaum, George, and Palmore 1985) or for both men and women (George, Fillenbaum, and Palmore 1984). Erdman Palmore (1981) found, in research conducted at Duke University between 1950 and 1976, that the elderly cohort under study (a sample of Durham County, North Carolina, residents) did not become completely inactive, isolated, or very lonely, nor did very many of them suffer from poverty or depression because of retirement. "Most appear," stated Palmore (1981:46), "to adapt to the 'crisis' of retirement with little or no negative effects."

Overall, it therefore appears that retirement in itself is not generally stressful. McGoldrick (1989) found that a growing body of evidence suggests that this situation is due to changes in attitudes toward work. Many people view their job primarily as a source of income and do not find the source of meaning of their lives from work alone. Family, friends, and personal pursuits providing pleasure, interest, and satisfaction are very important, and perhaps more important than work, in providing self-fulfullment. McGoldrick (1989:105) suggests that "as the concept of retirement becomes incorporated into a culture, the tendency to look on work as a temporary part of life increases, causing people to look elsewhere." As people enter late middle age and begin thinking about retirement, the possibility of satisfaction outside of their work situation may begin to take on greater importance. Problems associated with retirement appear due more to health, finances, and opportunities for enjoyment than to the act of retiring itself.

The Retirement Experience

Robert Atchley (1994) identifies eight possible phases of retirement. First is the "preretirement" phase in which, as retirement approaches and becomes near, the individual begins to prepare for the experience. Preparation consists of adjusting to the separation from one's job and the work environment and making plans about retirement activities. When retirement occurs, states Atchley, the person takes one of three paths toward either (1) the "honeymoon," (2) the immediate retirement routine, or (3) rest and relaxation. The "honeymoon" is a retirement phase marked by euphoria, in which retired people are busy doing all the things that they "never had time for before." Extended periods of travel are very common in the honeymoon phase, for example. This phase requires money and good health, and some people skip it altogether. But, for those who go through it, they eventually leave this phase and settle into a less hectic routine that will characterize the remainder of their retirement days. Other people will move instantly into an "immediate retirement routine," which will most likely stabilize over time. In this phase, they will adopt a schedule of activities at a regulated pace, which will likely turn into a more or less permanent lifestyle. Still other individuals, after retirement, will enter the "rest and relaxation" phase, which consists of a very low level of activity. Many people just "take it easy" for a while, but eventually, Atchley notes, they get restless and become more active.

After experiencing one of the three phases in the initial postretirement period, movement into other phases takes place. Some people go into a "disenchantment" phase, as they find that retirement is not enjoyable and does not live up to their expectations. Disenchantment, however, may be rare, for few people were found in Atchley's earlier studies (Atchley 1976, 1982) to be unhappy with retirement. Another possibility is a "reorientation" phase in which retired persons change their approach to retirement. Perhaps they become more involved in activities with friends and family, after initially pursuing their interests more or less on their own. But eventually the great majority of retired persons enter into the phase of "routine," in which they know what they want to do and what they are able to do; thus they develop a set of stable activities that becomes their own particular retired lifestyle. Finally, some may even adopt a "termination" phase and go back to their old job or find a new one. They do this because they prefer working or find that they have to work in order to support themselves in old age. Eventually, however, essentially all older people adopt the phase of routine as they settle into a particular pattern of living out their remaining years.

Who Retires?

Practically all Americans employed outside the home retire at some point when they reach old age. There are, however, some differences among people in the retirement process. According to Palmore (1981), the majority of people have retired in the past because of mandatory policies and health. With mandatory age limits on employment being eliminated, people still appear to view the sixties as the age in which retirement is appropriate. Women are more likely to retire than men, and married women, in contrast to single, widowed, or divorced women, tend to retire earlier. Married men, on the other hand, tend to retire later than their nonmarried counterparts. Palmore suggests that the reason for the greater likelihood of female than male retirement is that, in the current generation of workers, the work role is more important for men than for women. Yet he notes that, with greater sexual equality in the labor market, retirement rates of men and women are beginning to converge.

Education is also an important factor in retirement, in that the highly educated tend to retire later than the less educated. The reasons for this, states Palmore, are these: (1) the better educated are more likely to have jobs not affected by the physical decline that accompanies old age; (2) the work of the better educated tends to be more interesting and more rewarding; (3) the skills of the educated are likely to be in greater demand; and (4) better-educated persons are more likely to be self-employed, so they can decide for themselves how long they wish to continue to work.

For persons under the age of 65, Palmore explains that it is either poor health, or disability, or the attractiveness of a pension plan that draws them toward retirement. The greater the physical strain and demands of the job, coupled with lesser rewards, as is the case for blue-collar or manual labor workers, the more likely retirement is the preferred option for the older employee. Persons in lower skilled jobs are also more likely to retire earlier than persons in higher skilled positions. However, regardless of a person's physical abilities or demographic characteristics, such as gender, level of education, type of occupation, or even a particular age, Palmore concludes that there is something about aging itself that markedly increases the desire for retirement. In other words, most people in advanced societies reach a point in life when they feel—for whatever reason (declining energy, pressure from others, eligibility for a pension, age discrimination, desire to pursue personal interests)—that it is time to retire.

Retirement and the Aged Family

Retirement can mean both positive and negative changes in family relationships. Free of occupational demands and childrearing duties, older husbands and wives can have more time to spend with each other, with children and grandchildren, and in leisure activities—including recreation, travel, hobbies, and social occasions. Retirement also means adjustment to circumstances that may be negative, such as decreased earnings, loss of status, and dependence on one's children. However, current studies suggest that status and family income tend to show only modest downturns in old age (Pampel and Hardy 1994). And, despite a normative emphasis on self-sufficiency in the United States, aged parents are more likely to turn to their adult children for advice, emotional support, and household assistance in both emergency and nonemergency situations (Hogan and Eggebeen 1995). The older and more frail or unhealthy the aged person becomes, the greater the dependence on children and the greater the potential for moving in with a child or being placed in a nursing home. As Harold Cox (1996) explains, dependence on one's children in old age is a role reversal. The child becomes responsible for the parent, and it is the parent who is counseled and cared for by the child.

In a nationwide study of American families, Dennis Hogan and David Eggebeen (1995) found that children are more readily accessible to their aged parents than popular images suggest and are the most responsive in situations of need. More distant kin tend to be much less important if children are available. Elderly persons without children typically substitute other sources of support, such as relatives or friends, so that their level of support is not distinctly inferior to those of people with adult children. Consequently, the older an individual becomes, the more vital the family or someone serving in a familylike role becomes to that person (Brown 1996). The maintenance of family relationships after retirement is an important feature of late life.

The Future of Retirement

The Social Security Act firmly established the concept of retirement on a national scale. But, as Morrison (1986) explains, despite the general consensus about the value of retirement and its apparently positive consequences, there are serious social and economic questions about whether it can continue in its present form in an aging society. The social uncertainties, notes Morrison, revolve around the fact that retirement has both positive and negative consequences for the older person. The positive aspects of retirement are—provided one has sufficient income—the capability to pursue one's interests and not have to work. The negative consequences are that the retired person loses his or her work status and moves into a less socially important role.

The economic questions have to do with the ability and willingness of society to continue providing Social Security benefits and health insurance

(Medicare) through contributions of the active labor force. In the past, it has been necessary for the U.S. Congress to reallocate funds to prevent both the Social Security program and Medicare from becoming bankrupt. As Morrison points out:

> It has taken national legislation to forestall the insolvency of the Social Security retirement program and the Medicare program in the United States, and although the measures enacted or proposed appear to remedy fiscal problems for the time being, few informed observers believe today's benefit levels can be maintained in the future without further program modifications that would involve additional taxation of workers and the retired themselves, and/or substantial reductions of benefits.[4]

What is likely to happen, given the political influence of older voters and the national commitment to provide for the needs of the aged, is additional taxation with little or no reduction in benefits. In fact, pressure is likely to mount, as the age structure of society becomes older, to increase benefits for the elderly. In the future, the aged will likely take up an increasingly greater share of the federal budget. The projected increase in the elderly population is virtually certain to require increased government spending for health and social services for the aged, because the alternative—holding expenditures constant or decreasing them—could seriously erode levels of health and quality of life available to old people (Lusky 1986).

One trend that counterbalances this situation is the likelihood of older workers remaining in the labor force for a longer period of time. With an increase in older persons and a decline in the proportion of younger adults, employers may begin to offer incentives to older workers to delay retirement or return to work after retirement. Morrison (1986) observes that, with increasing numbers of people entering retirement and living longer in a retired status, retirement takes on the attributes of a separate life stage in which people are not generally productive. He suggests that it might not be good social policy to limit the overall productivity of as much as 20 percent of the total population. Therefore, changes may come about in both policy and practice that encourage the aged to continue their contributions to social, cultural, and economic life. This will mean allowing older persons the flexibility to remain productive, the elimination of ageism in the workplace and the larger society, and public promotion of the skills, talent, and experience

---

4. Malcolm H. Morrison, "Work and Retirement in the Aging Society," *Daedalus* 115 (1986): 270.

the elderly can provide to the economy and the cultural life of the country. In short, notes Morrison, a new social conception of productive roles for older persons is needed. No longer can old people be cast in the public eye as a social and economic burden, or excluded from major participation in the ongoing activities of the wider society.

Retirement is a stage of the life cycle in developed societies that appears to have evolved into a basic right and a normative outcome in the lives of employed persons. Although current trends point to tendencies toward earlier retirement in Western nations, this situation may be modified. Increased numbers of people may opt for early retirement if they are financially secure, but inducements are likely to be forthcoming in the twenty-first century to promote later retirements or to have phased retirements in which the older worker bows out of the workplace slowly. Phased retirement would consist of reduced work schedules, prorated salaries, and health and retirement benefits that are either continued or prorated as well. Partial pension payments may also be allowed at this time. Or retirees may be rehired as part-time workers or become independent contractors who provide their services to their former employer in return for a negotiated fee. Therefore, the retirement pattern in the future is likely to be one that is highly variable, as aged persons adopt different approaches to dealing with the period of life in which retirement has been common. All of this suggests that the aged will be closer to the social, cultural, and economic mainstream of society than ever before in modern history.

SUMMARY

Negative attitudes toward the aged extended to the workplace, especially as elderly workers were discriminated against during the industrialization of the United States. But this situation has improved, for older workers now have legal protection from discrimination and guaranteed benefits from Social Security and other retirement plans. Retirement is now a normative expectation in the lives of most working people. Older workers are pushed by retirement policies to retire from the labor force to make room for younger workers, and they are also pulled toward retirement by pension benefits. Because retirement is typically an expected event, it is not especially stressful or negative. Other people, primarily males, are retiring from the labor force in greater numbers and at earlier ages. Attitudes are such now that most older people do not consider it a privilege to work past retirement age; instead, retirement is perceived as a desirable phase of old age that provides the opportunity to seek self-fulfillment in late life.

However, with a decline in the proportion of younger workers and an increase in the number of elderly in the twenty-first century, older people are likely to be in greater demand for employment. Thus there is likely to be greater variation in the retirement years, as older people opt for either retirement or full-time or part-time employment.

Chapter 10

THE AGED AS A SOCIAL FORCE

A major theme of this book is that the elderly population in the United States, as well as in other developed countries, is in an advantaged position compared with past generations of old people. In the twenty-first century, the elderly will be a more important and powerful segment of society than ever before because of their large numbers, longevity, experience with the political system, and enhanced levels of health, education, and income. In this chapter, we explore the manner in which the elderly are emerging into a major political force. Initially, we discuss why the aged are more of a political interest group than a minority group in American society. Then we review the development of the welfare state in Western society in relation to old age politics.

THE AGED: A MINORITY GROUP?

Do the aged constitute an emerging minority group in American society, and, if so, is it in a minority group context that they will play a political role? According to Louis Wirth (1945:67), "We may define a minority as a group of people who, because of their physical or cultural characteristics, are singled out from the others in the society in which they live for differential and unequal treatment and who therefore regard themselves as objects of discrimination." It has been pointed out that many older people have experienced negative stereotyping, relegation to an inferior social status, discrimination, and segregation from younger people (Levin and Levin 1980; Rosow 1974). A common reaction of people exposed to these social and psychological stresses is the formation of a group identity with a specific belief and value system reflecting the needs and goals of group members. It has therefore been proposed that such a group identity may have developed among the aged in the form of a subculture, and the emergence of this subculture among old people marks them as a distinctive minority group (Rose 1965).

But is there really a subculture of the aged? The norms of older people tend to be middle-aged. That is, most old people judge themselves on the basis of how closely they reflect middle-age norms (Fontana 1977). They also like to think of themselves more or less as they always have—except that they are just older (Gove, Ortega, and Style 1989; Kaufman 1987). All of this would suggest that elderly people do not necessarily focus on age as the basis of their distinctiveness. This tendency undermines claims that old people are a subculture in their own right.

This becomes especially clear when one considers the definition of a subculture. A *subculture* is a system of values, attitudes, modes of behavior, and lifestyles of a social group that is distinct from, but related to, the dominant culture of society (Abercrombie, Hill, and Turner 1984:312). Aged persons, accordingly, do not appear to qualify as a subculture, because the values, attitudes, behaviors, and lifestyles they pursue are not especially different from those of middle-aged adults. Old age may cause a modification in an individual's behavior and lifestyle (because of reduced finances and energy and increased leisure time), but usually there is not a drastic change from the past unless the aged person's health fails. And, if the personality has continuity, as indicated by continuity theory (Neugarten 1964), the older person's lifelong values and attitudes are not likely to change a great deal either.

Thus, to describe elderly people as a minority group on the basis of a subculture of old age does not appear to be accurate, nor do the aged appear to be a minority in the same sense that blacks, Hispanics, American Indians, or Asians constitute minority groups in the United States. For instance, Gordon Streib (1965, 1976) points out that membership in a minority group is usually permanent and exclusive. Most people who are part of a minority group begin life in a minority status because of their race, ethnicity, or religion—and remain there. Yet *everyone* becomes old; no one starts out life that way. True, some people may choose to be a member of a minority group by changing their situation, such as changing from a majority to a minority religion. But most minority group characteristics cannot be changed, such as race or ethnicity, because people are born with these traits, and the biological or cultural imprint is permanent. The only way to change such minority status is to move geographically to where the particular traits are those of the majority. Being elderly, on the other hand, is something that happens to people for only part of their lives if they live long enough, and it takes place regardless of where they reside. Thus, to become old is not something that is exclusive only to some people, because anyone may reach old age.

Furthermore, the extent of prejudice and discrimination against the aged as a group falls far short of the manner in which prejudice and discrimination have historically affected racial, ethnic, and religious minority groups. Such groups have been persecuted throughout much of human history because of their minority traits, but old people have not been singled out for persecution—killed, imprisoned, tortured, enslaved, or denied participation in the political process—simply because they became older. In fact, elderly people still enjoy relatively high status in Japan and developing countries of the third world, and there is evidence that their status is improving in the developed nations of the West (Binstock 1983). Streib (1965) notes that, in the United States, elderly persons have never been denied (because of their age) the right to vote, own property, or hold political office, as has happened to blacks and women. It is therefore difficult to make a case demonstrating that elderly people suffer from prejudice and discrimination to the same degree experienced by blacks, Hispanics, and other racial or ethnic minorities.

Thus it does not seem appropriate to depict old people as either a subculture or a minority group. The most apt description of the elderly is that they are a segment of society composed of people from varying backgrounds who have old age in common. Whatever sense of collective identity the elderly have most likely derives from being old, and this circumstance promotes age-specific similarities, feelings, and consciousness but does not eliminate racial, social, and economic differences among them. The collective nature of the elderly seems best expressed within the context of being an *interest* group. An *interest group* is a voluntary association of citizens who attempt to influence public policy. Senior citizens' groups have become one of the most important political lobbies in the nation and have been highly successful in obtaining benefits for all older persons. What provides a sense of social solidarity and cohesion in such groups is an awareness of common problems and interests and the desire to work together to achieve a better life for themselves and the elderly who follow them. Thus it is in the context of an interest group, rather than a minority group, that the elderly in American society influence the political process.

THE AGED AS AN INTEREST GROUP

Senior citizens' groups are organized throughout the country and are set up to provide various services, such as social activities, recreational opportunities, and assistance in the form of delivering hot meals, helping with household duties, and securing the delivery of health services. Many of these groups are also involved in politics at all levels of government, as they work to elect politicians who will support their interests and goals. Because these groups tend to keep abreast of public affairs and to vote, they are a potent force in elections. Therefore, politicians usually pay attention to them and do not openly oppose their interests. The tendency of older persons to vote is shown in Table 10–1, which depicts voting patterns in American presidential elections by age group for 1964 through 1992. Table 10–1 shows that persons age 65 and over usually equaled or surpassed the percentage of voters in other age groups in each election. For 1992, for example, some 70.1 percent of persons age 65 and over voted, compared to 70.0 percent for those 45 to 64, 58.3 percent for persons 25 to 44, and 42.8 percent of the youngest age category of 18 to 24 years. Data like these suggest that older people have a greater propensity to vote than the young (Posner 1995).

The most influential organization speaking for older persons on the national level is the American Association of Retired Persons (AARP). In 1978, AARP had 10 million members, but in 1995, there were 33.3 million members. Thus the influence of AARP rests in the fact that it can claim it represents one-fifth of all voters in the United States. The cost of membership is modest. Dues, only $5 annually, provide a third of the association's income; other money is obtained from selling products to assist aged persons, health insurance, home and automobile insurance, a pharmacy service, and advertising in their magazine *Modern Maturity*. In 1994 AARP had a budget of $430 million, an eight-story office building in Washington, D.C., ten regional offices, and a staff of 1,807. Membership is open to anyone 50

TABLE 10–1　Percentage Of Each Age Group Voting in Presidential Elections, 1964–1992

Age	1964	1968	1972	1976	1980	1984	1988	1992
18–24	50.9	50.4	49.6	42.2	39.9	40.8	36.2	42.8
25–44	69.0	66.6	62.7	58.7	58.7	58.4	54.0	58.3
45–64	75.9	74.9	70.8	68.7	69.3	69.8	67.9	70.0
Over 65	66.3	65.8	63.5	62.2	65.1	67.7	68.8	70.1

Source: Jerry T. Jennings, "Voting and Registration in the Election of November 1992," *Current Population Reports, Population Characteristics,* Series P30-466 (Washington, D.C.: U.S. Government Printing Office, 1993).

years of age and older, and nearly 50 percent of all Americans in this age bracket belong to AARP.

AARP was organized in 1958 under the leadership of Ethel Percy Andrus as a nonprofit association intended to enhance the quality of life of older persons. Initially, its primary function was to provide inexpensive health insurance for the aged, rather than to become politically powerful. But, in working with members of Congress to support the well-being of the aged and in representing their views to lawmakers, AARP has become one of the most effective lobbies in Washington. Moreover, AARP has its own Public Policy Institute for analyzing policy issues and its own legislative division to support its lobbyists, whose job is to influence lawmakers. AARP conducts its own research, works with its membership in contacting their government representatives about important legislation, and produces a large volume of publications discussing the needs of old people. AARP does not donate money to politicians or political groups; rather, its influence comes from its size (in voting power) and the nature of its constituents (the aged). To oppose the needs of the elderly is not only a generally unpopular position for a politician to take, but also one that is likely to present serious problems for remaining in office. With an organization like AARP, older people exert an important influence in the nation's politics; and with increasing numbers, this influence is likely to become even greater. Consequently, elderly people have evolved in the late twentieth century into one of the most influential segments of American society, and it is organizations like AARP that have helped them do it.

Although AARP is the most powerful of today's lobbies for the elderly, this organization is only one of several groups that have worked for the benefit of the aged and influenced legislation. There are, for example, some 30 organizations based in Washington, D. C., that directly represent the interests of the elderly (Achenbaum 1985). Besides AARP, the most important organizations are the National Council on Aging (NCA), which represents nearly 2,000 separate health care, social work, and social service agencies and sponsors a national center for aging policy; and the National Council of Senior Citizens (NCSC), with strong ties to labor unions. AARP, NCA, and NCSC are the so-called Big Three organizations for the elderly (Achenbaum 1983). Other important organizations include the American Association of Homes for the Aged (AAHA), the American Nursing Home Association (ANHA), and the National Association of State Units on Aging (NASUA), which support the interests of the aged and manage the delivery of specialized services. There are other groups, such as the Gray Panthers (a politically militant organization), the National Caucus on the Black Aged, the Asociacion Nacional Por Personas Mayores, which helps older Hispanics, and the

National Association of Retired Employees, which helps protect the interests of federal workers.

The first major organization of importance for older people was the Townsend Movement, which began in the 1930s in California with physician Frances E. Townsend as its founder. The Townsend Movement claimed over 5 million members at its peak in 1935 and was important in influencing the enactment of the Social Security Act. Another group in the 1930s was the American Association for Old Age Security, which espoused not only pensions for the elderly but also a redistribution of the nation's wealth. The American Federation of Labor likewise supported old age benefits as a means to protect workers after retirement, and another labor group—the American Association for Labor Legislation—worked to have old age benefits included in the collective bargaining process between labor and management (Achenbaum 1983).

The Townsend Movement, labor unions and councils, business associations, and various state organizations and interest groups all vied for influence on Congress and President Franklin D. Roosevelt in relation to a federal program of old age benefits in the 1930s. With the nation suffering the Great Depression, the plight of the elderly was particularly acute, because they had the highest rates of unemployment, and private pension plans were not widespread (Achenbaum 1983; Graebner 1980). Considerable disagreement existed among many of the interested parties, as organized labor sought to tie old age benefits to labor force participation, agricultural and political interests in the South wanted to minimize or avoid regulation of a national pension plan by the federal government, and various business interests demanded that taxes to support any form of social security be kept low (Quadagno 1984, 1988a). State managers of pension plans in private industry were under pressure to respond to the economic hardships of the Great Depression and deal with labor discontent. Various members of Congress also had ideas about welfare for the aged.

In the meantime, the Townsend Movement advanced its own plan, which caused a political furor by demanding that every person over the age of 60 be given $200 a month and be required to spend the entire amount within that month in order to stimulate the depressed economy. The Roosevelt administration claimed that the plan was simply unworkable, and President Roosevelt created a Committee on Economic Security, which functioned to mediate between the various interest groups. Eventually, compromises were reached, and the Social Security Act marked the beginning of the welfare state in the United States. Labor received what it wanted in linking Social Security eligibility and benefits to participation in the work force, the states acquired administration of the program's public assistance services, and all persons 65 years of age and older received entitlement to a pension from the federal government.

According to Jill Quadagno:

> What was at stake in the debate surrounding the Social Security Act was the nature of the state itself. Organized labor, nonmonopoly capital, and Southern agricultural interests were struggling to keep social-welfare measures outside the jurisdiction of the state, whereas a core group of influential monopoly capitalists, national state managers and various citizens coalitions argued for increased centralization. The outcome of this battle was a reorganization of the state in a manner that expanded its role and incorporated interest groups more fully in its jurisdiction.[1]

With the passage of the Social Security Act, the federal government assumed the role and the duty of guaranteeing a minimum level of income to all elderly citizens. However, Quadagno (1984, 1988a) points out that the Social Security Act did not happen by itself, and she notes that it was the Townsend Movement of elderly persons that provided the pressure for reform. Since the Social Security Act, and continuing until the present, the driving force in obtaining old age benefits has been organizations representing the aged (Pampel and Williamson 1985). Before 1920, the elderly in the United States were unable to engage in collective action to solve the social problems of growing old; now the aged have all the earmarks of a "modern" force in society, and a potent lobby exists to support their cause at the national level (Achenbaum 1983:169).

THE AGED AND THE WELFARE STATE

With the Social Security Act of 1935, the elderly played a major role in influencing the federal government in the United States to adopt a welfare state approach to assisting old people. Since then, the aged have been able not only to influence the continuation of the program, but also subsequently to enhance it. However, in both the United States and Western Europe, public demand for social security programs for the aged was initially centered in labor movements, because the elderly themselves lacked political power. It was principally in the United States, not Western Europe, that the elderly pressured the national government as a major interest group to begin providing old age benefits. Social welfare programs had begun in the late nineteenth and early twentieth centuries in most countries of Western Europe, but

---

1. Jill Quadagno, "Welfare Capitalism and the Social Security Act of 1935," *American Sociological Review* 49 (1984): 646.

they were brought about through maneuvering for political influence over the working class between conservative governments, liberal and socialist political parties, trade unions, and wealthy capitalists. Thus the *origins* of the welfare state in Western society are generally located in problems of the labor force in a capitalist economy, not the problems of the aged.

Evolution of the Welfare State in the West

Behind the development of the welfare state in Western Europe was the desire of many European governments and industrialists for a healthy population whose productivity could be translated into economic power. Greater economic power, in turn, meant an enhanced capability of projecting greater political and military power, as well as securing a higher standard of living for the nation and increased profits from trade and manufacturing. In some countries, providing state-sponsored welfare was also a means to reduce political discontent and the threat of revolution from the working class. Social insurance programs were essentially devised to protect the income of workers when sick, disabled, unemployed, or old. Private pension plans from business corporations had been unable to provide adequate coverage in the scope and quality necessary for all of a country's labor force, and it therefore fell to national governments to take greater responsibilities for the welfare of the governed (Hugman 1994; Myles 1984).

Initially, social insurance was provided by many of the Western European governments only to wage earners below a certain income level, but gradually benefits were extended to all or most of the population. In most of these countries, social insurance was provided first in the form of national health insurance and the protection of income lost to workers through sickness or disability. Old age pensions tended to follow shortly thereafter. Germany established the first system of social insurance in 1883 and added old age benefits in 1889. Austria initiated social insurance in 1888 and began providing old age pensions in 1906. Denmark, in 1891, and Great Britain, in 1908, both initiated social welfare programs that included old age pensions at the beginning. Some form of national pensions eventually became available for the elderly in the Netherlands in 1913, Italy in 1919, Belgium in 1924, and Switzerland, which had a national health insurance program in 1911 but waited until 1946 for a national pension system. France waited until 1930 to lay the legal foundation for a national-level social insurance program that included old age benefits, although various nonprofit organizations were allowed to provide social security insurance as early as 1901. Elsewhere, old age pensions for the general population began in Canada in 1927 and, as previously noted, in the United States in 1935.

The advent of the welfare state in the West, as British sociologist T. H. Marshall (1964) explained, is actually a culmination of processes that began in the eighteenth century. Marshall pointed out that the establishment of the welfare state is the latest phase in an evolution of citizens' rights in Western society. To *civil* rights (gained in the eighteenth century), like freedom of speech and equality before the law, and *political* rights (acquired in the late eighteenth and the nineteenth centuries), such as the right to vote and participate in the exercise of government, were added the *social* rights (achieved in the late nineteenth and the twentieth centuries) of protection from economic insecurity and the provision of at least a marginal level of economic welfare. The emergence of these various rights of citizenship, all promoting equality, stated Marshall, is a paradox, because they came during the same historical period as the rise of capitalism, which essentially is a system of inequality. Inequality in the capitalist system stems from the fact that it is based on private ownership of property and the gearing of economic activity to profit in the marketplace. Individuals are not equal in the amount of property they own or acquire, their position in relation to the production of goods and services in the marketplace, and the amount of profits (or losses) they derive from their work. As John Myles (1984:30) comments, "This marriage between a protective state and a capitalist economy was a union of opposites, for it required an accommodation between two opposing logics of distribution—one that attached rights to the possession of *property* and another that attached rights to *persons* in their capacity as citizens."

Essentially, what had taken place, in Marshall's (1964) view, was a "war" between the rights of citizenship considered inherent in a democratic society by the general populace and the capitalist social class system. In the modern welfare state, individual rights of citizenship, not ownership of property, emerged as the basis for political representation and entitlement to public programs.

Old Age Pensions: Labor and the Aged

In this war between citizens' rights and the capitalist economic system, what role did workers play as potential retirees? In the United States, large corporations, rather than workers, were initially the most influential in establishing the principle of retirement. This was done in order to reduce unemployment during the Great Depression, maintain high worker productivity with a young labor force, and lessen production costs by hiring younger workers at lower salaries and placing older workers on pensions (Graebner 1980; Haber 1978). Consequently, it was in the vested interest of management in the

United States to have a social security system (Brents 1986; Graebner 1980). Other studies show American, British, and French workers and their labor unions resisting proposals to create government-sponsored pension plans for older workers as a method to bind workers' loyalties to the state and reduce the influence of the unions; yet some labor unions worked to establish national pension plans (Myles 1984). Marxists often opposed such measures because they increased the power of capital over labor.

However, since the 1940s, labor organizations have generally supported public pensions for the elderly. This development was aided significantly by the economic boom that followed World War II and influenced the current orientation of modern welfare states. Western governments during the postwar era began assuming increasing responsibility for distributing the national income, and the elderly were the major beneficiary of this development. Myles (1984) shows in his analysis that the traditional concept of providing public support for the elderly changed during the postwar era from that of providing social *assistance* to one of providing social *security.* That is, the intent of government was no longer to provide a safety net for old people unable to meet their financial needs; instead, the goal became that of providing a retirement income sufficient to replace wages from work. Old age benefits thus turned into a method to support a standard of living for elderly persons that was not significantly lessened because of retirement. Private pensions were negotiated at the bargaining table between labor and management, but public pensions tended to be a consideration in this wage-setting process as well, because they were an important source of income after retirement. Old age pensions, especially in Western Europe, became, in Myles's (1984:77) view, part of the "social contract" between government, employers' associations, and labor organizations—to exchange wage demands for improved benefits. Myles found in his research on the politics of public pensions that a cohesive labor movement that is able to elect its candidates to public office and sustain political control for an extended period was the means by which adequate pensions for retired workers were achieved in many Western European countries after World War II.

Although the influence of labor unions on the provision of old age pensions has been significant in the modern welfare state, the dominant influence today is the political power of the aged population. This is aptly demonstrated in research such as that by Fred Pampel and John Williamson (1985). Pampel and Williamson investigated, in some 48 nations, whether class politics (the power of the working class) or old age politics (the power of the elderly population) was more important in influencing state expenditures for public pensions at different levels of political and economic development.

They found that, the more democratic a nation and the larger its aged population, the greater the political power of the aged in increasing pension expenditures. Social class variables, in contrast, had little or no effect on pension increases, thereby indicating the greater importance of age politics over class politics in national expenditures for old age benefits.

Pampel and Williamson noted that, over time, age variables tend to become more important than class variables. The reason is that rises in public pensions can be correlated with changes in the age structure: state-funded pensions rise the most when the proportion of the aged increases in the general population. Countries like Sweden, Norway, and Austria are among those with the highest percentage of aged persons and highest pension expenditures. In countries like the United States, Canada, and Switzerland, labor unions have not been strongly centralized or exceptionally powerful, and socialist and liberal politics have also tended to be weak, yet expenditures for public pensions have nonetheless increased dramatically, as has the size of the aged population.

Key variables in old age pension expenditures, other than the size of the aged population, include the extent of democracy in a country and its level of economic resources. Affluent nations, of course, can spend a higher proportion of their income on old age pensions than can less affluent countries. Pampel and Williamson also found that age has no influence in nations with low levels of democracy. But in both developing and developed industrialized democracies, increases in the size of the aged population are correlated with increases in pension expenditures, with the highest increases coming in those countries having the highest levels of income and political democracy. In sum, the highest old age pensions are found in those nations with the greatest (1) aged population, (2) levels of democracy, and (3) economic resources.

The strength of old age politics and the difficulty of legislators in opposing plans to limit spending on the aged is based on the special nature of public pension expenditures. "Unlike nearly all other social welfare programs," state Pampel and Williamson (1985:782), "pensions benefit a large and easily identifiable population with ascribed characteristics and a high rate of voting." Pampel and Williamson point out that both the aged and the nonaged view pension benefits as a legitimate entitlement after decades of work and financial contributions. The large numbers of elderly persons who vote and feel deserving of pensions make them a strong interest group that can influence public policy in ways that mothers on welfare, the unemployed, children, and the poor cannot. Pampel and Williamson thus draw the appropriate conclusion that, whereas other social welfare programs may be influenced by the power of the working class in highly democratic societies, pensions appear to be more strongly influenced by the political power of the elderly population.

Differing Welfare Ideologies

Tension between the competing ideologies of the capitalist economic system and the rights of citizenship continue in the welfare states of the West, particularly in the United States. As Myles (1984) reminds us, a basic tenet of capitalist social relations was that whatever social benefits were to be provided outside of the marketplace should be a mirror image of the relative prices (wages) assigned by the market to the worth of an individual's labor. In other words, welfare benefits should not be out of line with the earning power of individual workers. Also, the amount of entitlements for measures such as old age pensions should, under a capitalist-oriented system, be determined by the individual's work history instead of through a system that provides everyone with the same level of support. Nor should welfare become so attractive that it motivates people not to work, or increases tax burdens on employers or the public to the extent that it undermines the economy. Hence, social insurance in a capitalist system needs to be based on labor force participation, and this is exactly what happened in the United States with respect to Social Security benefits (Quadagno 1984, 1988a).

Entitlements based on citizenship, however, have a different orientation. They are aimed at providing people with a normal standard of living, regardless of their position in the labor market. The welfare system of Western Europe is more advanced in this regard than that of the United States. Many Western Europeans receive allowances for child support, comprehensive health insurance, and protection for lost income due to sickness or injury. These benefits accrue to *all* qualified citizens, regardless of their income or position in the labor market. For example, in Sweden, West Germany, and elsewhere in Western Europe, all families with children receive an allowance intended to supplement family expenses for children's clothing, school lunches, and the like. The amount of the allowance paid by the state is based on the number of children in the family. Income is not a criterion, and both affluent and nonaffluent families receive the same amount for the same number of children.

Welfare programs in the United States, in contrast, are not as extensive, and benefits are generally based on income. When most Western European governments were introducing social welfare programs around the turn of the century, the U.S. government was not deeply involved in regulating the economy, nor was there a significant threat of social revolution from discontented workers. Moreover, Americans have traditionally been less committed to government welfare programs and more in favor of private enterprise's dealing with economic and social problems. Except for the elderly, participation in the welfare system is not considered at all normative in the United States, and nonretired Americans who receive welfare tend to be especially stigmatized and socially devalued (Mead 1985). But, in Western Europe, providing welfare and social security for the general population, not just the elderly and the poor, has evolved into a normal feature of the state's role. This situation implies a fundamental difference in the social values of Americans and Western Europeans, with Americans stressing individualism and Western Europeans viewing government in a more paternalistic fashion.

For example, Erwin Scheuch (1989), in discussing the results of a 1985 International Social Survey Programme (ISSP) question that asked whether it is the responsibility of the government to reduce differences in income between people with high incomes and those with low incomes, found that the results could be correlated by welfare state indicators. The more extensive the development of the welfare state, the more persons living in those countries believed the government should reduce differences in income. In Italy, some 67 percent of the respondents stated agreement with the government's responsibility in reducing income inequalities; in other Western European countries, those agreeing were 66.3 percent in Austria, 56.4 percent in West Germany, and 52.2 percent in Great Britain. In the United States, however, only 29.5 percent of the population sampled were in agreement. Other research, by Bernice Pescosolido, Carol Boyer, and Wai Tsui (1985), investigated public evaluations of government performance in providing medical care in eight Western welfare states, including the United States. Great Britain and the Netherlands had the highest public evaluations, followed by West Germany and Austria. The United States ranked seventh, just ahead of Italy, where the populace was particularly dissatisfied with government planning in health care. Those governments with the most positive evaluations overall were those whose system of health benefits was considered by the population as the most innovative in *guaranteeing* health care.

Consequently, there are differences in orientation between welfare states, with Western European nations generally ahead of the United States in providing social welfare as a right of citizenship. This difference is important, because greater proportions of the gross domestic product (GDP) are spent on old age benefits in many countries of Western Europe than in the United States.

The Coming Crisis in Paying for Social Security

On the negative side, Western society's social security system is going to be in great difficulty in financing its old age assistance programs in the twenty-first century, and this is especially the case in Western Europe. Western Europe has a more generous welfare state tradition, and there is strong resistance to cutting benefits, as Italy, France, and Germany found in the early 1990s. Unemployment is about twice as high in Western Europe than in the United States. Because it is politically difficult to encourage people to retire earlier, younger people are prevented from taking their place in the labor force. Additionally, Western Europeans are more dependent, on the average, on their state-supplied old age pensions than are Americans. In many Western European countries, such pensions range from 80 (Sweden) to 51 (the Netherlands) percent of an individual's income, compared with an average of about 45 percent in the United States. The welfare states of Western Europe not only typically provide greater financial support to their older citizens than does the United States, they also collect a greater proportion of income from workers and employers to finance their system. For instance, in 1995 the social security contributions of West German workers and matching funds paid by employers amounted to 18.6 percent of a worker's monthly wages or salary, compared with less than 11 percent in the United States. Greater benefits mean greater taxes—something many Americans do not desire.

Western Europe appears headed for a major fiscal crisis earlier than the United States, largely because its population is aging more rapidly and the number of workers paying into the system is decreasing faster. What is likely to come is either an increase in the age for entitlement to social security, a reduction in the amount of paid benefits, or allocations of even larger proportions of expenditures to support the elderly.

For the time being, Western Europe's old age pensions and services for the elderly remain more generous than those of the United States. But there are signs of adjustments, as Germany, for instance, which has the lowest birthrate in the world, began a restructuring of pension plans in the 1980s and continues to do so today in anticipation of having significantly fewer people paying into the system in the twenty-first century. The financing of old age pensions gives every indication of remaining a major issue of public concern among Germans. The guiding principle behind the German pension system is that persons who have retired from working will be able to maintain an adequate standard of living; therefore, old age benefits are likely to remain relatively high. In the early 1990s, the average retired German at age 65 received a monthly pension from the government of approximately $1,100 to $1,600 (compared with $674 in the United States), depending on the individual's earnings and residence (East or West).

In the United States, the commitment from the federal government is also well established, and the increasingly important problems of how to pay for public old age pensions remain. Such benefits are taking up larger proportions of the budgets of private companies and federal agencies. Nearly 21 percent of the federal government's entire budget in 1993 was allocated to Social Security. A particular problem with Social Security is that it pays out more money than it takes in, which resulted in increases in payroll deductions for Social Security during the 1980s to the current level of 7.65 percent on the first $61,200 earned. Taxes paid by the baby boom generation will keep the Social Security system adequately financed until the early twenty-first century, when the baby boomers start retiring. With a smaller population of workers following them, fewer workers will be available to support the largest number of retirees ever, and a crisis is likely to loom.

This situation is depicted in Figure 10–1, which shows the declining number of taxpayers per Social Security beneficiary for the years 1955 through 2065. In 1955, Figure 10–1 shows 8.6 taxpayers (workers paying into the fund through payroll deductions) for one Social Security beneficiary; between 1975 and 2005, the number of contributors to Social Security will drop to 3.3 per beneficiary. By 2015, the number of taxpayers per beneficiary will decline to 2.8, followed by further decline, beginning in 2035, to about 1.9 taxpayers per beneficiary in 2055; in 2065, Figure 10–1 projects another drop to 1.8 workers per retiree. Figure 10–1 also shows that the Social Security Trust Fund is expected to rise to $4 trillion (in 1989 dollars) by 2030. But, at that time, the surplus will begin to decrease rapidly because of the large number of beneficiaries resulting from the baby boom generation and the much smaller ratio (about 2 to 1) of workers to retirees. Between 2035 and 2055, a period of only 20 years, the amount of the trust fund will drop from $4 trillion to $1 trillion—clearly indicating a future crisis in the funding of the nation's Social Security program as the low ratio of workers to retirees continues.

At present, the commitment of the welfare states of Western Europe to the well-being of their older citizens is somewhat more advanced than that of the United States, where the individual's responsibility for his or her own welfare, including old age, remains an important social value. Yet the general trend in the welfare states of the West, including the United States, is that the

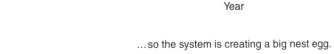

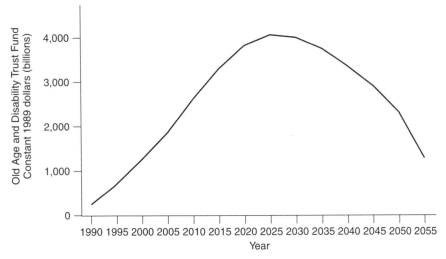

FIGURE 10–1   Planning for retirement in the United States

Source: Social Security Board of Trustees Report, 1989.

rights of citizenship—civil, political, and social—have evolved into basic entitlements for the general population. Although crises in the funding of old age benefits appear forthcoming, entitlement to those benefits on the basis of citizenship has been firmly established. The principal issue in the future will not be whether to continue such benefits, but what is the best method to finance them.

SUMMARY

This chapter has examined the role of the aged as a social and political force in society. The elderly do not appear to be a minority group in the political process along the same lines as blacks, Hispanics, and others. Rather, the aged constitute a political interest group and are supported by several influential organizations like the American Association of Retired Persons. The AARP and other senior citizens' groups are highly effective in lobbying for benefits for old people at all levels of government.

Through the enactment of the Social Security program in 1935, the United States became a welfare state. The welfare state in Western society evolved out of the struggle for the civil, political, and social rights of citizenship in which equality based on these rights surpassed the ownership of property and capital as the basis for political representation and entitlement to public programs. Much of the struggle in Western society to secure an adequate level of subsistence for the elderly was fought by labor organizations in the past, but the dominant influence in the present is the political power of the aged population. The more democratic a nation and the larger its aged population, the greater the political power of the elderly. Despite the American tendency to have more individualistic attitudes about the responsibility for security in old age and for Western Europeans to invest more responsibility in their government for providing such security, the clear tendency in Western society is toward guaranteeing an adequate level of well-being for old people. Although Western nations will face a financial crisis in paying for old age benefits in the future, the right of entitlement to such benefits on the basis of citizenship has been established and is highly likely to continue.

Chapter 11

AGING AND SOCIAL POLICY IN SELECTED COUNTRIES

This chapter examines social policy toward the aged in selected countries. The purpose of most social security programs worldwide is identical in that they are intended to protect people from loss of income in old age, as a result of disability, illness, widowhood, or other problems. Abram de Swaan (1988) points out that what distinguishes modern social security arrangements is their nationwide, collective, and compulsory character. They are nationwide in that they apply to everyone; collective in that resources are accumulated and paid out of a common fund; and compulsory in that benefits are defined, funds collected, and eligibility determined whether the individual wishes to join and contribute or not.

However, hardly any two social security systems in the world are alike. They vary from country to country in the manner in which they are organized, staffed, and financed, as well as in the amount of benefits they provide, the coverage they offer, and the historical, social, economic, and ideological factors that influenced their development. Yet comparing social policies toward the aged in various countries is an excellent way to determine general trends, assess differences, better understand the situation in any one particular country, and obtain ideas about the advantages or disadvantages in the various approaches. In this chapter we review social policy toward the aged in several selected countries. Included is a comparison of the North American nations of the United States and Canada,

Great Britain (the first Western country to offer free medical care to its entire population), Sweden (the country with the largest proportion of elderly), Germany (the first nation to enact a social welfare system), France (which has a highly decentralized system of social insurance), Japan (with the fastest growing population of aged persons), and China (the nation with the largest number of elderly).

UNITED STATES

Some 33 million persons, or 13 percent of the total population of the United States in 1993, were age 65 or over. In 2025 the number of aged should be about 58.7 million, or 19.5 percent of the total population. Thus the United States, like most other Western nations, will have about one aged person out of every five people in the general population in the early twenty-first century.

As noted in previous chapters, the United States is fully committed to supporting the elderly. The key legislation was the Social Security Act of 1935, in which the federal government assumed the responsibility for helping ease the financial burden of old age by providing monthly payments to qualified persons at age 65, the disabled, and widows and their dependent children. Other important legislation includes: (1) the Older Americans Act of 1965, which underscores the nation's commitment to older persons by providing a legal basis for coordinating and monitoring social services for the elderly through Area Agencies on Aging, and authorizing funding for various old age assistance programs, such as multipurpose senior citizens' centers in local communities; (2) the passage of Medicare in 1965, which authorizes payment for most health care expenses for old people; and (3) the Age Discrimination in Employment Act of 1967 and its subsequent amendments, which end forced retirement for most Americans and prohibit denial of employment on the basis of age.

Eligibility and the amount of benefits provided to old people under the nation's Social Security program is based on prior participation in the labor force. Persons without such participation, or who are not disabled or surviving dependents of deceased workers, are not included. Nevertheless, it is extremely rare for an elderly person not to have some type of government-sponsored financial support in old age. The average monthly Social Security check in 1993 was $647. Funds to support Social Security are collected through contributions of 15.3 percent of a worker's earnings. Half (7.65 percent) is paid by the employee on the first $61,200 of annual salary, and employers pay the other half.

But in comparison with most other Western nations, the United States was relatively late in embarking on a national welfare program. And, although the elderly are the prime beneficiaries in modern welfare states, including the United States, the American system of social welfare is not as comprehensive as those found elsewhere. As shown in Table 11–1, which lists the dates of the introduction of various social welfare programs on a national level in Germany, Great Britain, France, Canada, and the United States, not only was the United States slow (1935) to provide old age pensions, but it is the only nation not currently providing sickness benefits (coverage for wages lost because of illness), family allowances (allowances for child care and housing for the poor), and health insurance for the entire population. What this signifies is that there are gaps in coverage for the social welfare of all citizens, including younger persons. As Robert Hudson (1988:67) points out, "Many Americans will continue to arrive in old age with histories of low wages, poor health, limited education, and marginal family and social supports."

As also discussed in the preceding chapter, social welfare is not considered normative in the United States for anyone but the elderly. Therefore, if one is economically dependent on government assistance prior to old age, that person tends to be socially devalued and arrives at old age with a lifetime history of disadvantages. Programs to intervene in that person's life course at a younger age are limited to unemployment benefits and some educational and job-training opportunities. Health care coverage is available only for the most economically disadvantaged younger persons through Medicaid. Therefore, although the United States is a welfare state, its welfare system is clearly not as extensive as those found in Western Europe or Canada.

This is seen in the fact that, when we speak of a welfare state in the United States, we are referring primarily to programs for the disadvantaged.

TABLE 11–1   Dates of Introduction of National Social Welfare Programs in Selected Western Countries

	Old Age Pensions	*Health Insurance*	*Sickness Benefits*	*Family Allowances*	*Unemployment Insurance*
Germany	1889	1883	1883	1954	1927
Great Britain	1908	1948	1911	1945	1911
Sweden	1913	1955	1955	1947	1934
Canada	1927	1972	1971	1944	1940
France	1930	1945	1930	1932	1914
United States	1935	—	—	—	1935

There are government programs for the welfare of the general population, of course, such as public health, environmental protection, education, highway construction, and the like. But the term *welfare,* as used in the United States, generally refers to assistance for those living in poverty. To a somewhat lesser extent it applies to those who are old; but many elderly are not poor, and the notion of being "on welfare" would not accurately represent their social situation. Rather, Social Security payments supplement their income and represent partial replacement of lost wages or salaries due to retirement. However, regardless of the popular meaning of the term *welfare* in the United States, the American welfare state evolved to a large extent as a response to the needs of the elderly.

The development of the nation's Social Security system for the aged was reviewed in the last two chapters and will not be repeated here. Essentially, this system arose out of compromises between government, private industry, organized labor, and the lobbying of the aged themselves during the Great Depression of the late 1920s and early 1930s (Quadagno 1984, 1988a; Skocpol 1994). Prior to this time, there was no particular social policy regarding the elderly. Old people were generally on their own. Financial support (which was uncommon in the early twentieth century) came from savings and pensions, from families, or from whatever resources were available in the local community, such as churches or charities. For many elderly (perhaps a majority), to be old also meant to be poor. However, passage of the Social Security Act in 1935 signified the assumption of responsibility on the part of the federal government to provide at least a basic level of subsistence to the elderly. Subsequent revisions in the Social Security program, including an expansion of coverage and cost of living increases—along with the provision of Medicare to pay for most medical expenses and the spread of pension programs for full-time, permanent employees—have significantly assisted older people.

As the nation moves into the twenty-first century, the most pressing social policy issue for the aged will be the financing of the Social Security system and Medicare. Medicaid will also be affected because it pays a large share of the costs of nursing home care for the aged poor. The more affluent among the elderly have been required to pay income taxes on their Social Security allotments, and payroll deductions from the wages and salaries of active workers have been increased to the current 7.65 percent level. Individual out-of-pocket costs for participating in Medicare have risen, and cost containment measures for Medicare have been instituted by congressional legislation. A fixed schedule of fees (known as Diagnostic Related Groups, or DRGs) establishing limits on the amounts paid to hospitals for Medicare patients was passed in 1983. A major overhaul of Medicare fees (the Physicians Payment Reform Act), passed in 1989, set fixed fees for physicians as well. This legislation lowered the amounts (by 20 percent) usually paid to physicians providing specialized services, such as those provided by surgeons and radiologists, while increasing amounts paid (by 40 percent) for family practitioners and internists for preventive care. Thus the focus of Medicare was to be oriented more toward prevention and health maintenance than toward treatment per se, especially treatment involving very expensive medical procedures. The amount physicians can charge patients in excess of payments they receive from the government was also limited to 25 percent in 1992, 20 percent in 1993, and 15 percent thereafter.

Thus the pattern of social policy for the aged in the near future is likely to be one that preserves support for old people in the area of health and Social Security, but does so within a context of cost containment. Payroll deductions to maintain Social Security appear to be adequate until the early twenty-first century because of the large baby boom generation in the active labor force. By 2030, when the baby boomers have retired, however, there will be a major decline, as previously noted in other chapters, in the funding of Social Security, due to the smaller population of active workers. This will likely mean changes in policy for the aged, such as financial incentives for older workers to remain in the labor force. Increased payroll deductions for Social Security are also likely to take place.

Whatever measures are taken by the federal government with respect to old age benefits are likely to be done in conjunction with lobbying by the elderly, who form a powerful political constituency. In late 1989, for example, political pressure by the elderly resulted in the repeal of the 1988 Medicare Catastrophic Coverage Act, which funded long-term hospital care for old people. This act was repealed because of objections to a $4 monthly premium and a surtax (as high as $800 annually for some individuals) affecting about 40 percent of Medicare beneficiaries. The act also was opposed because it failed to cover the costs of long-term nursing home care. This development helps demonstrate that a unique policy situation in the United States—in comparison with other nations—is the immense political influence of the elderly. Social policy toward the aged is influenced more strongly in the United States by older citizens and the organizations representing them than elsewhere in the world. To a large extent, social policy toward the aged is shaped, within the context of fiscal restraints, by the influence of the elderly on Congress. The elderly are able to do this because they are well organized, vote in large numbers, keep in contact with their legislators, and have effective organizations lobbying on their behalf. With a large and relatively healthy population of aged persons in the twenty-first century, the central task of policy makers will be to find the financial resources to meet the social and health needs of the elderly without compromising opportunities for the young.

CANADA

In 1994 some 12.0 percent, or 3.4 million, of Canada's total population of approximately 28.5 million people were age 65 or over; by 2025 Canada's population is expected to reach 33.2 million, and the proportion of elderly will increase to 6.2 million, or 18.8 percent, of all Canadians. In comparison with other countries, especially those of Western Europe, Canada is still relatively youthful in demographic terms; but this will change by 2025, for the number of older people will have increased significantly. In monetary terms, this will mean, according to John Myles (1988), a *graying* of the nation's budget, because in Canada, as in other modern welfare states, public programs for the elderly comprise the largest single category of expenditures. With significantly larger numbers of older people, the aging of Canadian society will be an increasingly important aspect of public policy (McDaniel 1986; Novak 1993).

Canada's initial step in the direction of social welfare for the aged was the passage of the Old Age Pensions Act of 1927. As Myles explains, this act was neither universal nor generous. It provided a pension of just $20 a month only to persons over the age of 70 with very low incomes; by 1951, this pension had been increased just marginally to $40 monthly, and one had to be very poor to get it. The first major change came in 1951 with the Old Age Security Act, which affirmed the benefit level of $40 per month but extended the pension to include everyone, regardless of income, at age 70. By 1970, eligibility for the basic pension had been reduced to age 65, where it remains today, and the amount of the benefit has been raised significantly. Funds to support this basic pension are derived primarily from general taxation.

As of 1995, an elderly Canadian received a flat rate, in Canadian dollars (about 85 percent of an American dollar), of a maximum of $381.60 monthly as a basic pension. This amount is generally not enough to support an adequate standard of living for most retired persons, so it has been necessary to adopt a second tier of pension benefits—as has been the case in Great Britain—based on contributions from earnings. This additional earnings-related plan, known as the Canadian Pension Plan (which covers all of Canada but Quebec province) and the Quebec Pension Plan (which covers Quebec), both of which were passed in 1965, provides employees with a pension in addition to the basic plan. The Canada and Quebec Pension Plans pay the retired worker a maximum of 25 percent of his or her contributory average lifetime adjusted pensionable earnings. The employee and the employer each contribute to the plan 2.7 percent of the worker's wages or salary; self-employed persons contribute the full 5.4 percent by themselves. In 1995, the maximum amount paid to a retiree entitled to full benefits under these plans was $713.19 monthly. When a retired worker dies, the surviving spouse is entitled to a portion (up to 60 percent) of the earnings-related pension.

For those persons who retired soon after 1965 and were therefore not eligible for full benefits, an income supplement was provided in 1967 and remains in force today for elderly persons with low incomes. In addition to these public pensions, employed persons have access to pension plans established by their employers and to personal savings plans. Canada thus offers a safety net for all its citizens by providing all the aged a flat rate of monetary support regardless of the level of their participation in the labor force; they receive some supplemental pension of varying amounts as well.

Therefore, although the eligibility for Social Security benefits and the level of payments is determined in the United States by the length and amount of a person's contributions to the system from wages and salary, all Canadians receive a basic pension. Supplements to this basic pension are then determined by the person's history of contributions from employment. Persons lacking sufficient past contributions because of low incomes are still provided for, however, in Canada's approach. Myles explains that low-income persons actually fare slightly better than more affluent persons in the Canadian system of state pensions, leaving those persons with relatively greater financial resources to depend more on private pensions and savings, instead of the state, to maintain their standard of living.

Also, the Canadian government provides family allowances (1944), sickness benefits (1971), and national health insurance (1972) to all citizens. Canadian physicians, like those in the United States, are generally private, self-employed, fee-for-service practitioners; but, unlike those in the United States, doctors' fees in Canada are paid by government-sponsored national health insurance according to rates negotiated with the provincial government. Most hospitals also operate on a budget negotiated with government officials at the provincial level. Private health insurance is generally prohibited except for covering some supplemental benefits, such as semiprivate room accommodations. Thus Canada essentially has a private system of health care delivery paid for almost entirely by public funds. The money to pay for this system is obtained from public tax revenues. The Canadian government is able to exercise greater control over the costs of care than can the United States government, because the former buys basically all the care provided and is in a strong position to determine how much it is willing to pay for it (Evans 1986).

With a relatively rapid increase in the proportion of its elderly population in the future, Canada will be faced with increased financial requirements to continue providing for the health and social welfare of its aged citizens. Canada's approach to dealing with the needs of the elderly is not likely to change from the current system of providing a basic level of support to the general population as a right of citizenship. No longer is it the situation that old age benefits provided by th   go only to the poor, for all elderly receive a pension and free medi(

GREAT BRITAIN

The total population of Great f   is expected to stabilize around 58 million in the years between 199≤   )25, but the number of elderly is going to increase from 9.0 million t   10.5 million during this same period. The proportion of aged perso'   general population will increase from 16.0 percent in 1992 to 18.7 ʒ   in 2025, although the overall number of people in Britain will remain about the same. Although the growth of the elderly population in Britain is relatively modest compared with that in many other countries, the increase is nonetheless significant because it will mean a substantial demand for health and social services as the nation moves into the twenty-first century.

State-sponsored old age pensions were instituted by the Pensions Act of 1908, but the pensions provided only a minimum level of subsistence, for they were primarily intended to support only those aged who were quite poor. However, with the victory of the British Labour party in 1945, Britain became a leading welfare state. This was accomplished with the passage of legislation beginning in the late 1940s which provided family allowances and rent or property tax supplements for housing for the poor, old age pensions, sickness benefits, unemployment benefits, national health insurance, and the provision of a national health service—all intended to guarantee freedom from want as a right of citizenship. Thus the provision of social welfare in Britain was transformed from providing benefits just for the poor or for the working class, to that of helping all citizens in need. As Myles (1984:40) explains, "The state, acting on behalf of all its citizens, would provide a safety net below which no member of the community would be allowed to fall."

When it came to health care, the National Service Act of 1948 allowed the British government to become the owner of hospitals and the employer of physicians, nurses, and other health care workers. Medical services, in turn, are provided free of charge to patients. About 15 percent of the funds to support the National Health Service is derived from payroll deductions and employers' contributions; most of the remaining revenue comes from general taxation.

General practitioners, or family practice physicians, are paid a set fee by the government for each patient on their patient list (up to 3,500 patients for a solo practice or 4,500 patients in a partnership, as long as the average number of patients per doctor does not exceed 3,500). A higher fee is paid for patients who are 65 years of age or older. General practitioners are the first line of medical care for all patients. If care by a specialist (known as a "consultant" in the British system) or hospitalization is warranted, the patient must be referred by a general practitioner. Generally, specialists are the only physicians who treat patients in hospitals, and they are paid a salary by the government. Other legislation includes a supplement to income for employed persons when they become sick or injured and death benefits for survivors.

As of 1995, men at age 65 and women at age 60 without dependents have a right to a basic state retirement pension of approximately $355 monthly, a small Christmas bonus, free medical care, free health service drug prescriptions, and free dental and eye checkups. A retired person with a spouse or other adult dependent receives a basic monthly pension of about $565. Qualification for the pension depends on the number and level of contributions over a specified period. In addition to the basic pension, there is an additional earnings-related pension based on the amount of earnings paid into the state retirement system; there is also a supplementary pension for persons whose basic and earnings-related pensions do not give them sufficient resources to live on. Although the state remains responsible for the basic pension, to which all qualified persons are entitled and which generally pays the same amount to everyone, employers are allowed to remove their employees from the state's additional earnings-related pension plan if their program equals or betters the state's plan. Moreover, the Social Security Act of 1986 gives the individual the right to choose between participation in either the state's earnings-related plan, the employer's plan, or a retirement plan sponsored by a bank or other financial institution.

In general, the elderly in Britain are more financially secure than ever before and are supported by an extensive system of supplementary benefits and free medical care. Nevertheless, important problems remain. The majority of the elderly (over 54 percent of married couples and 63 percent of single pensioners) in Britain have below-average incomes and are dependent on their state pensions as their largest source of income (Abercrombie et al. 1994; Pilcher 1995; Wells and Freer 1988). For example, in 1993 42.7 percent of the income of all heads of household between the ages of 65 and 75 came from the state retirement pension, 26.3 percent from earnings-related and private pensions, and 30.2 percent from other sources, such as wages and salaries or investments. For heads of household over age 75, 54.4 percent of income came from the state pension, 24.5 percent from other pensions, and 21.1 percent from other sources.

Although the economic position of the elderly has improved during the twentieth century, old people still make up a large proportion of the poor in modern Britain (Pilcher 1995). Poverty among the aged remains a particular problem which adversely affects both the length and the quality of life. The British government, although continuing to emphasize the right of social security in old age, is faced with coping with the rising costs of the aging of its population in much the same manner as in other developed countries. However, they must do so with less financial resources than some of their more affluent neighbors, such as Germany. Consequently, in Great Britain the relatively rapid increase in the elderly population is a major social problem, for the aged consume an increasingly larger share of the nation's limited budget for health and social welfare.

SWEDEN

Sweden not only has the highest proportion of elderly people in the world today, but it is perhaps the most developed welfare state as well. Out of a total population of 8.7 million people in 1993, over 1.5 million, or about 17.7 percent, were age 65 and older. The number of aged persons is not expected to change significantly in the 1990s, but between 2000 and 2020 it is forecasted that Sweden's elderly will increase to about 1.9 million people, comprising 20.7 percent of the population. Thus, relatively early in the twenty-first century, one in five Swedes will be age 65 and older, as is the case in the United States. Yet an interesting development in Sweden that is likely to affect the composition of the aged population is that the average life expectancy of men is growing more rapidly than that of women. In 1993 life expectancy was 75.5 years for men and 80.8 for women; however, between 1984-1993, women added only 1.2 years to their lives compared to 1.9 years for men. This trend appears likely to continue and will result in increasingly larger numbers of men at the oldest ages.

Although Sweden has had a tradition of social welfare services dating back to the Middle Ages, the Swedish welfare state was not fully established until after World War II when the Social Democrats took power and made the social protection of citizens a foundation of government. The Swedish model of social welfare became characterized by the provision of extensive benefits to the entire population, not just the aged or the poor. The general goal was to reduce social and economic inequality, with the stipulation that: (1) no Swedish citizen should suffer from need and (2) government-sponsored benefits will be provided to all as a universal right, not a form of charity. Consequently, every Swedish citizen, regardless of socioeconomic position, receives welfare benefits, including old age pensions (1913), unemployment insurance (1934), family allowances (1947), health care (1955), and sickness benefits (1955) in the form of protection from lost income when ill or injured.

An initial measure affecting the life of every Swede was the provision, beginning in 1913 and followed by subsequent improvements, of pensions for the elderly by the national government. There are two categories of pensions, the basic pension (*folkpension*) and a supplemental pension (ATP). The basic pension is based on residence in Sweden, while the ATP pension is based on income from earnings. The basic pension is financed by the state and contributions from employers and self-employed persons. In order to receive the basic pension, a person must have lived in Sweden for 40 years, beginning at age 16, and have worked and earned credit (points) toward the ATP pension for at least 30 years. Persons who have not lived or worked in Sweden the required number of years may still receive a basic pension, but it will be reduced by the number of years which fall short of the requirement for receiving a full pension. The normal retirement age is 65, but a person may choose to retire at age 60 or delay retirement until age 70. The amount of the basic pension is less if received earlier or higher if started later. In 1994, the average basic pension was the equivalent of about $589 a month.

The ATP pension is based on contributions from employers for their employees and from self-employed persons for themselves according to their earnings. The amount of the pension is determined by the contributions paid into the pension system on behalf of the individual during his or her period of earning income. In 1994, the average ATP pension was $945 monthly. The elderly may also qualify for a housing allowance, disability pension, survivor's (of deceased spouse) pension, widow's pension, wife and child supplements, and other allowances.

Whereas overall responsibility for the aged and the payment of pensions rests with the national government, Sweden's smallest units of local government—the municipalities—provide day-to-day assistance to the elderly, including housing, home health care, home help services, and supervision of nursing homes. Under the 1982 Social Services Act, all individuals are entitled to receive municipal services at all stages of life. A guiding principle in the care of the elderly is that a person should be able to continue to live in his or her home as long as possible. Therefore, most elderly people (92 percent) live in ordinary houses and apartments and generally enjoy a high standard of living arrangements.

Sweden, like Great Britain, has a system of socialized health care delivery and a National Health Service in which health care providers are government employees. Enrollment in the national health plan is mandatory for the entire population. Health care is provided with little or no cost to patients and guaranteed by the 1983 Health and Medical Services Act, which stipulates that health services will be available to all members of society on an equal basis. Medication is either free or inexpensive. The provision of health care is generally regulated by county councils who employ physicians and other health care workers, while hospitals are owned by municipalities or county councils. Hospitals receive relatively little funding from the national government, but rely largely on local tax revenues. Altogether, the health care costs in Sweden are met by contributions of approximately 70 percent from county taxes, 15 percent from the national government, and the remainder from various other sources.

Although there is much to admire about Sweden's social welfare system, the Swedes are heavily taxed to pay for it. Sweden's taxes have been the highest in the world, but the public demanded tax reform in 1991, which reduced the highest income tax rate from 72 to 51 percent. Tax reform has not helped the government's fiscal situation in the face of increased welfare expenditures. The major problem is pressure on the national budget as a result of the maturing of the welfare state—including the provision of full pensions, high health care costs, and other rising welfare expenses—along with a slowdown in economic growth. Currently, all major social programs, including those for the elderly, are under scrutiny. A reorganization of the pension system, transfer of home health care from county councils to municipalities, the phasing out of large nursing homes, and the establishment of group dwellings for the aged are some of the most important measures affecting older people.

As Sweden moves into the twenty first-century, it is likely to face a continued level of fiscal difficulty as increased numbers of people reach old age and the proportion of younger workers paying taxes to support the welfare system shrinks. Throughout its modern history, Sweden has functioned as an independent and neutral nation. But in 1995 Sweden joined the European Union in order to participate in an integrated European economy. This measure was in recognition of the fact that the key to Sweden's ability to continue to support its generous welfare state is international trade competitiveness.

GERMANY

The Federal Republic of Germany is growing older, like other Western nations; however, when it comes to the age structure of German society, the country represents a special case, because the decline in Germany's birth rate is one of the steepest of any advanced nation in modern history. The German population is decreasing because births are not keeping up with deaths. For example, in 1985 West Germany had a birthrate of 9.6 births per 1,000 persons, but the death rate was 11.5 per 1,000 persons. So in the mid-1980s, more people were dying than were being born. However, the birth rate rose to 10.3 per 1,000 in 1987 and continued to rise after unification with East Germany in 1990. By 1992, there were 11.3 births compared with 11.1 deaths per 1,000 in the western states of unified Germany; consequently, the situation was actually improving, with births exceeding deaths in the west—although the margin was slight (0.2 percent). In eastern Germany, the opposite pattern appeared after unification: births dropped from 13.4 per 1,000 in 1986 to only 6.8 per 1,000 in 1992. The death rate also fell somewhat, from 13.4 deaths per 1,000 in 1986 to 12.7 deaths in 1992, but the great disparity in births (6.8) compared to deaths (12.7) per 1,000 residents signifies a steep population decline in eastern Germany. The sharpest decrease has been in states like Brandenburg, where the number of births fell from 38,000 in 1989 to only 12,000 in 1993, causing the state to pay a family allowance of $650 monthly for every new child.

The population in the western part of Germany rose from 61.0 million in 1986 to 64.5 million in 1991. Many East Germans moved west, as did over 1 million ethnic Germans from the former Soviet Union, in one of Europe's greatest population shifts in the 1990s, while the number of people in the eastern German states fell from 17.0 to 15.9 million during the same period. The overall population of Germany is projected to become smaller in the future as the low birthrate—especially in the east—continues. Since January 1, 1993, the number of ethnic Germans accepted by Germany has been limited by law to 220,000 a year—because of the high cost of unification and the rebuilding of eastern Germany; high unemployment, which reached 11.1 percent in early 1996 (9.6 percent in the west and 17.5 percent in the east); an economic slowdown; and the strain on the government's ability to pay old age pensions and other welfare benefits to the migrants. The elderly among the migrants receive pensions of about $900 monthly (30 percent less than average), to which they have not contributed.

Not only is the German population headed toward fewer numbers, but it is also getting older. In 1985 there were 8.7 million persons over age 65, constituting 14.5 percent of the population in West Germany. In 1991 some 9.9 million people, or 15.9 percent of the population, in western Germany were over age 65, as were another 2.2 million persons, or 13.7 percent of the population, in eastern Germany. The increase in elderly Germans will be especially dramatic in the twenty-first century. As shown in Table 11–2, there were 24 persons age 65 and over for every 100 persons between the ages of 20 and 64 in Germany in 1995. There will be 26 elderly per 100 younger adults by the year 2000; however, in 2040 there will be 56 aged persons for every 100 younger adults.

This situation signals a major problem for Germany's social security system, because it means that considerably fewer persons are available in the working-age population to provide income to fund welfare benefits and old age pensions. The problem facing the German welfare system is not just the declining percentage of workers, but also rising costs because an increasingly older population means a different mix of illnesses (more diseases associated with aging) and greater demand for health services to cope with these diseases.

The costs associated with the aging of its population are likely to be particularly high in Germany because of a tradition of paternalism on the part of the government, which dates back to the 1880s and the social policies of old imperial Germany. Unlike the United States, Germany has a comprehensive system of social welfare services, including the provision of free health care for the vast majority of its citizens. What this means is that all Germans, as members of one of the most affluent societies in the world, can demand and receive an extensive array of social benefits from their government.

TABLE 11–2 Number of Persons Age 65 and over in Germany, 1995–2040

Year	Number of Elderly Per 100 Adults Age 20–64
1995	24
2000	26
2005	30
2010	34
2015	34
2020	36
2025	41
2030	48
2035	55
2040	56

Source: Verband Deutscher Rentenversicherungsträger, 1996.

As Myles (1984) explains, Germany and the United States differ in attitudes toward welfare entitlements in general and old age benefits in particular. Germany was the first country to introduce a system of universal health insurance and old age pensions in the late nineteenth century, whereas the United States was one of the last to provide old age benefits and, as noted, still lacks coverage for health care on a national basis. Except for the aged, participation in a government welfare system is not considered a normative practice in the United States. Those Americans who receive welfare tend to be stigmatized and socially devalued (Mead 1985). In Germany, in distinct contrast, providing welfare and social security for the general public, not only the poor and the aged, is a normal feature of the state's role. This contrast implies a fundamental difference between the value systems of the two countries: Americans emphasize individualism, whereas Germans manifest a high regard for the state.

The study by Bernice Pescosolido, Carol Boyer, and Wai Tsui (1985) on public evaluation of health care in eight countries, including West Germany and the United States, illustrated this difference. West Germans rated government performance lower if they believed that the government was taking less responsibility for providing medical services, but the Americans were not as prone to do so. A distinctive psychological orientation on the part of Germans, in comparison with Americans, helps us understand the different approaches to welfare. The German word *anspruchsdenken* cannot be translated literally into English, but essentially means "mentality of entitlement." It signifies a readiness on the part of the individual to claim and use the welfare benefits to which he or she is entitled by law. As Erwin Scheuch (1987) explains, the current welfare system in Germany makes it possible for its citizens to demand the most in all welfare programs. Thus Germans, on the average, appear to have a different mentality about the welfare state. They can use its services whenever and for as long as necessary; therefore, Germans can approach the social welfare system for health care, pensions, and other benefits with an exceptionally strong sense of personal entitlement. The fact that *anspruchsdenken* has no equivalent in English underscores the lack of a corresponding mentality in American society (Cockerham, Kunz, and Lueschen 1988).

The historical basis for this orientation began in 1883, when Germany's Chancellor Otto von Bismarck introduced a series of social reforms. These reforms were intended to thwart the influence of socialist politicians, secure the loyalty of the working class, and espouse the paternalistic view that the state has the duty to provide for the welfare of its subjects. There is little doubt that Bismarck was aware of the advantage that might be gained from a social insurance program in his struggle against socialism (Craig 1982). Bismarck was a Prussian by birth, and Prussia—the leading state of imperial Germany, which Bismarck had helped establish in 1871—had a tradition of state responsibility for the welfare of its citizens in return for their obedience and allegiance. Not only was a program of social insurance for all of Germany consistent with this tradition, but it offered Bismarck the opportunity to promote the national government at the expense of socialist politicians and workers' trade unions. Socialist members of the German Reichstag, or parliament, were caught in a dilemma and were forced by political and public pressure to support Bismarck's plan in order to avoid being accused of disregarding the needs of the working class.

As Myles (1984) observes, Bismarck's measures were both a response to democratization and an attempt to suppress it. In other words, Bismarck wanted to defuse the demands for political rights from an increasingly well-organized and leftist-oriented working class by providing them with social rights that linked workers to the state rather than to trade unions or socialist politicians. Included in Bismarck's reforms (national health insurance was provided in 1883) was a national compulsory old age insurance program initiated in 1889. As David Childs and Jeffrey Johnson (1981:99) aptly summarize the outcome: "Whatever view we might now take of Bismarck's motives in introducing these schemes, there can be no doubt that they were excellent for their time and they became a model both for subsequent German governments and for foreign governments."

Following Germany's defeat in World War II and incorporation of its eastern lands into a separate Communist state, West Germany became a multiparty republic in 1949. The West German constitution, the Basic Law, guarantees the social welfare of its citizens, continues the comprehensive social security system developed by Bismarck, and now includes East Germans. The program that was established included health insurance, old age pensions, sickness benefits for income lost to illness or injury, unemployment insurance, and family allowances in the form of child benefits, rent allowances (especially for the elderly), and public funds for the construction of low-income housing.

Participation in the state-sponsored health insurance program is compulsory for most Germans. Employees, the unemployed, foreign workers, students, farmers, household workers, and old age pensioners are all required to be insured by one of several hundred health insurance organizations that are supervised by the federal government. Some 13.5 percent of a worker's monthly gross earnings in the west and 13.1 percent in the east goes to pay for health insurance, with half the contribution made by the employee and half by the employer. Approximately 10 percent of the German population is excluded from coverage—namely, civil servants, employees with high salaries, and the self-employed—but they can take out private insurance or voluntarily join the state program. Health care is free to the individual and covers medical and dental treatment, drugs and medicines, and hospital care for an indefinite period of time. In the event of illness, the employer must continue to pay the employee's full wages for six weeks, and then the health insurance fund provides the individual with his or her approximate take-home pay for up to 78 weeks. If the illness is more protracted, benefits are continued under a welfare plan unless the person is permanently incapacitated and is entitled to a disability pension. Since 1983, retired persons have been required to pay part (about one-sixth) of the cost of their health insurance from their pensions, with the remainder financed from contributions paid into the government's compulsory health insurance program by members of the labor force.

Participation in the statutory old age pension plan is also mandatory for all wage and salary earners and farmers; self-employed persons and housewives may voluntarily join the program. Additionally, widows and orphaned children of insured persons are entitled to a portion of the insured's pension. Retirement normally takes place at the age of 65, but anyone who has contributed to the statutory pension fund for 35 years may retire at age 63; women may opt to retire at age 60 if they have made contributions for 15 of the last 20 years prior to their application. The amount of the pension depends on the size of the individual's contributions and the number of years he or she was a member of the active workforce. The pension contribution in 1995 stood at 19.2 percent of a person's gross monthly earnings—again, half paid by the employee and half by the employer. In 1988 the average monthly pension from the government-sponsored program was about $1,379 in the west and $1,036 in the east. In addition to the "normal" old age pension—that is, the one based on the state's statutory pension plan—many employees also receive a pension from a plan set up by their employer. The amount of this additional pension generally depends on how long the pensioner worked for the employer involved and the amount contributed to it.

Overall, German society has developed an effective "safety net" to provide for the welfare of its citizens, and this is especially true for the aged. The underlying principle of social security in Germany is that the gainfully employed will support those who are unable to work for reasons of old age, sickness or disability, or unemployment. The employed, in turn, can expect similar support when they need it. The general social welfare of its population is guaranteed by the nation's Basic Law enacted in 1949; thus the basis of government is clearly that of a welfare state. Nevertheless, in the future, Germany, like other welfare states, will face serious problems in funding its social welfare system as costs rise and the labor force shrinks.

FRANCE

Nearly 8.5 million people in France, representing some 14.6 percent of the nation's total population of 58 million, were age 65 and over in 1994. By 2025, the number of elderly in France will have increased to 11 million people, comprising 14.8 percent of the overall population. This will be a relatively large gain in the percentage of elderly in a Western European country. However, the projected growth in the percentage of old people in France will be considerably below the increases of 200 to 300 percent in developing countries in Asia and Latin America and the increases of over 100 percent in developed nations such as Japan, Canada, the United States, and Australia.

Unlike Germany, which began its social security system in the late nineteenth century, France did not have similar developments until 1930. As a result of a law passed in 1901, there were numerous private organizations offering health and pension plans on a nonprofit basis to specific occupational groups. But the 1930 legislation laid the legal foundation for a truly national insurance program, which provided assistance for children and subsidized housing, health care, and old age benefits for low-income families. The system was reorganized in 1945 after the second world war and expanded to include practically the entire population.

However, there is no single organization providing insurance coverage nationwide, nor do all individuals belong to the same organization. Rather, the French social insurance system remained divided among occupational groups. For old age benefits, wage and salary earners in commerce and industry have their own organization, as do farmers and agricultural workers. Businesspeople, craftspeople, professionals, and employees in the public sector are represented by several different organizations. As Anne-Marie Guillemard (1986:1321) notes, "The universal right to retirement was split up into as many pieces as there were funds." For health and family benefits, a similar system exists. Thus there is only a minimum level of centralization in France's social welfare system. All of the various insurance organizations are nonprofit, supervised by the government, and responsible to their members. As Isidor Wallimann (1986) points out:

> Germany, Switzerland, the U.S.A. (and as a rule all or most modern welfare states) tend towards having one insurance system covering all citizens irrespective of their occupational or class location. This is also true for health insurance where states—such as Sweden, Great Britain, Germany, however not the U.S.A. or Switzerland—intend to provide coverage against illness for the entire population. It must be concluded, therefore, that the French welfare state is very unique in that it covers the entire population against such things as old age and illness by means of an insurance system which is not only more

decentralized but also organized around the occupational or class location of individuals.[1]

With so many different insurance organizations involved in the French system of social welfare, how can uniformity and equality in covering the entire population be achieved? The answer is that the welfare system, including state-sponsored pensions, is not uniform or equal (Guillemard 1986; Wallimann 1986). Everyone is required to belong to an insurance organization, and all such organizations are controlled by various government agencies. The Department of Agriculture, for example, supervises the insurance organization for farmers and agricultural workers, and the Department of Social Affairs and National Security controls the salary and wage earners' insurance organization. These agencies all follow national policy, which provides some uniformity and coordination; otherwise, there are many differences and inequalities in coverage. Different organizations have different rates of contributions and levels of benefits. This situation tends to violate the principle of equity on which welfare states are based. In contemporary France, as Wallimann (1986:1308) notes, "Those better off (such as the self-employed) maintain some of their privileges also in the social insurance system by virtue of the fact that they are permitted to quite autonomously form and shape their own insurance organization and its policy." Farmers and agricultural workers, on the other hand, are at a relative disadvantage with respect to the amount of premiums they can afford to pay to their own organization and the level of benefits they receive. Consequently, France's social welfare system is divided along socioeconomic lines and is subject to greater class conflict than similar systems in other Western welfare states. Nevertheless, as Wallimann observes, there is no evidence at present that the basic structure of France's social insurance system is going to be changed.

France also differs from other Western states in its method of financing social insurance. The French depend less on taxes and more on personal income to meet their social needs than any other developed country (Wallimann 1986). Instead, about 42 percent of the funds comes from contributions made by employers and employees, and 39 percent from property tax and taxes on goods and services. Income taxes provide only 19 percent of welfare spending in France, compared with about 45 percent in the United States and Canada, 40 percent in Great Britain, and 36 percent in Germany. Employer contributions to health and retirement benefits are 20.2 percent of their payrolls, whereas employees contribute about 13.3 percent of their wages and

---

1. Isidor Wallimann, "Social Insurance and the Delivery of Social Services in France," *Social Science and Medicine* 23 (1986): 1307.

salaries. Thus "France is unique in that employers pay an unusually high share of all contributions into the social insurance system" (Wallimann 1986:1310). Other countries, such as the United States, Canada, Great Britain, and Germany, tend to have equal percentages of contributions from employers and employees. But, in France, employers are required to contribute more heavily to social welfare because of the political success of socialists and labor unions in attempting to reduce or eliminate altogether the contributions of workers.

Another important difference between France and other Western nations was its increased spending on social insurance in the late 1970s and early 1980s, which only recently lessened because of a slowdown in the economy. Until the 1970s, old age pensions, as John Ardagh (1987) observes, were so low that many elderly lived in poverty unless they were able to obtain assistance from their families or religious charities. However, following the victory of the Socialist party in France under François Mitterrand in 1981, the minimum pension for retirees was increased by 25 percent. In 1995 the retirement minimum guaranteed by the government was about $619, and the maximum was $1,293. The official age of retirement is 65 years. Higher pensions and longer life expectancy have meant a considerable strain on France's current budget for social welfare. Like other developed nations, France is confronted with serious problems in financing its welfare state. According to Ardagh (1988:423), "Old people are at last quite well protected by the State: but officialdom has not worked out how best to pay for this new largesse."

JAPAN

Defeated by the United States and its allies in World War II, Japan has recovered to become a giant in the world economy. With a 1994 population of over 125 million people, Japan has advanced to the first rank of world trading nations. In fact, Japan emerged in the late twentieth century as the world's leading creditor nation, exporting billions of dollars each year in loans and overseas investments. The Japanese government, however, does not engage in massive welfare expenditures, including generous pensions, for its own population, nor does it require high income taxes from them. The Japanese people are encouraged to save money for use in old age, and over 20 percent of all personal income goes to savings accounts. Private companies, in turn, are encouraged to establish their own welfare programs for their employees, which includes providing retirement plans, helping retired employees find postretirement work, and providing health insurance.

The problems facing Japan in relation to the aging of its population are not fundamentally different from those in other developed nations, with the notable exception that the Japanese are growing older at a faster rate than any other country. Some 15.6 million people or 12.6 percent of the Japanese population was age 65 or over in 1991. But by 2025, the proportion of elderly will reach 25.8 percent, which represents a pace of aging unexceeded elsewhere in the world at present. In the twenty-first century, China will replace Japan as the most rapidly aging society, but until then Japan will hold that position. There has been concern that Japan's social security system would go bankrupt, because the number of younger workers paying taxes to support the system is shrinking. In 1970, there were 8.5 workers paying taxes into social security for every person over age 65; by 1991, there were 6.0 workers per elderly person; and in 2020 it is expected that there will be only 3.0 workers.

Unlike the situation in the United States, the aged in Japan do not have effective organizations to lobby on their behalf with the national government. Thus government measures with respect to social security usually do not become political issues to the extent found in the United States. With the exception of national health insurance, elderly Japanese have traditionally not relied on their government for extensive old age benefits. Although there were various pension plans for government employees and workers in private businesses prior to World War II, it was not until 1960 that Japan created a national pension and health insurance system for all of its citizens, including the self-employed. Japan has three public pension plans: the National Pension, which provides a basic pension to all Japanese and a supplement to the self-employed; the Employees' Pension Fund, which supplements the basic pension of private-sector employees; and the Mutual Aid pension, which supplements the basic pension of public-sector employees. Retirement age under the National Pension is 65 years, with the supplemental plans allowing retirement at age 60 for men and 58 (to be raised to age 60 in 1999) for women. Some Japanese can retire as early as age 55 (miners and seamen) or 57 (police). The basic pension is paid by the government, and the supplemental plans require contributions ranging from 14.50 (private-sector employees) to 19.08 percent (for railroad workers), shared equally between employers and employees. Initially, benefits were lower than those available in most public and private pension plans already existing both in Japan and in the welfare states of Western Europe. But, with the economic growth beginning during the 1960s, Japan increased its spending on social security from 5 percent of the national income in 1960 to 13.7 percent in the 1990s. Allowances for children (beginning with the third child), completely free medical care for older persons at age 70, and greater equality in the level of old age pensions, especially for employees in the private sector, became part of the overall welfare system in the early 1970s. Prior to age 70, those persons without health insurance from private employers are generally covered by public insurance, but they must pay 30 percent of the cost out of their own pockets.

However, publicly funded old age benefits in Japan have never equaled the entitlements available in many Western European nations. For example, when Japanese social security spending in 1990 was 13.7 percent, several Western European nations had expenditures between 22 (Great Britain) and 44 (Sweden) percent. As Joji Watanuki (1986) and others (Kobayashi and Reich 1993) explain, a Japanese welfare state has never been fully realized. Rather, public pensions were intended to supplement pensions from private employers, and old persons were also expected to be taken care of to a large degree by their family. Thus the Japanese system of old age security consists largely of three institutions: the government, private business, and the family—with the government making the least contribution.

In 1991, an employee of a large corporation in Japan with 30 years on the job received a lump-sum payment at retirement of approximately $160,000 on the average. The retired employee also received a monthly pension of about $1,360. This may seem generous, but Japan is one of the most expensive countries in the world to live in, and the cost of housing is particularly high. Consequently, nearly 80 percent of all Japanese continue to work after the customary retirement age, which, in most large corporations, is between the ages of 55 and 60. Of those who continue to work, half are self-employed as farmers and shopkeepers; the remainder usually work full or part time in lesser jobs for the same company or for some other firm. Some 40 percent of retired Japanese who continue to work do so because of financial necessity. This is a larger percentage than is found in either the United States, Great Britain, or France (Palmore 1985). But there is also a strong work ethic among elderly Japanese, and younger persons tend to accord older workers considerable respect; in addition, as Erdman Palmore (1985) observes, the elderly generally have job opportunities in Japan, and those aged persons in the highest leadership positions in business, politics, education, and religion usually do not retire until they are very old or their health fails. The proportion of working elderly declines from nearly 80 percent between the ages of 60 and 64 to just under 20 percent at age 80 and above. Nevertheless, there is an important normative distinction between Japan and America when it comes to retirement. As Palmore (1985:51) explains, "In the United States retirement usually means the end of employment; in Japan it usually means reduced work and responsibility, but continued employment."

The Japanese not only are more likely to be employed in old age than in either the United States or Western Europe, but are also more likely to be living with one of their adult children. Although not as large a proportion of Japanese elderly live with their children as is the case in some developing Asian nations like the Philippines and Singapore (Martin 1988), more elderly live with their children in Japan than in any other developed nation in Western Europe or North America (Hermalin 1995; Watanuki 1986). According to Watanuki (1986:266), "If we only compare industrialized societies, we can say that a high ratio of elderly people living together with their children is peculiar to Japan, and this is the Japanese advantage to be encouraged in order to promote security for the aged." What the aged gain is social support, and what their adult children gain is a residence usually in their parents' home—in a nation where housing is expensive and space for homes is scarce. They also gain assistance with household tasks and an enhanced opportunity for young wives to be employed outside the home, because child care facilities are not extensive in Japan. In addition, maintaining a residence with one's aged parents is consistent with the traditional care and respect given to the elderly in Asian societies. According to S. Philip Morgan and Kiyosi Hirosima (1983), living with one's parents is not an anachronism, but an adaptive strategy for many in Japanese society. Morgan and Hirosima state:

> Extended residence is an accepted tradition in Japanese society supported by strong intergenerational ties, by an emphasis on duty to parents, and by less emotional interdependence between spouses than in Western settings. Also, the Japanese economic system more heavily rewards senior employees so that interfirm moves, which entail geographical mobility, are less frequent. Finally, the extremely expensive housing in Japan, inadequate child care facilities, and less extrafamilial support for the aged make extended residence more attractive in Japan. In short, extended residence seems to fit better with modern Japanese society than with similarly modern nations of the West such as the United States.[2]

Attitudes toward co-residence may be changing somewhat. Watanuki (1986) notes that there can be strain from co-living with aged parents, especially for daughters-in-law who are expected to care for their aged parents-in-law. Linda Martin (1988) also observes a growing preference among better educated elderly to live apart from their children. In 1950, some 87 percent of all elderly Japanese lived with their children, but the percentage

2. S. Philip Morgan and Kiyosi Hirosima, "The Persistence of Extended Family Residence in Japan: Anachronism or Alternative Strategy?" *American Sociological Review* 48 (1983): 280.

had declined to 60 percent by 1989 (Hermalin 1995). However, despite this decline, the practice of extended residence is not likely to disappear in Japan (Morgan and Hirosima 1983); the proportion of aged Japanese living with their adult children is likely to remain at about 50 percent (Martin 1988). In the United States, for example, in 1994 only 13 percent of the aged lived with a family member other than their spouse; however, this figure includes persons who live with their children and those who live with siblings or other relatives.

Another feature of aging in Japan that differs from that in Western societies is the respect accorded to old people. Palmore (1985) suggests that the high proportion of elderly living with their children indicates a continuing high level of respect and affection for the aged by their families. Palmore also notes features of the Japanese language (the honorific form) that are used in speaking to elders to show the proper degree of respect or deference. In addition, aged family members have special places to sit (a seat of honor) at family gatherings and meals, and they are served first at mealtime with the choicest portion of food. The aged also, according to custom, pass through doors before younger persons and bathe first in family baths. Japan also has a special holiday for the aged, Respect for Elders Day, which involves public ceremonies and family activities honoring old people. And Japan has a National Law for the Welfare of the Elders, passed in 1963, guaranteeing a "wholesome and peaceful life" for the aged as a matter of government policy. Although the status of the aged may have declined somewhat in modern Japan, as compared with pre–World War II conditions, Palmore finds that the status of the elderly is returning to relatively higher levels and has traditionally remained higher than in Western countries.

Palmore concludes that the disengagement theory of aging does not apply in Japan, where the elderly are not pushed out of the social mainstream when they are old, nor do the aged themselves wish to withdraw completely from participation in social and economic matters. Palmore also finds that industrialization has not resulted in low status for the aged, as modernization theory would claim. Rather, Palmore finds that the activity theory of aging applies best to the Japanese situation in that the older Japanese tend to maintain high levels of activity if their health permits, and the more active Japanese elders tend to be the most satisfied with their lives.

Japan, as discussed in Chapter 3, has the highest life expectancy in the world. According to 1991 figures, the average Japanese male lives 76.4 years, and the average female, 82.8 years. Americans, in contrast, had a life expectancy in 1991 of 72.0 years for males and of 78.9 years for females. The traditional Japanese diet, featuring foods like fish, soybeans, and vegetables, has been found to be effective in preventing heart disease (Yamori et al.

1989). Also, as Palmore observes, elderly Japanese are relatively happy and healthy; they have free medical care beginning at age 70; and the status and respect accorded to them by their family and the general public are among the highest in the world at present. Japanese elderly, more than those in other industrialized nations, also tend to be more socially integrated into their families. Japan thus appears to be one of the best countries in the world in which to experience old age.

But this does not mean that Japan is a paradise for aging. The approach of the Japanese government to aging is to stress self-reliance. Aged Japanese do not receive lavish old age pensions from the government but are required to rely strongly on pensions from employers and savings in one of the most expensive countries in the world. This situation helps explain why the Japanese have one of the highest rates of savings in the world. It also helps explain why a majority of older Japanese continue to work in old age. As Palmore (1985:55) points out, "In Japan most men continue to work at least until age seventy despite 'retirement' at age fifty-five." Many older Japanese no doubt work in order to remain active in late life and because of the strong work ethic in the country, but for many older Japanese, it is necessary for them to work in order to supplement their old age benefits.

CHINA

Unlike the other countries discussed in this chapter, the People's Republic of China is a Communist society with one-party rule. The Communists came to power in China in 1949 following a civil war with Nationalist forces. The country remained isolated from non-Communist nations until 1972, when government, cultural, and business contacts were reestablished with the United States and other Western countries in order to further economic development. Although showing tendencies toward allowing greater individual freedom and expression among its population in the 1980s, the Chinese government ruthlessly crushed a student-led prodemocracy movement in 1989 and retains its Communist government.

China is of particular interest to gerontologists because of its large and rapidly aging population. With over 1.2 billion people in 1995, representing over 20 percent of the world's entire population, China has more people in general and more older people in particular than any other country on the globe. In addition, China is going to overtake Japan in the early twenty-first century as the world's fastest-aging society. What this means is that by the middle of the twenty-first century, China will have a higher proportion of older people in relation to its total population than any other country. According to U. S. Census Bureau projections, some 40 percent of China's population will be over age 65 by 2025. In terms of absolute numbers, China's elderly population is expected to increase from 68 million in 1991 to over 179 million in 2020. Clearly, China is facing a major demographic and social evolution with respect to aging.

The greatest increase in China's older population is due to declines in fertility and increases in life expectancy that are characteristic of aging societies everywhere. What makes China different is that the large size of its population is in the process of producing greater numbers of older people at a faster pace than elsewhere. According to Jersey Liang and his associates (Liang, Tu, and Chen 1986), China's birthrate fell 50 percent between 1950 and 1982, whereas life expectancy rose from 42.2 years for males and 45.6 years for females during 1953–1964 to 61.6 years for males and 63.2 years for females in 1964–1982. By 1991, overall life expectancy in China was 69.4 years.

Liang and associates point out that about 80 percent of all workers in urban areas are employed in the public sector, which consists of government and Communist party employees and persons working in education, science, industry, and cultural enterprises. Age 60 is the average retirement age for men, and age 55 is the average retirement age for women. However, mandatory retirement is often not required for persons with special skills and positions of political leadership. In order to qualify for a pension, which pays from 60 to 100 percent of the individual's preretirement salary, the person needs to have been employed in the public sector for at least 10 years. The amount of the pension is based on years of service and credit for revolutionary work. Workers in the public sector have the best retirement situation in China, in that they receive the largest pensions and free medical care. Other urban workers in light industry and handicrafts receive pensions that are not as generous as those given state workers, and they do not receive health insurance benefits. They must work 20 years to receive a pension that is 45 to 50 percent of their last wages. Workers in the few private businesses in China do not receive any public pension at all. Old age pensions, in fact, are not widespread in China. Less than 25 percent of all persons of retirement age receive a pension, and pensions are especially rare for rural dwellers. Nor does reaching old age bring any special entitlement to health insurance; health insurance benefits when one is elderly are dependent on earlier coverage.

The majority of Chinese elderly depend on their family for support in old age. The government requires that families be responsible for their aged parents under a 1980 marriage law; thus most old people live with their children and depend on them for financial support as well (Hermalin 1995; Ikles

1991; Liang, Tu, and Chen 1986; Martin 1988; Olson 1988). The bulk of China's population is provided for this way, especially in rural areas where 80 percent of all Chinese live. Some 82 percent of all elderly Chinese live with their family, with a range of 73 percent in cities and 89 percent in rural areas (Hermalin 1995). Under Chinese law, farm workers are to be provided "five guarantees" by their collective farm, which include food, clothing, medical care, housing, and burial expenses. "However," Liang and associates (1986: 1359) point out, "it soon became apparent, such guarantees were to apply only to old people who had no pensions or grown sons to support them." Thus aged persons without pensions or family support from a son are provided welfare from either their neighborhood committee in cities or their production brigade on collective farms. Many elderly men also find postretirement jobs to provide them with income. It is apparent that a transition of support for the elderly from the responsibility of children to that of the local community is taking place in China, because the one-child-per-family policy limits such support (Shi 1994).

Historically, China, like Japan and other Asian societies, has been characterized as according the elderly relatively high status. Confucian teachings stressing parental authority, the extended family, ancestor worship, and veneration of the aged were influential in China for much of its recorded history (Sher 1984). However, in reality, only upper socioeconomic groups had the economic resources to support large extended households, practice ceremonies associated with Confucian ancestor worship, and consolidate power in the senior family heads (Yin and Lai 1983). Under Communist rule, the status of aged landholders, members of upper and middle socioeconomic groups, and rich peasants was curtailed. But this was primarily a form of social class rather than age discrimination, as the Communists under Mao Tse-tung sought to destroy the influence of China's elderly capitalists. Peter Yin and Kwok Lai describe the circumstances for the aged bourgeoisie:

> Hence, compared to what their situation might have been in traditional China, this bourgeoisie subcohort of elderly adults lost the most social and parental status, and power. In traditional China they would have been venerated by the young, but under the Maoist state, they were despised. Within the family, the same situation prevailed: In traditional China they would have had a large multigenerational household, control of property, and near absolute obedience from the younger generation; under Maoism, they had small families, no property, and little control over their children. Although the literature has noted the decline of older people in Maoist China, it applies almost exclusively to this subcohort of the elderly adults.[3]

3. Peter Yin and Kwok Hung Lai, "A Reconceptualization of Age Stratification in China," *Journal of Gerontology* 38 (1983): 611.

Thus criticism directed against the elderly was motivated by reasons of ties to capitalism rather than age itself. Other aged persons—namely, workers and less affluent peasants—maintained a higher degree of status in China, whereas the greatest status and power in society accrued to the Communists in general and to its political leadership in particular. As Yin and Lai (1983) explain, although the new government deliberately diminished the status of the aged, respect for parents was still emphasized, and obedience to parents was to continue unless it conflicted with the demands of the state. Moreover, youth did not come to power in China under Mao; the most powerful persons in both the central and regional governments were elderly and remain so in the post-Mao period. China's government, with very few exceptions, is controlled by very old men.

The position of the aged in Chinese society has slowly returned to the point that old people generally now have higher status and respect than in the immediate aftermath of the Communist takeover (Sher 1984; Yin and Lai 1983). Whether such status will continue, however, remains an open question, because modernization like that taking place in China in the late twentieth century often lessens the social value of the aged (Cowgill 1986). Whether this will happen is not clear, because the leadership of the Chinese Communist government is elderly; some educated older people, trained in capitalist business methods prior to 1949, have technical and managerial skills needed for modernization; and veneration for the aged is a Chinese cultural tradition, just as it is in Japan, where modernization did not result in diminished status for the aged. Furthermore, with nearly 40 percent of its population over the age of 65 in 2050, China cannot afford to diminish the respect and position of such a large segment of society. Aging is going to be a dominant factor in Chinese life in the twenty-first century, regardless of its politics.

SUMMARY

This chapter has examined the social policies pertaining to the support of the elderly in the United States, Canada, Great Britain, Sweden, Germany, France, Japan, and China. Each country is unique in its provision of income and medical care to the aged. Yet there are some common features: (1) the percentages of elderly are increasing rather than declining or remaining stable; (2) the cost of supporting increased numbers and percentages of the aged in the future remains a social policy problem, and no clearly superior method has yet been discovered to increase revenues significantly; (3) national governments are generally supportive of assisting the elderly in maintaining a positive standard of living; and (4) there is likely to be a worldwide crisis in the twenty-first century about national spending for the elderly as their numbers increase and those of younger persons decrease.

Moreover, among Western welfare states, the link between welfare benefits and poverty has tended to be severed, for the United States and the Western countries discussed in this chapter have clearly expanded their support for the aged to include all social classes. Thus the right of citizenship, rather than social class position, has evolved as the basis for extending state-sponsored benefits to all old people. In non-Western societies, as seen in Japan and China, traditional aspects of Asian society emphasizing family responsibility for elderly parents still prevail to a large extent. A major difference between the West and Asia is that the family remains more of a pillar in Asia for support of the elderly. Family support seems particularly pronounced in China. The vast majority of old people in China have no pension and must depend on their family.

The aged worldwide share problems of declining health and decreased income, but—as the development of social security for the aged in the countries discussed in this chapter indicates—the clear trend is toward the continued allocation of state resources to support the elderly. There are almost as many different ways to accomplish this as there are countries, yet national governments have committed themselves to this end at various periods during the twentieth century. Consequently, increased national resources for the elderly appear to be the norm in modern twenty-first century societies—provided the means can be found to pay for them without sacrificing the future of the young.

Chapter 12

DEATH AND DYING

Death comes to everyone, and all human societies have developed social arrangements for containing its impact on the living. Yet attempts to define death as something so indeterminate that it can be denied or easily avoided have not been successful strategies in coping with both the meaning and the process of dying, on either an individual or a societal level. Death is an inevitable biological and social experience of all people and represents the final stage of the aging process.

Beginning in 1965 with Barney Glaser and Anselm Strauss's seminal work, *Awareness of Dying,* social scientists have become increasingly interested in studying the process of death and dying in contemporary society. The study of attitudes toward death has made that topic one of the most recent sources of significant theoretical and applied insight into human behavior. Initially, most of the research concerning death dealt with the problem of death as a solitary and perhaps cruel experience in modern hospitals, where the dying patient was often found to be socially and psychologically isolated. Hospital staff and the dying patient's family appeared inhibited in their attempts to interact with the patient in an open and socially meaningful manner. The process of dying was itself hidden as much as possible, to minimize the effect of death on all concerned, especially the living. Now it seems that our attitudes toward death may be changing, not only in the academic disciplines, but in American society generally. Although it remains to be confirmed that we are actually in a period of "death revolution," which some writers suggest will see the elimination of the fear of death in advanced industrialized societies, the contemporary approach to death is to deal with it as a natural part of the human condition. It is hoped that this approach will help us to understand our own lives and ease our fears about the inevitability of mortality in a more open, honest, and satisfying manner.

DEATH AND THE INDIVIDUAL

The basic problem that humans have in dealing with death is fear. In a review of the literature on attitudes toward death, Elizabeth Kübler-Ross (1969), one of the most noted scholars on death and dying, pointed out that death has been and remains a fearful event for most human beings and that fear of death is universal throughout the human species. Many studies in psychology and psychiatry have documented the fact that this strong, deep-rooted fear motivates many people to seek secure environments and to avoid activities and situations that could result in premature death (Kammerman 1988; Weisman 1985). Sigmund Freud, for example, believed that fear of death was a primary motivation for social cohesion, as people sought security and strength from group membership. Even though some people may not overtly express a fear of death and dying, Herman Feifel and Allan Branscomb (1973) suggested, nearly everyone fears death. In a survey, Feifel and Branscomb noted that over 70 percent of their respondents verbally denied that they were afraid of death. However, at a second level of testing, which involved reactions to images of death, the respondents began to demonstrate ambivalent attitudes. At a third level of testing, involving word and color-word associations, nearly 95 percent of the respondents revealed a subconscious fear of death. Even people who characterized themselves as extremely religious indicated "a demonstrable fear of death" on the subconscious level.

Fear of Death and Dying

Although many fears have been identified in connection with death, the primary fear is fear of the unknown—the dread of not knowing what happens as you die and when you are dead. Glaser and Strauss (1968) say that, when death occurs slowly, the dying patient is forced to cope with death by overcoming the fear of loss of self and the fear of dying as physical, and perhaps mental, disintegration. Avery Weisman (1985) indicates that a fear of dying evokes ideas about decay, destruction, and obliteration. No one can share his or her experiences of death with the living; yet reports are available from people who have nearly died of a heart attack or from an accident of some kind. Although such reports do give clues about the experience of life's final moments, the reader should be cautioned about accepting the validity of such accounts because they obviously cannot be verified.

A study by Russell Noyes, Jr. (1972), of the process of dying found that many people who report being close to death have similar experiences. Using descriptions of dying experiences, both autobiographical and clinical, Noyes developed a model of the death experience consisting of three stages: resistance, review, and transcendence.

The initial stage of *resistance* to death begins when a person struggles for survival, realizing that death may be imminent. This resistance is characterized by marked anxiety but not disabling panic. If even the slightest possibility of survival remains, the person often feels an enormous surge of energy that may enable him or her to survive by alert mental activity and feats of strength. But, conversely, this upsurge of energy is countered by a powerful desire to surrender, and the person is caught between the impulse to fight and the impulse to surrender. If the person is dying gradually, Noyes claims that, as energy wanes, life seems to be dependent on an inner struggle to maintain it. He (Noyes 1972:177) states, "it is as though their will to live sustains them and as though without it they might simply let themselves go and, in a sense, will their deaths."

The second stage of *review* appears after all hope of survival has apparently disappeared and the person surrenders to his or her fate. Death is faced calmly, perhaps with a sense of tranquility. At this particular point, Noyes says that the person begins to review past life experiences from a detached perspective, as if the ego had become an entity capable of observing itself act out the past. The present author has interviewed people who reported similar experiences after being close to death as a result of automobile and industrial accidents. These people believed that they, in fact, left their hospital beds and "hovered" about the room, able to view themselves and others as a detached consciousness. Parapsychologists term this experience an "out-of-the-body" phenomenon, which may be a negation of death on the part of the dying person. Here the subject views his or her body as near death, but exists outside it, thus becoming a detached witness. Some people, according to Noyes, report viewing scattered scenes or all the important events in their lives in this "detached" state. He suggests that the certainty of loss of one's future may necessitate a return to the past to make one's existence real in a final grip on life. The phenomenon of the ego splitting from the body may also lessen personal anxiety by reducing death to solely bodily annihilation.

The final phase is *transcendence*. Here the person's perspective becomes more distant, and one experiences oneself as outside of time or beyond the past and future. This altered sense of time represents complete immersion in the present moment. Another characteristic feeling is a sense of loss of control, as if one is held by a superior power. At this point, the person experiences feelings of oneness or unity with other human beings and the universe. Death is near.

Although providing some interesting insights, Noyes's analysis of the death process cannot be considered conclusive by any means. His descriptions were rendered by people generally in good health who were suddenly threatened with death. We do not know if these experiences are typical or how accurately most people identify their dying moments. Then, too, the mystical state of consciousness reported during transcendence may not be shared by all dying people, but just those who have a tendency toward such modes of perception. Not all people near death report such experiences (Kastenbaum 1981). "If they did," states Jack Kammerman (1988:105), "you would expect all people coming close to death to have them, which they don't." Other variables, such as age, sex, personality, and culture, may also be very important in influencing near-death experiences. Still, the similarities among those cases reported by Noyes and other researchers (Moody 1976; Ring 1980) suggest important guidelines for future research into the experience of dying.

Research by Raymond Moody, reported in his book *Life After Life* (1976), suggests that the out-of-the-body phenomenon and the review of one's past life are especially common elements of the dying process. Moody, a physician, interviewed several people who were supposedly near death at some time in their lives, and he described the typical experience of death as follows:

A man is dying and, as he reaches the point of greatest physical distress, he hears himself pronounced dead by his doctor. He begins to hear an uncomfortable noise, a loud ringing or buzzing, and at the same time feels himself moving very rapidly through a long tunnel. After this, he suddenly finds himself outside of his own physical body, but still in the immediate physical environment, and he sees his own body from a distance, as though he is a spectator. He watches the resuscitation attempt from this unusual vantage point and is in a state of emotional upheaval.

After a while, he collects himself and becomes more accustomed to his odd condition. He notices that he still has a "body," but one of a very different nature and with very different powers from the physical body he has left behind. Soon other things begin to happen. Others come to meet and help him. He glimpses the spirits of relatives and friends who have already died, and a loving, warm spirit of a kind he has never encountered before—a being of light—appears before him. This being asks him a question, nonverbally, to make him evaluate his life and helps him along by showing him a panoramic, instantaneous playback of the major events of his life.[1]

Moody goes on to explain that the dying man is caught up in intense feelings of joy and peace, but somehow he realizes that it is not time for him to die. Reluctantly, he returns to his physical body and lives. Kenneth Ring (1980) followed up Moody's research in a study of 102 people to determine if they had near-death experiences. Half did not, and the other half experienced some five stages, consisting of (1) the affective component (sensing peace and well-being); (2) body separation; (3) entering darkness; (4) seeing light; and (5) entering the light. Parallel to stages 2 through 4 was a decision-making process on whether to return to life; this process included the life review, encounter with a "presence," encounter with deceased loved ones, and the making of the decision. Not everyone passed through all five stages, but the respondents who experienced all or part of this process reported that it was a positive situation. Martha and Rainer Baum (1980) likewise reported that their review of near-death experiences showed the process of dying to be blissful and devoid of fear. They also noted that the experiences of dying took place in stages, in this case, three stages: resistance, life review, and transcendence.

The stage of resistance raises an important sociological question regarding death. This question concerns the extent to which the "will to live" is responsible for length of life. Although researchers are not aware of what physiological mechanisms may be at work in this process, a body of literature in psychology suggests that perhaps rats, chickens, monkeys, human beings, and even cockroaches become unusually susceptible to death when they discover that they have no control over what is happening to them and that further action is futile (Seligman 1974). The experience of American prisoners of war during the Korean and Vietnam wars who simply laid down and died, although apparently in good physical health, are examples of this phenomenon.

Research by David Phillips and Kenneth Feldman (1973) found evidence that there are fewer deaths than usual before important ceremonial occasions such as a birthday, a presidential election, and the Jewish Day of Atonement. Using data derived from biographies of famous people, Phillips and Feldman suggest, in accordance with Émile Durkheim's (1961) description of social integration and ceremonies, that people who are strongly integrated into a society feel an obligation to participate in the ceremonies of that

---

1. Raymond A. Moody, *Life After Life* (New York: Bantam, 1976), 121–122.

society. Thus people strongly attached to society postpone death in order to be alive during meaningful social ceremonies; people detached from society and uninvolved with its ceremonies may die earlier by just "letting go." Admittedly speculative, this hypothesis does offer interesting possibilities for research concerning the will to live and the social processes that might either reinforce or possibly negate that will.[2]

Other research by Phillips supports this hypothesis. For example, Phillips and E. King (1988) found that mortality rates for Jewish men in California fell sharply below an expected level before the Jewish holiday of Passover and rose by an equal amount above the expected level immediately afterward. Non-Jewish control groups showed no significant fluctuation in mortality around Passover. In another study, Phillips and Daniel Smith (1990) found the same pattern among elderly Chinese women in California for the Harvest Moon Festival. Mortality dipped 35 percent before the Harvest Moon Festival and rose 34 percent in the week thereafter. Chinese men and young Chinese women did not show the same pattern in mortality, nor did a control group of Jewish men. However, the Harvest Moon Festival in Chinese culture is a ceremonial custom in which the central role is assumed by the senior woman of the household, who is responsible for preparing special foods. Research such as this suggests that people may be able to prolong living in some cases in order to reach particularly important social events.

The other major fear of the unknown is fear of what happens after death. Beliefs about existence after death are common in most cultures, and one of the primary functions of religion is to reduce anxiety by providing answers concerning life after death. However, research about the effects of religion in allaying fear of death has either been inconclusive (Dumont and Foss 1972) or found to have a positive influence on reducing anxiety (Rasmussen and Johnson 1994). The more certain people are about life after death, the less anxiety they express. However, Kübler Ross (1969) found in her research with terminally ill patients that religious patients seemed to differ little from those who were not religious. Very few patients could be identified as being truly religious or as confirmed atheists. Most held beliefs

---

2. An interesting example of the possible relationship between a significant social event in a person's life and the will to live is found in the biography of Thomas Jefferson. Jefferson died on July 4th, 50 years to the day after he signed the Declaration of Independence. Jefferson's physician described the scene as follows: "About seven o'clock of the evening of that day, he [Jefferson] awoke, and seeing my staying at his bedside exclaimed, 'Oh Doctor, are you still there?' in a voice, however, that was husky and indistinct. He then asked, 'Is it the Fourth?' to which I replied, 'It soon will be.' These were the last words I heard him utter" (Peterson 1970:1008).

somewhere between the two extremes, and their philosophical perspectives were usually not strong enough to relieve them of the fear of dying. Kübler-Ross observed that people with less education, little sophistication, and few professional obligations or social ties had the least difficulty facing death. Those persons experiencing the greatest difficulty were characterized as ambitious, attempting to strive for control of their environment and for accumulation of material goods. Although they had many social ties, they exhibited few meaningful personal relationships and usually faced death alone.

But fear of the unknown is not the only fear related to the experience of dying. At least five other significant fears have been identified: (1) fear about not being able to pursue or to complete certain goals; (2) fear of what will happen to dependents; (3) fear of the loss of self-mastery or control over one's destiny; (4) fear of punishment for sins; and (5) fear of isolation and separation from loved ones and treasured objects. All of these fears, either singly or in combination, can produce a considerable degree of anxiety in an individual concerned about death.

Strategies for Dealing with Death: Childhood, Adolescence, Adulthood

Because fear of death tends to be universal—defined by existentialist philosophers as the human being's "most profound awareness"—numerous strategies have been employed by individuals and society for coping with death anxieties. In very early *childhood*, there is generally no conception of what death means, and the discovery of the phenomenon of death is not usually accompanied by great emotion (Anthony 1968, 1972). Often the child's discovery of death occurs as a simple incident in day-to-day living when the child explores his or her environment and perhaps finds a dead object such as a bird or insect. Sylvia Anthony (1968) tells us that usually there is a definite interval between a child's first questions about death and the arousal of emotion connected with the idea of dying. Death is commonly associated with the child's understanding of his or her world and may be reviewed as going to sleep, going on a trip, or going up in the sky.

Anthony suggests that anxieties regarding death do not appear until around the ages of three to five, when the child realizes the possibility of loss of someone on whom the child depends or the loss of one's own self. D. G. Prugh and associates (1953), for example, found that, among hospitalized children, types of death anxiety varied according to age; children under the age of six were thought to be highly anxious about separation from other people. Thus death seems to disturb the very young child mostly due to the thought of separation, loneliness, or abandonment.

Many young children, however, do not develop death anxieties. They are usually able to control their fears about death perhaps because they do not perceive death as the end of life. The dead may be viewed as being simply another category of the living who are less than alive or who live somewhere else, such as in heaven. As a defense against death anxiety, many children are taught that there is an afterlife. Often the perception of young children regarding death may involve a close relationship between death and birth; someone dies and then returns as a baby. Many games that children play also include a death theme in which death is not defined as a permanent or finite state. Children who are "killed" while playing "soldier" or "cowboys and Indians" are expected to come back to life at an appropriate time. This view of death is reflected in children's literature, where death is seen as an event that can be undone; the dead hero can be returned to life by magic or through the intervention of good fairies and spirits.

Although there is general agreement in the research literature concerning three- to five-year-olds' fears of death as separation, there has been serious disagreement about the characteristics of death anxieties in the six- to ten-year-old age group. Much of the initial research consisted of data collected from observations of terminally ill children, which found that this age group lacked the intellectual ability to develop an extensive concept of death (Debuskey 1970). These children apparently experienced little anxiety about dying unless adults intervened to point out to the child the seriousness of the illness. Other research suggested that, although six- to ten-year-olds could not fully conceptualize death, they were nonetheless aware that something very serious was wrong with them (Easson 1970). John Spinetta (1974) has strongly criticized this research, however, on the grounds that its conclusions rested largely on observations of parents and hospital staff rather than on direct observation of the children; also, when the studies were based on observations of the child, they lacked objective measures, with little or no use of control groups for comparison.

Other studies strongly suggest that six- to ten-year-olds are aware of what death means. E. H. Waechter (1971) asked a set of four matched groups of children who were fatally ill, children with chronic but not fatal illnesses, children with temporary illnesses, and normal, nonhospitalized children to construct stories about themselves using a set of pictures. Waechter found a greater number of overtly expressed death themes among the fatally ill children. She concluded that this age group is not only subjectively aware of dying, but also able to express that awareness objectively.

Spinetta, Rigler, and Karon (1974) tested Waechter's conclusion in an experiment involving a group of 25 children fatally ill with leukemia and a control group of 25 chronically ill children with nonfatal diseases. The six- to ten-year-olds were matched not only by age group, but also by sex, race, grade in school, and amount of medication. The children were asked to tell a story about a sick friend by placing in a model of a hospital room dolls representing a sick child and significant adults (nurse, doctor, mother, father) in their *usual* places. Later the children were asked to repeat the story by putting the dolls in places they would *like* them to be. Because the dying children placed the adult dolls at such a significantly greater distance from the doll of the sick child, Spinetta and associates inferred that the placement of the dolls by the dying children reflected a growing sense of psychological separation from both the people and the circumstances of the hospital environment. In interviews with parents and hospital staff, they found additionally that adults reported a decrease in the frequency, intensity, and quality of interaction with the dying child. Although the parents wished for the child's recovery and attempted to provide great affection, they also wished to withdraw from the child to protect themselves emotionally when the child died. The hospital staff likewise reported a reluctance to become emotionally involved for similar reasons.

Accordingly, Spinetta and associates ask some important questions: Does the dying child reflect the unresponsive feelings of adults, or does the child try to prepare for death by separating from parents? Does the dying child prefer to be left alone for reasons of his or her own choosing or because he or she senses embarrassment on the part of adults? Spinetta does not provide answers to these questions, but he does suggest that, whatever the reason, the fatally ill child is aware of death and perhaps dies psychologically isolated from other people.

Spinetta concludes:

> It seems clear . . . that the fatally ill 6- to 10-year-old child is concerned about his illness and that even though this illness may not always take the form of overt expressions about his impending death, the more subtle fears and anxieties are nonetheless real, painful, and very much related to the seriousness of the illness that the child is experiencing.[3]

Once children near *adolescence,* around the age of ten or so, they develop adult concepts of death which recognize that death is not only inevitable, but also final. Yet adolescents generally fear death less than other age groups because death is not an immediate threat and they are reasonably sure of a full life. Actually, the outward aspects of death often appear very funny to them. They construct jokes and rhymes about death and enjoy

3. John J. Spinetta, "The Dying Child's Awareness of Death: A Review," *Psychological Bulletin* 81 (1974): 259.

laughing at movie and television scenes containing exaggerated expressions of bloody mayhem. Anthony (1968) calls the adolescent's mockery of death "a halfway house" to the defenses against death anxiety available to the adult.

Human beings like to think that somehow the individual personality is not meant to die and that something personal about themselves is able to survive death. However, the strategies that exist for use by the *adult* in the desire for eternal survival are limited to those of (1) sexual reproduction, (2) belief in an afterlife, or (3) belief in reincarnation. Sexual reproduction allows adults at least to imprint themselves genetically on succeeding generations. Belief in an afterlife is derived from either religion or a personal philosophy of existence. Some people embrace religion and try to live the kind of life that "qualifies" for life after death in heaven. Other people have their own, perhaps nonreligious, belief in a life or existence of some type after death, perhaps as a spirit or energy form in the cosmos, or the adult may believe in reincarnation. Several accounts have been written by people who are convinced they were born, lived, and died at a time in the past and have returned to the present to live another life. Otherwise, the adult must cope with the idea of death as the total end of experience and an eternity of nothingness.

Strategies for Dealing with Death: The Dying Patient

Despite the particular strategy an individual selects to contain the fear of death, the time arrives for most people (except for infants, comatose patients, or those persons dying sudden and unexpected deaths) to confront the process of dying in old age. Two of the most noted studies describing this process are those of Kübler-Ross (1969) and Glaser and Strauss (1965, 1968). Kübler-Ross identified five stages of coping with dying: (1) denial and isolation, (2) anger, (3) bargaining, (4) depression, and (5) acceptance. Not everyone may go through each of these stages or do so in the order prescribed by Kübler-Ross, but the sequence she suggests was typical of most patients in her study. The first stage of *denial and isolation* consists of the patient's shock and dismay at the disclosure of impending death. Often the initial awareness of death is accompanied by resentment against other people who are not dying or against fate itself. Sometimes patients in the stage of denial will "shop around" for another physician to disprove a previous diagnosis of terminality. Most patients, according to Kübler-Ross, demonstrate at least partial denial of their deaths at some point in their efforts to cope with the dying process.

Glaser and Strauss also found attempts at denial in their study of terminal patients. Some of these attempts included refusal to seek further information from physicians, refusal to discuss their illness and death with anyone, favorable comparisons of themselves with other dying patients, emphasis on the future, a state of being highly active, and the attempt to juggle time. This last strategy consisted of setting a particular point in time as a survival goal and, after reaching that time, selecting another future time, and so on.

Throughout all of the stages outlined by Kübler-Ross, dying patients expressed hope that death could somehow be averted. Usually this hope was based on the possible discovery of a new drug or sometimes on the skill of physicians. Stewart Alsop (1973), a journalist dying of cancer, said that such hope allowed the dying person to die more easily. Although the patient may be told he or she *may* die or *probably* will die, Alsop thought that the patient should not be told he or she *will* die.

Kübler-Ross observed that very few patients are able to maintain a "make-believe" world in which they are healthy up until the final moments of living. When denial of one's death can no longer realistically be maintained in the face of medical evidence, the second stage of *anger* appears. Often this anger is displaced on family, friends, the hospital staff, or God. Kübler-Ross said this can be a very difficult time for those who must interact with the dying patient. The next stage, *bargaining*, usually does not last very long. This stage represents an attempt to postpone death by good behavior or good deeds. Perhaps in return for some special service, dying patients hope they will be granted an extension of life. The fourth stage, *depression*, occurs usually prior to the acceptance of death. Here the patient knows definitely that absolutely nothing can be done to change his or her fate. The great majority of patients, according to Kübler-Ross and Glaser and Strauss, come to terms with their depression sufficiently to go on to the final stage of *acceptance*.

If the patient has had enough time and perhaps assistance in working through the other stages of reaction to dying, Kübler-Ross found, the patient usually reaches the stage of acceptance. During this stage, the patient is no longer angry or depressed, but recognizes the inevitability of death. This is not a happy period, but one characterized by Kübler-Ross as "almost devoid of feelings." Pain and struggle may be over, and all that usually remains is the wait for death. Glaser and Strauss, however, tell us that acceptance may be either active or passive. Passive acceptance consists of calm resignation as described by Kübler-Ross, but active acceptance involves preparing for death by becoming philosophical about life and death, settling personal and financial affairs, becoming very religious, or eliminating the distressing prospect of dying a painful and lingering death by committing suicide. Some patients accept the fact of their dying but decide to fight it by intensive living, by seeking out marginal or "quack" doctors for miracle cures, or by volunteering to participate in medical research and experiments that might produce a cure.

Alsop (1973) provided a particularly insightful account of the acceptance of death in his book *Stay of Execution*. Although he did not welcome the prospect of dying, it was difficult to accept a life of pain and weakness with a dependence on medication and blood transfusions. To be without the possibility of ever returning to a normal life and to feel very, very sick made the thought of dying far less terrible to him. Alsop (1973:23) finally reached the point where he believed that, just as a sleepy man needs to sleep, a dying man needs to die, and that a time comes when it is both wrong and useless to resist.

Another dying writer, Harold Brodkey (1996:52), expressed a similar view in a journal he kept to record, as he put it, his "passage into nonexistence." Brodkey states:

> Being ill like this combines shock—*this time I will die*—with a pain and agony that are unfamiliar, that wrench me out of myself. It is like visiting one's funeral, like visiting loss in its purest and most monumental form, this wild darkness, which is not only unknown but which one cannot enter as oneself. No one belongs entirely to nature, to time: identity was a game. It isn't cruel what happens next, it is merely a form of being caught. Memory, so complete, and clear or so evasive, has to be ended, has to be put aside, as if one were leaving a chapel and bringing the prayer to an end in one's head.[4]

DEATH AND SOCIETY

Like individuals, societies develop attitudes toward death that are reflected in the establishment of normative practices designed to contain death's presence. To assess the American perspective regarding death, it is useful to compare its evolution from social thought of western Europe during the Middle Ages to the present. According to Philippe Ariès (1974), the French social historian, death in Western society in the twelfth century could be characterized as "tamed death" because it seemed to lack the anxieties common to the twentieth century. People in the Middle Ages did not desire to die, or at least they were in no hurry to do so; but when they realized that death was near, the art and literature of the period suggest that people usually died simply, as if death were a familiar aspect of living. Death was supposedly viewed as the collective destiny of the species, and the simplistic, perhaps naive, acceptance of death was acceptance of the order of nature.

4. Harold Brodkey, "This Wild Darkness," *The New Yorker*, 5 February 1996, 52.

Except for sudden or unexpected death, the deaths that occurred during the Middle Ages usually involved a familiar ritual. First, the dying person was supposed to lie down in bed, if at all possible, in order to die. Then the actual process of dying consisted of a ceremony organized by the dying person, who was expected to follow a prescribed sequence of behaviors intended to conclude life. The dying person was supposed to express sorrow about the end of life and to recollect beloved persons, events, and things. He or she was expected to pardon for any disapproved acts the usually numerous companions who gathered around the deathbed; this was followed by a final prayer in which the dying person requested forgiveness of sins. After a priest administered absolution, all that remained was the wait for death. Dying was a public and familiar act, and the dying person's room was a social setting to be entered freely by relatives, friends, and neighbors. For example, as Ariès pointed out, no portrayal of the deathbed scene between the twelfth and eighteenth centuries failed to include the appearance of children. Usually there was no great show of emotion at the deathbed, because behavior was guided by the dying person in the formally prescribed death ritual.

In modern society, people no longer experience death in this simple ceremonial manner. Instead, the modern version of dying has been characterized by fear, anxiety, and social isolation. What happened? What caused our attitudes toward death to change? Ariès claimed that, from the Middle Ages on, death in Western society was subtly modified into a pervasive dread. One source of this change, as noted by Ariès, is found in Christianity. Inspired by the book of Matthew, the Christian death scene during the Middle Ages emphasized the idea of judgment; that is, the weighing of souls by Christ the Judge according to the deeds, both good and bad, committed during the person's lifetime. The eternal destination of heaven or hell for the dying person was at issue and, notwithstanding its cosmic essence, judgment was peculiar to each individual. Thus the security of death as a collective rite was joined by the anxiety of interrogation and personal trial.

Medieval Christianity was certainly not wholly responsible for the changing attitudes toward death, but it was influential. Another important factor in attitudes toward death in the Middle Ages, according to Ariès (1981) was a love of life among the more affluent social classes. At this time, Ariès (1981:138) stated, "Death was not only an end to being but a separation from having: One must leave behind houses and orchards and gardens." During the eighteenth century, romanticism, with its emphasis on love of nature and the expression of strong emotion, also viewed death as a painful rupture from the beauty of nature and the joy of living things. Acute anxiety over death was a norm sanctioned by a society strongly aware of the pain of separation from persons and objects that were loved and valued. Another important attitude that first emerged full-blown in the nineteenth century, the Age of Rationalism, was the notion of guilt about personal failure to accomplish certain goals. Ariès (1974:105) summarized this latter attitude as a "passion for being, an anxiety at not sufficiently being."

The twentieth century marked the efforts of society to control death by making it as unobtrusive a social process as possible. Emphasis was placed on the "acceptable" death, which was a death that could be tolerated by the survivors. This idea had its origin in the belief of the Middle Ages that there was a close relationship between death and an individual's personal biography. It was thought that each person's life flashed before his or her eyes at the moment of death; the dying person's attitude at that time would thus provide his or her biography with its conclusion and final meaning. Death was believed to be the occasion when human beings were most able to know themselves. Consequently, to die well or to experience a good death became very important. The twentieth-century interpretation of this attitude, however, was concerned not with the benefit for the individual but with society. The antithesis to an "acceptable" death was the graceless, fearful, and embarrassing death that caused strong emotions and revulsion among other people and a disruption of social life. Therefore, modern society sought to control death and to make it as acceptable as possible by hiding it.

Societal control of the impact of death was significantly assisted by two contemporary phenomena: (1) the occurrence of dying generally among people furthest removed from the mainstream of social life; and (2) the displacement of the traditional site of dying from the home to the hospital. Approximately two-thirds of all deaths in industrialized societies are the result of old age. Deaths associated with the aging process occur largely among people who have retired from work and who no longer have parental responsibilities. These deaths rarely interrupt the smoothly functioning society.

Hospitals have become the place to die, because the care provided there is usually not possible in the home. Today in American society, only a minority of people dies at home, and the number is decreasing rapidly. About 70 percent of all deaths occur in hospitals and nursing homes (Kammerman 1988). Fewer than one-third of the deaths in American society take place at home, at work, or in public places. The removal of most deaths from the home has caused the traditional death ritual to disappear. Death in the hospital is controlled not by the dying person or his or her family, but by the physician and the hospital staff, who define not only the circumstances of death but the exact moment of dying.[5] Access by family and friends to the dying patient can also be controlled by the hospital, so that death occurs under the jurisdiction of relative strangers to the dying person. Such a controlled death is disruptive to neither the general functioning of the hospital nor the society at large.

The Social Organization of Dying

Two major studies on death in sociology, those of David Sudnow (1967) and Glaser and Strauss (1965), provide illustrations of the death environment in American society. Sudnow (1967) studied the organization of dying by using participant observation in two hospitals: a large West Coast urban charity institution and a private general hospital in the Midwest. Most of Sudnow's observations took place in the charity hospital, which he described as a setting for the concentration of death. Three-fourths of the patients were over age 60, and there was an average of three deaths daily. Most of the deaths occurred on the medicine and surgery wards. The personnel on these wards encountered death so frequently that it was considered routine. The routinization of dying was made easier, both at the charity and the private hospitals, because almost all of the deaths were preceded by a coma. Comatose patients were regarded as being essentially dead, and they could be disattended as social objects.[6] Of the some 200 deaths he witnessed, Sudnow noted that not a single death was of the "Hollywood" variety, where the dying person's last sentence was interrupted by a final breath.

Those people having the most contact with death in the hospitals were generally lower-echelon employees. Once a patient died, except for the autopsy, the physician lost interest in the body. The higher one's position in the status hierarchy of the hospital as a nurse or a physician, the less likely

5. The medical and legal definition of death is no longer the traditional criterion of heart stoppage because of the possible restoration of heart action, even when there is no longer the remotest possibility of the patient's recovering consciousness and brain functions. The basis for defining death is that of a "flat" or isoelectric electroencephalogram denoting "brain death," which is taken after signs of respiratory and circulatory failure.

6. As suggested by Erving Goffman, Sudnow (1967:74–75) made a distinction between "clinical death" (signs of death based on physical examination), "biological death" (cessation of cellular activity), and "social death" (the point at which a person is treated like a corpse although still alive clinically or biologically). "Social death" was not simply the asocial treatment of a dying patient by the hospital staff, but was the beginning of social activities commonly associated with death: planning the autopsy, grieving, preparing the obituary notice, contacting insurance companies, disposing of personal effects, arranging for the funeral, and so forth.

was one to witness dead bodies or to physically handle corpses. The handling of corpses was considered "dirty work" in the value system of the hospital, and whenever possible ward personnel would leave a body to be processed by the next work shift.

Sudnow saw the hospital as an environment of occurrences, with deaths being an occurrence mainly definable in reference to its similarity to other deaths experienced by the personnel. Although any given death could give pause for retrospective comment by staff members, the mention of deaths was usually routine except for those involving unusual events, such as obtrusive settings or styles of dying, accidents, diagnostic or treatment errors, or the high social status of a patient. The age of the dead person could also cause comment, especially the deaths of children. General philosophical consideration by the staff on death and dying did not naturally occur.

Although the staff sought to minimize and routinize death as much as possible for themselves, the organization of dying was constructed in such a way as to hide the fact of dying from patients and visitors. Most hospitals, for example, locate the morgue in a relatively inaccessible part of the hospital basement. Sudnow (1967:51) quotes a text in hospital administration: "The hospital morgue is best located on the ground floor and placed in an area inaccessible to the general public. It is important that the unit have a suitable exit leading onto a private loading platform which is concealed from hospital patients and the public." Often the patient whose death was imminently expected was moved to a private room to avoid troubling other patients, and bodies were not removed from these rooms during visiting hours to avoid upsetting visitors.

There was, however, a difference between the charity and private hospitals in the presence of family and friends at the dying patient's bedside. At the private hospital, relatives were considered entitled to be present at the bedside at the moment of death. The dying person did not preside over the gathering, as in the traditional death ritual; nonetheless, the experience of death was not solitary, as it was in the charity hospital. Dying patients were shielded from relatives at the charity hospital in order to minimize disruption of hospital routine and processing of the body. The justification for this action was to protect the relatives from the "unpleasantness of seeing someone die." If death was regarded as imminent, family members were urged by the staff to go home and await further news or to wait in waiting rooms or in the corridors, not in the patient's room. The result was that relatives were usually not present at the time of death and were summoned only after the staff had completed its processing duties.

Awareness Contexts

Glaser and Strauss developed a typology of awareness contexts based on both participant observation and personal interviews in six hospitals in the San Francisco Bay area. These awareness contexts—closed awareness, suspected awareness, mutual pretense awareness, and open awareness—were all derived from observing the social settings and the control of information about dying in the hospital. Glaser and Strauss found that the physicians were reluctant to disclose impending death to the patient, and nurses were not expected to do so without the consent of the responsible physician. Thus patients were generally required to take action to get information about the extent of their illness and were often prevented by the staff from asking questions about dying. Awareness contexts were not relevant if the patient was comatose, an infant, or someone whose knowledge of death was not important to the staff, or in emergency situations. Awareness contexts pertained when the patient was conscious and the staff managed knowledge of the patient's dying.

Closed awareness is a social condition in which the staff knows the patient is dying but the patient is unaware of the fact. It is based on the following structural conditions: (1) inability of the patient to recognize the signs of dying; (2) reluctance of the staff to discuss dying with the patient; (3) reluctance of family members to discuss the patient's condition with the patient; (4) organization of the hospital itself, which is designed to conceal information; and (5) lack of anyone to help the patient find out the facts, including other patients. When any of the above conditions was lacking, other awareness contexts were possible. *Suspected awareness* is a situation in which the patient is suspicious but does not know that an illness is terminal. The patient is then forced to draw information from whatever sources are available to confirm his or her suspicions. *Mutual pretense awareness* is a somewhat more comfortable situation; the patient is aware of a terminal condition and refuses to talk about it, and the staff is under no obligation to discuss dying. This arrangement usually worked to contain emotions unless either party to the interaction broke down while trying to maintain the pretense. *Open awareness* is a condition in which everyone knows and openly acknowledges the terminal situation. The patient is held responsible for his or her behavior and is expected by the staff to face death with dignity, to sustain responsible ties to family and friends, and to cooperate with the staff. This last condition was most acceptable to the staff. Although there are no formal norms for the "ideal" death, Glaser and Strauss make the important point that people just cannot help judging other people.

The Glaser and Strauss study differs somewhat from Sudnow's research because most of the patients observed by Glaser and Strauss were not comatose, paid for their own hospital care, and were of a higher social status. Unlike patients in the Sudnow study, they were in a better position to negotiate the dying process. Nevertheless, in both studies the staff saw death as inconvenient and managed interaction with the dying patient so as to minimize disruption.

Desensitizing Death: Coroners and Physicians

The implications of the Sudnow and the Glaser and Strauss studies contribute to an understanding of the social psychology of those people whose occupations and professions require routine exposure to death. The findings of other attitudinal studies should also be noted. For example, Kathy Charmaz (1975) reported that county coroners' deputies employed self-protective strategies to avoid the emotion of the death scene and to maintain the routine character of their work (ascertaining the cause of death, establishing the identity of the deceased, protecting the property of the deceased, and locating the relatives of the deceased to whom the announcement of death could be made). In making the announcement to relatives, most deputies expressly avoided using the word *dead* and substituted the words *fatally injured* or *passed away,* if they made any direct reference to death at all. Sometimes they just gave progressively meaningful cues in the conversation so that the relatives would realize what had happened and would themselves say the word *dead.* The deputies were also prompt to turn the situation around by asking about funeral and burial arrangements, so that the responsibility for the occasion was thus symbolically shifted to the relatives.

According to Charmaz, one of the most striking features of the attitudes shown by the deputies was the extent to which they reflected typical cultural taboos. The deputies demonstrated an avoidance of death, were uncomfortable during the expression of grief by survivors, and showed an absence of personal philosophy either about death in general or about their own deaths in particular. Instead, they subjectively interpreted death as being a by-product of their work rather than the focus of it. This approach was exemplified by the comment of one deputy (Charmaz 1975:304), who stated, "That's not a body lying there. It's an *investigation.* You have to look at it as an investigation, not as a person lying there." The deputies supported an occupational ideology that prevented them from becoming involved in the situation, on the grounds that they would then be unable to perform their work properly. Robert Clark and Emily LaBeff (1982) found, in a study of physicians, nurses, law enforcement officers, and clergy, that death telling was an aspect of their jobs that they strongly disliked. Typically, they would try to prepare the next of kin for the worst before delivering the news. In an earlier study of over 200 physicians on the staff of Michael Reese Hospital in Chicago, Donald Oken (1961) found that 90 percent of the doctors stated a preference for not telling cancer patients that their condition was terminal. In discussing their diagnosis with the patient, the use of euphemisms was the general rule. Patients would be told they had a "lesion," a "mass," or perhaps a "tumor," but terms like *cancer* and *malignancy* were avoided.

Despite the strong reluctance to inform a cancer patient of his or her diagnosis, there was essentially unanimous agreement among the physicians that some family member must be told. Not only were legal and ethical considerations important in disclosing the diagnosis to some relevant person but, Oken believed, the physician had a strong need to share the burden of knowledge that someone was going to die. The primary reason cited by the doctors for not wanting to tell the patients they had terminal cancer was "clinical experience." "Clinical experience" consisted of the physicians' opinion that most people did not want to know, that they knew already, or that they should not be told so that they should not give up or become depressed. However, Oken found that the real determinant for avoiding the disclosure of a terminal diagnosis was an emotion-laden, a priori judgment related to a fear of how the patient would react to the information (become angry, commit suicide) and the physician's underlying feelings of pessimism and futility about cancer.

Oken further explained that the physicians interviewed generally agreed that patients feared cancer because its diagnosis was equated with suffering and certain death. What was impressive was that the physicians themselves felt very much the same way, and these feelings were in conflict with their strong desire to prevent suffering and save lives. Oken stated:

> Situations of this kind, associated with intense charges of unpleasant emotions, call forth a variety of psychological defenses which reduce the intensity of feelings to manageable proportions. Among such defenses are those which involve the avoidance, negation, or denial of the existence of some unpleasant fact, and acting as if it were not real.[7]

Oken's research took place in the 1960s, when physician-patient communication about death tended to be highly indirect (Glaser and Strauss 1965). A major argument by physicians against informing patients of their death is that it interferes with compassion. This seems to be the case particu-

---

7. Donald Oken, "What to Tell Cancer Patients: A Study of Medical Attitudes," *Journal of the American Medical Association* 175 (1961): 1127.

larly in Japan (Hattori et al. 1991). Some doctors may believe that, in order to maintain hope or avoid unnecessary suffering, especially for patients with a terminal illness, the patient should not be informed about his or her condition. The question of whether or not to tell terminally ill patients the truth about their condition has significant ethical, as well as legal, complications. There is a body of opinion in the United States that physicians must use discretion in communicating the truth to patients, regardless of their situation (Meyer 1991). The primary reasons for withholding the truth about a terminal illness include the patient's inability to cope with the news and the potential for suffering great stress and anxiety. There is also the notion that sick, dying people know they are dying and do not have to be told.

Other opinions maintain that it is ethically wrong for doctors to withhold or manipulate medical information; a decision to deceive must be a very unusual step in caring for a patient (Bok 1991). This view takes the position that harm resulting from disclosure is outweighed by the benefits, including the option to choose among treatments. Furthermore, research on this subject shows that patients become more cooperative, more capable of dealing with pain and discomfort, and more responsible when they are told the truth (Garrett, Baillie, and Garrett 1989; Rosoff 1981). Regardless of ethical issues or opinions involved in withholding the truth, the law requires informed consent from patients concerning the treatment available to them and the reason for it. Consequently, terminally ill patients in the United States are typically informed of their situation.

This trend is reinforced by the Federal Patient Self-Determination Act of 1991, which requires hospitals to inform patients of their right to make their own decisions about their medical care. The law requires physicians to inform patients about their medical condition and the available courses of treatment, and to obtain consent to proceed with treatment from the patient or his or her lawful surrogate (such as next-of-kin) if the patient is unable to consent. Exceptions involve emergency situations in which the patient is unable to consent and no lawful surrogate is available. Therefore, doctors today commonly tell their patients their diagnoses, regardless of how dire the consequences are for the patient. They may prepare the recipients for the news by approaching the subject indirectly in the beginning but nevertheless move toward making sure the patient understands the situation. An example of such a conversation is related by Jeffrey Clair (1990). The setting is Mr. Henderson's hospital room in the cancer ward of a hospital as the results of the X ray of his tumor are being related to him by his physician Dr. Winfield.

Mr. Henderson states to Dr. Winfield: "You said the x-ray looked better, what exactly does that mean?" Dr. Winfield responds: "It means that it is a little better." Mr. Henderson asks again, "What do you mean better?" And Dr. Winfield replies: "I mean smaller, which is good." Mr. Henderson is laying supine in his bed while the doctor is writing in his chart. After about ten seconds of silence Mr. Henderson asks: "For how long?" Dr. Winfield looks up from the chart and says: "Well, I don't know, you're asking me to be a sorcerer." Mr. Henderson immediately responds: "No, not quite." He pauses and says: "I know it won't be very long." Dr. Winfield then asserts: "Well you never know, it could be for quite sometime." Mr. Henderson quietly states: "I hope so." At this time Dr. Winfield closes the patient's chart and starts speaking: "Now, I don't want to be—there also is always the chance that you could have complications within the next three to four months. This isn't our plan of action but it is possible. But at the same time, you should, if your affairs are not in order, get them that way."[8]

Differences in styles of death telling also exist among professionals, and it appears that physicians tend to be rather elaborate when they announce deaths to next-of-kin. Police officers, for example, tend to be more direct than physicians in telling about death; physicians, on the other hand, take a more technical approach by relying on a large repertoire of explanations and giving what is essentially a detailed, orderly, blow-by-blow description of the situation (Clark and LaBeff 1982).

Robert Coombs and Pauline Powers (1975) have characterized medical school and the teaching hospital as the locale in which medical students and physicians learn to cope with death in an objective manner (while at the same time denying its subjective implications). Coombs and Powers identified five developmental stages in this process: (1) idealizing the doctor's role, (2) desensitizing death symbols, (3) objectifying and combating death, (4) questioning the medical model, and (5) dealing with personal feelings. In the initial stage, medical students tend to demonstrate the same emotional attitudes toward death that are common among laypersons; for example, they found the "coolness" of the qualified physician's approach to death to be "offensive." Nevertheless, they generally realized that they themselves needed to control their emotions about death if they were to become good physicians. In the second stage, they began to become desensitized to the symbols of death as a result of their experience dissecting cadavers, attending autopsies, and working in the pathology laboratory. In addition, they began to acquire the knowledge and medical terminology that allowed them to adopt an intellectual perspective toward disease.

The third stage of objectifying and combating death came when the medical students started working in the hospital and were exposed to dead

8. Jeffery Michael Clair, "Regressive Intervention: The Discourse of Medicine During Terminal Encounters," *Advances in Medical Sociology* 1 (1990): 63–64.

and dying patients. They realized more fully at this time the necessity of detaching themselves from the trauma associated with death in order to protect themselves from their own personal feelings and be able to work effectively as doctors. One way medical students socialize themselves to deal with the emotional side of death, as found in another study by Frederic Hafferty (1988), is the telling of cadaver stories and jokes. Another important desensitizing technique found by Coombs and Powers (1975), which was modeled by the clinical faculty, was the student's denial of the subjective features of death. Coombs and Powers explained it this way:

> In other words, the clinician learns to view dying patients not as people with feelings, but as medical entities, specimens, or objects of scientific interest. By adopting a scientific frame of mind, utilized so effectively in their previous work with dead bodies, clinicians can effectively avoid the uncomfortable inner feelings which occur when they are exposed to dying patients.[9]

Some (but apparently not all) of the medical students and physicians in the Coombs and Powers study experienced a fourth stage of socialization to death, which questioned the medical model. As they perceived it, the medical (scientific) model of treatment tended to dehumanize patients and to define doctors as little more than technicians. From this perspective, it became unrealistic to think that all patients could be cured; thus in some cases it might be inappropriate to prolong life unnecessarily. Some physicians apparently did not experience this fourth stage; their ego was easily inflated when they were cast in the role of a healer who had powers over death. "When his self-esteem was involved," stated Coombs and Powers (1975:262–263), "it is imperative that he prevent death from occurring, for death makes him feel vulnerable. But if he can keep the 'corpse' alive for a few more days or weeks, his mastery over death is demonstrated." This so-called God complex, regarded by many physicians as incompatible with good medical practice, was nonetheless an observable phenomenon.

What socialization had generally accomplished up to the time of the fifth stage of dealing with their own personal feelings about death was that the doctors had been conditioned to repress their personal anxieties and fears. However, Coombs and Powers (1975:263–264) found: "Our interviews with physicians revealed rather dramatically how much repressed emotionality exists among medical practitioners." When pressed to discuss their own feelings about death and dying, both on a professional and a personal level, the most common strategy employed by the physicians to cope with their own

---

9. Robert H. Coombs and Pauline S. Powers, "Socialization for Death: The Physician's Role," *Urban Life* 4 (1975): 258.

fears was avoidance. In a comment reminiscent of the Sudnow (1967) and Glaser and Strauss (1965) studies, Coombs and Powers stated:

> Typically every effort is made in the hospital to shield oneself from mourning relatives. In the emergency room quiet crying is tolerated, but if any kind of emotional outburst occurs, relatives are usually hustled off to the chapel as fast as possible. "We isolate them so that their grief is not so obvious," a physician said. "It isn't done cruelly, but frankly, it is done more to protect the emergency room staff than to help the family."[10]

This situation has led Clair (1990) to introduce the term *regressive intervention* to describe physicians' tendency to withdraw—either gradually or abruptly—from interaction with dying patients once their skills become useless and they are unable to prevent death. Hence, efforts to intervene or delay dying lessened (regressed) as the certainty of death increased. This process was not one of abandonment on the part of doctors; rather, it was an emotional withdrawal and a refocusing of their efforts on other patients they could still help.

What is suggested by these studies is a tendency of people who confront death regularly to develop a self-protective psychology that consists of a behavioral and cognitive pattern of avoidance and negation of the death experience through the process of objectification. Dead and dying people come to be defined as "cases" or "investigations" rather than as people. Meanwhile, personal fears and anxieties about the subjective meaning of death are suppressed. The objectification of death is justified on the grounds that the professional be able to carry on—to "do a good job." Yet, despite an outward appearance of control over emotions, the process does not always function smoothly. Some physicians and others who deal with death experience a considerable amount of subjective stress because of it (Clark and LaBeff 1982; Coombs and Powers 1975; Oken 1961).

CHANGING ATTITUDES TOWARD DEATH

Death in the wider context of American society has not been socially disruptive because, as Robert Blauner (1966) explained, the impact of death has been controlled through bureaucratization. Hospitals care for the terminally ill and manage the crisis of dying; mortuaries attend to the problem of disposal of the dead and the transition ritual of the funeral. The handling of death by these specialists and the isolation of the dying experience in hospi-

---

10. Ibid., 265.

tals and nursing homes have minimized the average person's exposure to death. Blauner described the modern hospital as a "mass reduction" system because it tends to reduce the individuality of its dying patients.

Yet, as Blauner noted, this system cannot be fully achieved because of the tension between death and bureaucracy. Bureaucracies are committed to routine and unemotional administrative procedures. Death, on the other hand, is laden with considerable emotionality, not only the deep-rooted fear of one's own dying, but also the grief and bereavement of survivors, which can elicit some of the strongest emotions of human existence. Several studies have found grief, mourning, and bereavement for a deceased person to be long-lasting; it can cause decreased appetite, weight loss, difficulty in concentration, sleep disturbances, and depression (Carr 1985; Lund et al. 1986; Lund 1987). No matter how much effort and control is exerted by a society to contain and routinize death and dying through bureaucratic procedures, such procedures are not in themselves satisfying alternatives for handling a strongly emotional and personal event.

However, an exception is found in Victor Marshall's (1975) study of a retirement community on the eastern seaboard of the United States. Marshall observed that the residents organized themselves as a community of dying to legitimize death as an appropriate (although not necessarily positive) event, because they had "lived their lives." The residents were able to socialize each other to their impending deaths through frequent conversations about it and the presence of role models with whom to anticipate their own dying. All in all, when a death occurred, the residents managed a "low-key" approach to the way in which that death was observed. Marshall agreed with Arlie Hochschild (1973) that individuals are better able to face their deaths if they can observe, in a kind of role-modeling process, that the deaths of others take place within a taken-for-granted framework.

Attitudes toward death in American society had reached a point of change in the late twentieth century. The fundamental cause of the change was the recognition of the failure of efforts to hide and deny the process of dying, which had resulted in death's becoming a depersonalizing and lonely experience. The humanistic approach appears to be slowly but steadily returning. Also, as Diana Crane (1975) observed, there is an increasing desire to exercise autonomy in areas where formerly the individual had allowed others to make decisions. Consequently, many individuals desire to control not only their own life but also their own death and the factors contributing to it. Crane further noted that the development of certain life-sustaining machines and techniques, such as dialysis for kidney disease and organ transplantation, have stimulated questions about the use of medical technology and the quality of the lives that are thus prolonged.

There is considerable evidence to support the contention that attitudes toward death in American society are changing. A tremendous amount of material on death has been produced and presented in the mass media, particularly in the form of books. Colleges, universities, and schools of medicine, nursing, and public health are adding courses on the social and psychological aspects of death. Practically none of these courses existed 25 years ago; in fact, medical schools offered courses dealing only with clinical facets of death. There has also been recognition in the last few years that large general hospitals have not been very good places to die. To cope with this problem, numerous clinics and seminars have been established to train in-service hospital personnel to handle dying patients more humanely. One particular approach is to encourage physicians and nurses to deal with the reality of their own deaths and their own personal philosophies about life and death. If health practitioners are unable to change the medical outcome of a disease, yet have faced the possibility of their own deaths, it is believed that they can perhaps be supportive of the dying patient in that patient's search for meaning during the remaining portion of his or her life.

Crane (1975:10) has summarized changing attitudes toward death as providing the context for the emergence of a loosely coordinated, norm-oriented social movement with two major goals: (1) improvement in the quality of interaction between dying people and those who come into contact with them; and (2) enactment of legislation to support the patient's right to refuse treatment. In line with this second goal, there is growing interest in euthanasia, as evidenced by increasing numbers of people who have joined organizations advocating the legality of "mercy killing."

WITHHOLDING CARE

Another important issue in terminal care concerns the decision to withhold care. In Boston, in 1995, a physician refused to take extraordinary measures to keep alive a comatose patient suffering from irreversible brain damage. The family sued the doctor and the hospital over the decision. The patient, a 71-year-old woman, had entered the hospital for surgery for a hip fracture, but had suffered a seizure and became *status epilepticus* (suffering repeated and uncontrollable seizures). When the seizures ended, the patient was comatose with irreversible brain damage. Her doctors consulted with the hospital's optimum care committee which authorized a not-to-resuscitate order. When the family objected, the order was withdrawn. But a month later, a new attending physician requested the same order from the committee, and it was given. The family claimed it was unaware of the second order and would have opposed it if it had known. The hospital maintained that it makes every effort to resolve disputes with family members about withholding care, but when there is inappropriate denial on the part of families, which cannot be broken through, doctors' decisions should prevail. The hospital maintained that providing care for no positive end adversely affects the health care team and is a waste of expensive resources in times of cost containment.

Lawyers for the family maintained that the hospital should have gone to court to obtain permission not to treat; however, courts typically decide for patients in these matters. Furthermore, such cases are not tried in a timely fashion because it often takes months for lawyers to prepare and argue the cases. Therefore, the hospital and the doctors involved decided to terminate care instead of spending time and money on more useless treatment and the financial costs of court action.

This situation has caused renewed debate over *who* has the right to withhold care when further care is futile. On one side are doctors, who feel they should not be required to provide treatment for no positive end simply because it is demanded by the patient or the patient's legal surrogates. On the other side is the question of protection for society's terminally ill and how it decides which lives are worth preserving. Decisions about terminating care are usually decided in discussions between the physician and the patient or the patient's family. Some patients sign statements rejecting the use of extraordinary measures to prolong their lives. But when doctors and a patient's family disagree, and there are not advance directives from the patient, no simple solution exists for quickly resolving the issue. The case in Boston was not decided as this book was being published, but will be among the first to decide this issue.

Most states in the United States (43 out of 50) require some type of advance directive for hospital patients—either a living will (indicating under what conditions a person does not want medical support continued), a value inventory (stating what the patient values in life, thereby helping the health care team and the family to make decisions about terminating care), or durable power of attorney (granting someone else the right to make financial and life or death medical decisions if the patient is incompetent). The power of attorney is the most powerful means of protecting the rights of terminally ill people.

The two most famous legal cases in withholding care are those of Karen Quinlan (1975) and Nancy Cruzan (1990). Both cases involved moral disagreements about the protection of vulnerable incompetent patients. Quinlan spent more than 10 years in a coma. After the first several months, when it was clear there was not hope of recovery, the family decided to remove their daughter from life support systems. The hospital, a Catholic hospital, and doctors on the case decided they had a moral duty to continue care. The case went to court, where the issue was the right to privacy—the right of the individual to decide purely personal issues. The court held for the hospital because the patient's wishes were unknown. The Quinlan decision was appealed to the New Jersey Supreme Court, which found for the parents. This court held that the right to privacy implied in the U.S. Constitution is broad enough to allow the family of a dying incompetent patient to decide to let the patient die by disconnecting life support.

The Cruzan case is a landmark decision in American law decided by the U.S. Supreme Court. This case, also involving a comatose patient, recognizes the rights of dying patients by requiring *clear and convincing evidence* of the patient's wishes, not just a preponderance of the evidence. Thus a higher standard of evidence is needed to terminate life. New testimony from the patient's friends supported the standard of clear and convincing evidence in a lower court, and life support was terminated and the patient allowed to die.

The widespread use of advanced directives and the American Medical Association's 1986 policy statement support the position that it is "ethically" possible to allow "irreversibly" comatose patients to die after consulting with the family. The question remains, however, as previously stated, what happens when the family and the doctor disagree?

THE RIGHT TO DIE AND EUTHANASIA

As for the right to die, such as the refusal of food and medicine by terminally ill patients, U.S. courts have held that the right of a competent adult to refuse medical treatment is a constitutionally guaranteed right which must not be violated (Pence 1995). Not every life must be preserved against the will of the person who is subject to great pain and suffering. Consequently, in the United States there is a right to die for competent adults. A person who has not been proven incompetent therefore has the right to make decisions about ending his or her life.

Until 1996 there was not a right to assist people to commit suicide (euthanasia) in the United States. Legal euthanasia did exist in the Netherlands, provided the request was voluntary and the patient was well informed, had a lasting wish to die, was experiencing unacceptable suffering, and administered a fatal drug to themselves. Consultation between doctors, one of whom has experience with euthanasia, was required, along with a signed document that all rules had been met. In the United States, in contrast, 32 states in 1995 had formal bans against assisted suicide, and virtually all other states prohibited the act through criminal statutes or court decisions. Two cases from the late 1980s illustrate this situation. One case involved an elderly physician who was charged with manslaughter for assisting his terminally ill wife, who wanted to die, in taking an overdose of drugs. The other concerned a father who disconnected his young brain-dead son from a life support system while holding hospital staff members at gunpoint. Both men were acquitted, but these cases illustrate the moral and legal dilemmas associated with mercy killings.

The national debate in the U.S. about physician-assisted suicide has been provoked by the activities of Dr. Jack Kevorkian who helped several chronically ill people take their own lives in the 1990s. As of 1996, Kevorkian has been tried and acquitted five times on criminal charges in Michigan after the state supreme court ruled that assisted suicide was a common law felony. Michigan juries, however, have been unsure about whether or not helping a person who willingly wants to die actually constitutes a criminal act and Kevorkian has not been imprisoned. At the core of this dilemma is the position of the physician, who has a special duty to preserve life. Physician-assisted suicide is typically based on the requests of patients to end their suffering by helping them to take their own lives, but legal support for this action has been lacking until recently. In a statewide referendum in 1994, Oregon became the first state to authorize physician-assisted suicide, but the Oregon law was found to be unconstitutional by a U.S. District Court in 1995. The court stated that the measure would unfairly discriminate against the dying, because there was little assurance that only competent terminally ill persons will voluntarily die—leaving open the possibility that others could be killed through error or abuse.

However, in 1996 there was a historic shift in legal opinion by U.S. Appeals Courts in San Francisco and Manhattan. The San Francisco court held that a State of Washington ban on physician-assisted suicides deprived people of their personal liberty and was therefore unconstitutional. The Manhattan court ruled that doctors could legally assist terminally ill patients commit suicide in certain circumstances. This ruling, which applies only to doctors in New York, Vermont, and Connecticut, and not to others who might help a person commit suicide, holds that—if terminally ill patients have the right to refuse treatment—they should also be free to terminate their lives by requesting appropriate medication in the final stages of a terminal illness. Bans on physician-assisted suicide were considered to deprive people of personal liberty without due process and denied them equal protection under the law. The subsequent effects of these cases has yet to be determined, but what was once a settled and consistent body of law is now unsettled and open to wider interpretation by the courts.

In contrast, supporters of the "hospice" concept insist that the right to die involves a corresponding duty to kill and that euthanasia should not be allowed. Instead, the hospice, a hospital that specializes in the care of the terminally ill, offers an alternative approach (Paradis and Cummings 1986). Tried with some success in Great Britain and the United States, the hospice involves a complete change in the priorities of the physician and nurse. The aim is no longer to cure the patient, but to make the patient more comfortable and his or her dying days more meaningful. The hospice stresses companionship, sense of security, and control of physical symptoms through medical and nursing techniques. The control of pain is very important in order to allow the patient to be as active as possible for as long as possible.

Because modern society has attempted to be more open and intellectual concerning death does not mean that the fear and anxiety of dying can be rationalized away. It simply suggests that the process of dying may become less impersonal and dehumanizing. Perhaps death in the future will return to a modern version of Ariès' notion of "tamed death." In the final analysis, however, death will probably remain an experience characterized by various forms of fear.

SUMMARY

This chapter has examined death and dying from the perspective of both the individual and the society. The primary problem death presents for the individual is coping with the fear of death, particularly fear of the experience itself and of its consequences. Although everyone has difficulty managing these fears, most people eventually reach a stage of acceptance of death.

At present, death is contained by the larger social system in hospitals, nursing homes, and mortuaries by specialists who ensure that death is not disruptive for society. The result of these practices has been the dehumanization of death in modern society. Evidence is now beginning to mount, however, that attitudes in American society are evolving toward a more humanistic interpretation of the dying experience.

POSTSCRIPT: THE FUTURE OF AGING

The future of aging in the world appears to be generally positive. Good health and relatively high standards of living are not only possible but probable for the majority of elderly people in technologically developed societies. Although old age remains a period that many, perhaps most, people wish to avoid, it simply isn't possible to do so. Consequently, the optimal strategy for the individual is to approach old age with the idea of enjoying and finding personal satisfaction in the final stage of life. Current social policies are oriented toward providing a basic level of financial support and enhancing the quality of life through social programs in old age. There are no signs that these policies will be changed. Rather, national commitments to the aged are evident in governmental decisions throughout the world.

What is behind this trend is the fact that the world's population of old people, those 65 years of age and over, is increasing to levels never before attained in human history. Although some individuals may not be old at age 65, others are, and the use of age 65 as a general age at which regard someone as elderly appears likely to continue. Perhaps, at some future time, it may be adjusted upward, but for now age 65 remains the boundary of old age. The twenty-first century will be the first period of human existence when one out of every five persons is likely to be age 65 or over. By the midtwenty-first century, the United States, Canada, Australia, Western Europe, Japan, and several Asian countries will have populations of elderly people in excess of 20 percent, and some 40 percent of China's population—a simply incredible proportion—will be elderly if present trends continue.

In advanced industrial societies, old people will be more affluent, better educated, and more involved in politics than ever before. They are likely to be a highly potent social and political force in the world of the near future. Adequate old age pensions and health care delivery, along with government policies supportive of their needs, will be major features of modern welfare states. The option to continue working will be available to the elderly, and forced retirements are likely to be less common; however, many old people may continue to choose retirement over work. The point is that employment will be generally available for those who want it, and the option to work or retire will be largely the choice of the individual. In fact, incentives for older workers to stay on the job—in the form of increased salaries, greater retirement benefits, or shorter work schedules—may be common, with the expected decline in numbers and proportions of younger adults in the labor force. Thus older people are likely to have a greater range of choices about work, retirement, leisure activities, and continued education than ever before. Moreover, the elderly are likely to be relatively healthy throughout much of their old age, perhaps remaining fit until just prior to death. Both preventive care and treatment for illnesses of the aged will increasingly become a major medical specialty in the twenty-first century.

This is not to say that old age will be a time of contentment and satisfaction for all old people. Many will be frail and in poor health; hence, they will simply be unable to find enjoyment in the late stages of their life because of their ailments. The key to happiness in old age is health; without it, even vast sums of money will not be able to compensate for feeling ill and being unable to enjoy one's interests and usual activities of life. Being poor, on the other hand, signifies a life course of social and economic disadvantages culminating in significantly reduced life chances and opportunities for the aged living in poverty. Those who are both poor and sick will clearly be the most disadvantaged of all. Furthermore, there are signs in the 1990s of increased physical and mental abuse of the elderly, often by family members, as ageism and devaluation of the old continues—despite indicators of increased status and well-being for the aged in the future.

The elderly in developing countries will generally lack the quality of life of old people in developed nations, but they nevertheless are sharing in the greater longevity available to people in today's world. Diet, sanitation, health care, and lifestyle are prolonging lives throughout the world. High birthrates and relatively lower death rates in developing countries will result in large populations in general and greater proportions of old people in particular. The result is that—at the midpoint of the twenty-first century—some

69 percent of all aged persons on the globe will live in the less-developed states and regions of the world. Moreover, poor countries are likely to find it difficult to provide adequate health, social, and financial services for this large population.

As for the theories formulated to explain the social aspects of aging, no single theory provides a comprehensive explanation to date. However, disengagement theory works well in explaining those situations in which older people, having been moved out of their jobs and replaced by younger workers, are themselves opting for the retirement role. Some aged persons may not wish to become disengaged, and the option to remain employed is likely to be more available than in the past, but there comes a time when disengagement may be preferred by the aged individual. For many people, some form of disengagement is inevitable in old age, and disengagement theory helps us to understand this process. The theory is most applicable to those situations in which the aged are disengaged (pushed out) from the mainstream of society and at the same time disengage themselves (pull away) from society to pursue their own late-life interests.

Activity theory, another major theoretical approach in social gerontology, is actually a theory of successful aging. Activity theory is based on the premise that middle-aged norms of activity constitute the standards by which older people are judged; thus, the more active an elderly person, the happier and more satisfied that person will be with his or her life. Activity theory would lead us to believe that disengagement is not desired or inevitable for the aged. Rather, being involved in chosen activities and remaining an active part of one's social environment best depict what is important for old people. Of course, not every elderly person can remain active indefinitely, and activity theory does not really explain what happens when this occurs. Nevertheless, activity theory helps us recognize the value of activity in the lives of the elderly.

Another important perspective on aging is continuity theory, which posits that a person's personality in old age is generally consistent with his or her personality when younger. That is, elderly people typically retain the same overall personality they had earlier in their adult life; they are simply older. Although disengagement theory explains tendencies toward disengagement in old age and activity theory shows us the merits of being active when elderly, continuity theory indicates that personality is little changed, if at all, by the aging process. Each of these theories explains a selected aspect of aging. Two other approaches, age stratification theory and modernization theory, apply a broader interpretation to the aging experience. Age stratification theory, a relatively complex theoretical concept of aging, provides a method for analyzing age cohorts as they pass through the life course. People are seen as generations filling the same or similar roles of the cohorts in front of them who have passed on to another stage, yet are different from other generations because of different historical events and experiences. Modernization theory, in turn, explains how old people typically occupy valued statuses and roles in developing societies, but become devalued as the process of industrialization and modernization favors the skills and energies of the young. Yet Japan is an exception to this trend because of its cultural emphasis on honoring the aged and a family's ancestors. And, as modern societies mature and come to terms with large numbers of elderly in their midst, modernization theory maintains that elderly people regain higher status.

These theoretical perspectives represent important contributions to understanding social factors influencing aging. Other, more general theoretical approaches in sociology—such as conflict theory (which can explain how the elderly function as a particular interest group in competition with other interest groups for social resources) and symbolic interaction theory (which can contribute knowledge concerning the development of self-concepts and small-group interaction in old age)—have been underutilized to date. But each has considerable potential for theory construction in social gerontology. In sum, significant theoretical concepts have been made, but more remains to be done.

As the world moves into the twenty-first century, the various nations on the globe will become increasingly concerned with old age policy. Efforts to hold down the cost of health care and pensions for the elderly are not likely to be successful as the aged population expands. Unfortunately, a superior method has not yet been discovered to increase revenues significantly for government support of the aged. But the governments of the world will all more or less be required to expand and improve health and social services for old people. Therefore, although the elderly are headed toward a more positive life situation in the future, as compared with past generations of old people, their large numbers will require considerably more resources than were required previously. A major political challenge today is to prepare to meet the health, social, and financial needs of the elderly now and in the coming future. Exceptionally large populations of senior citizens will be a reality in the twenty-first century.

REFERENCES

ABERCROMBIE, NICHOLAS, STEPHEN HILL, and BRYAN S. TURNER. 1984. *Dictionary of Sociology.* Harmondsworth, UK: Penguin.

ABERCROMBIE, NICHOLAS, and ALAN WARDE, with KEITH SOOTHILL, JOHN URRY, and SYLVIA WALBY. 1994. *Contemporary British Society.* 2d ed. Cambridge. UK: Polity Press.

ACHENBAUM, W. ANDREW. 1983. *Shades of Grey: Old Age, American Values, and Federal Policies Since 1920.* Boston: Little, Brown.

—————. 1985. "Stitching a Safety Net." *Wilson Quarterly* 9: 126–136.

AKERS, RONALD L., and RICHARD HAWKINS, eds. 1975. *Law and Control in Society.* Englewood Cliffs, NJ: Prentice-Hall.

ALSOP, STEWART. 1973. *Stay of Execution.* Philadelphia: Lippincott.

ANTHONY, SYLVIA. 1968. "The Child's Idea of Death." In *The World of the Child,* edited by T. Talbot, 315–328. New York: Anchor.

—————. 1972. *The Discovery of Death in Childhood and After.* New York: Basic Books.

APPLEWHITE, STEVEN R., ed. 1988. *Hispanic Elderly in Transition: Theory, Research, Policy and Practice.* Westport, CT: Greenwood.

ARBER, S., and J. GINN. 1991. *Gender and Later Life: A Sociological Analysis of Resources and Constraints.* London: Sage.

ARDAGH, JOHN. 1987. *France Today.* London: Penguin.

ARIÈS, PHILIPPE. 1974. *Western Attitudes Toward Death.* Translated by P. Ranum. Baltimore: Johns Hopkins University Press.

——————. 1981. *The Hour of Death.* New York: Knopf.

ATCHLEY, ROBERT C. 1976. "Selected Social and Psychological Differences Between Men and Women in Later Life." *Journal of Gerontology* 31: 204–211.

——————. 1982. "The Process of Retirement: Comparing Men and Women." In *Women's Retirement,* edited by M. Szinovacz, 153–168. Beverly Hills, CA: Sage.

——————. 1994. *Social Forces and Aging.* 7th ed. Belmont, CA: Wadsworth.

BAKER, PAUL M. 1985. "The Status of Age: Preliminary Results." *Journal of Gerontology* 40: 506–508.

BARASH, DAVID P. 1983. *Aging: An Exploration.* Seattle: University of Washington Press.

BASSFORD, TAMSEN L. 1995. "Health Status of Hispanic Elders." *Clinics in Geriatric Medicine* 11: 25–38.

BAUM, MARTHA, and RAINER C. BAUM. 1980. *Growing Old.* Englewood Cliffs, NJ: Prentice-Hall.

BECERRA, ROSINA M., and DAVID SHAW. 1984. *The Hispanic Elderly.* Lanham, MD: University Press of America.

BELL, J. 1992. "In Search of Discourse on Aging: The Elderly on Television." *Gerontologist* 32: 305–311.

BENGSTON, VERN L., MARGARET N. REEDY, and CHAD GORDON. 1985. "Aging and Self-Conceptions: Personality Processes and Social Contexts." In *Handbook of the Psychology of Aging,* edited by J. Birren and K. Schaie, 544–593. 2d ed. New York: Van Nostrand Reinhold.

BERGER, PETER L., and THOMAS LUCKMANN. 1967. *The Social Construction of Reality.* New York: Anchor.

BINSTOCK, ROBERT H. 1983. "The Aged as Scapegoat." *Gerontologist* 23: 136–143.

BIRREN, JAMES E., R. BRUCE SLOANE, and GENE D. COHEN, eds. 1992. *Handbook of Mental Health and Aging.* 2d ed. New York: Academic Press.

BLAU, ZENA. 1956. "Changes in Status and Age Identification." *American Sociological Review* 21: 198–203.

BLAUNER, ROBERT. 1966. "Death and Social Structure." *Psychiatry* 29: 378–394.

BLUMER, HERBERT. 1969. *Symbolic Interaction.* Englewood Cliffs, NJ: Prentice-Hall.

BOK, SISSELA. 1991. "Lies to the Sick and Dying." In *Taking Sides: Clashing Views on Controversial Bioethical Issues,* edited by C. Levine, 92–101. Guilford, CT: Dushkin.

BOWDEN, CHARLES L., and ALVIN G. BURSTEIN. 1974. *Psychosocial Basis of Medical Practice.* Baltimore: Williams & Wilkins.

BRAITHWAITE, RONALD L., and SANDRA E. TAYLOR, eds. 1992. *Health Issues in the Black Community.* San Francisco: Jossey-Bass.

BRENTS, BARBARA G. 1986. "Policy Intellectuals, Class Struggle and the Construction of Old Age: The Creation of the Social Security Act of 1935." *Social Science and Medicine* 23: 1251–1260.

BRODKEY, HAROLD. 1996. "This Wild Darkness." *The New Yorker* (5 February): 50–52.

BROWN, ARNOLD S. 1996. *The Social Prices of Aging and Old Age.* 2d ed. Upper Saddle River, NJ: Prentice-Hall.

BULTENA, GORDON L., and EDWARD A. POWERS. 1978. "Denial of Aging: Age Identification and Reference Group Orientation." *Journal of Gerontology* 33: 748–754.

BUTLER, ROBERT N. 1985. "Geriatric Psychiatry." In *Comprehensive Textbook of Psychiatry,* vol. 2, 4th ed., edited by H. Kaplan and B. Sadock, 1953–1959. Baltimore: Williams & Wilkins.

CAFFERATA, GAIL L. 1987. "Marital Status, Living Arrangements, and the Use of Health Services by Ederly Persons." *Journal of Gerontology* 42: 613–618.

CAIN, LEONARD D. 1987. "Alternative Perspectives on the Phenomena of Human Aging: Age Stratification and Age Status." *Journal of the Applied Behavioral Sciences* 23: 277–294.

CARR, ARTHUR C. 1985. "Grief, Mourning, and Bereavement." In *Comprehensive Textbook of Psychiatry,* vol. 2, 4th ed., edited by H. Kaplan and B. Sadock, 1286–1293. Baltimore: Williams & Wilkins.

CHARMAZ, KATHY C. 1975. "The Coroner's Strategies for Announcing Death." *Urban Life* 4: 296–316.

CHILDS, DAVID, and JEFFREY JOHNSON. 1981. *West Germany: Politics and Society.* London: Croom Helm.

CHUDACOFF, HOWARD P. 1989. *Age Consciousness in American Culture.* Princeton, NJ: Princeton University Press.

CLAIR, JEFFREY MICHAEL. 1990. "Regressive Intervention: The Discourse of Medicine During Terminal Encounters." *Advances in Medical Sociology* 1: 57–97.

CLAIR, JEFFREY MICHAEL, DAVID A. KARP, and WILLIAM C. YOELS. 1993. *Experiencing the Life Cycle: A Social Psychology of Aging.* 2d ed. Springfield, IL: Thomas.

CLARK, ROBERT E., and EMILY E. LABEFF. 1982. "Death Telling: Managing the Delivery of Bad News." *Journal of Health and Social Behavior* 23: 366–380.

COCKERHAM, WILLIAM C. 1995a. *The Global Society: An Introduction to Sociology.* New York: McGraw-Hill.

————. 1995b. *Medical Sociology.* 6th ed. Upper Saddle River, NJ: Prentice-Hall.

————. 1996. *Sociology of Mental Disorder.* 4th ed. Upper Saddle River, NJ: Prentice-Hall.

COCKERHAM, WILLIAM C., GERHARD KUNZ, and GUENTHER LUESCHEN. 1988. "Social Stratification and Health Lifestyles in Two Systems of Health Care Delivery: A Comparison of the United States and West Germany." *Journal of Health and Social Behavior* 29: 113–126.

COCKERHAM, WILLIAM C., KIMBERLY SHARP, and JULIE WILCOX. 1983. "Aging and Perceived Health Status." *Journal of Gerontology* 38: 349–355.

COHEN, CARL I., JEANNE TERESI, and DOUGLAS HOLMES. 1985. "Social Networks, Stress, and Physical Health: A Longitudinal Study of an Inner-City Population." *Journal of Gerontology* 40: 478–486.

COHEN, DONNA, and CARL EISDORFER. 1986. *The Loss of Self.* New York: W. W. Norton.

COMFORT, ALEX. 1976. "Age Prejudice in America." *Social Policy* 7: 3–8.

COOLEY, CHARLES H. 1964. *Human Nature and the Social Order.* New York: Schocken.

COOMBS, ROBERT H., and PAULINE S. POWERS. 1975. "Socialization for Death: The Physician's Role." *Urban Life* 4: 250–271.

COULTON, CLAUDIA, and ABBIE K. FROST. 1982. "Use of Social and Health Services by the Aged." *Journal of Health and Social Behavior* 23: 330–339.

COWGILL, DONALD O. 1986. *Aging Around the World.* Belmont, CA: Wadsworth.

COWGILL, DONALD O., and LOWELL D. HOLMES, eds. 1972. *Aging and Modernization.* New York: Appleton-Century-Crofts.

COWLEY, MALCOLM. 1980. *The View from 80.* New York: Viking Press.

COX, HAROLD G. 1996. *Later Life: The Realities of Aging.* 4th ed. Upper Saddle River, NJ: Prentice-Hall.

CRAIG, GORDON A. 1982. *The Germans.* New York: Putnam.

CRANE, DIANA. 1975. *The Sanctity of Social Life: Physicians' Treatment of Critically Ill Patients.* New York: Sage.

CUMMING, ELAINE, and WILLIAM E. HENRY. 1961. *Growing Old: The Process of Disengagement.* New York: Basic Books.

CUNNINGHAM, W. R., and J. W. BROOKBANK. 1988. *Gerontology: The Psychology, Biology and Sociology of Aging.* New York: Harper & Row.

DAHRENDORF, RALF. 1959. *Class and Conflict in Industrial Society.* Stanford, CA: Stanford University Press.

DAVIS, KINGSLEY, and WILBERT MOORE. 1945. "Some Principles of Stratification." *American Sociological Review* 10: 242–249.

DEBUSKEY, M. ed. 1970. *The Chronically Ill Child and His Family.* Springfield, IL: Thomas.

DENZIN, NORMAN K. 1970a. "The Methodologies of Symbolic Interaction: A Critical Review of Research Techniques." In *Social Psychology Through Symbolic Interaction,* edited by G. Stone and H. Farberman, 447–465. Waltham, MA: Ginn-Blaisdell.

—————. 1970b. "Rules of Conduct and the Study of Deviant Behavior." In *Deviance and Respectability,* edited by J. Douglas, 120–159. New York: Basic Books.

DESJARLAIS, ROBERT, LEON EISENBERG, BRYON GOOD, and ARTHUR KLEINMAN. 1995. *World Mental Health: Problems and Priorities in Low-Income Countries.* New York: Oxford University Press.

DESWAAN, ABRAM, 1988. *In Care of the State.* New York: Oxford University Press.

DEVINEY, STANLEY, and ANGELA M. O'RAND. 1988. "Gender-Cohort Succession and Retirement Among Older Men and Women, 1951 to 1984." *Sociological Quarterly* 29: 525–540.

Diagnostic and Statistical Manual of Mental Disorder (DSM-IV). 4th ed. 1994. Washington, DC: American Psychiatric Association.

DOHRENWEND, BRUCE P. 1975. "Sociocultural and Social-Psychological Factors in the Genesis of Mental Disorders." *Journal of Health and Social Behavior* 16: 365–392.

DOWD, JAMES J. 1980. *Stratification Among the Aged.* Monterey, CA: Brooks/Cole.
————. 1984. "Beneficence and the Aged." *Journal of Gerontology* 39: 102–108.

DOWD, JAMES J., and VERN L. BENGSTON. 1978. "Aging in Minority Populations: An Examination of the Double Jeopardy Hypothesis." *Journal of Gerontology* 33: 427–436.

DREVENSTEDT, JEAN. 1976. "Perceptions of Onsets of Young Adulthood, Middle Age, and Old Age." *Journal of Gerontology* 31: 53–57.

DUMONT, RICHARD G., and DENNIS C. FOSS. 1972. *The American Way of Death.* Cambridge, MA: Schenkman.

DURKHEIM, ÉMILE. 1956. *The Division of Labor in Society.* New York: Free Press.
————. 1961. *The Elementary Forms of Religious Life.* New York: Collier.

EASSON, W. M. 1970. *The Dying Child.* Springfield, IL: Thomas.

EDWARDS, E. D. 1983. "Native-American Elders: Current Social Issues and Social Policy Implications." In *Aging in Minority Groups,* edited by R. McNeely and J. Cohen, 74–82. Beverly Hills, CA: Sage.

EKERDT, DAVID, J., LYNN BADEN, RAYMOND BOSSÉ, and ELAINE DIBBS. 1983. "The Effect of Retirement on Physical Health." *American Journal of Public Health* 73: 779–783.

EKERDT, DAVID J., RAYMOND BOSSÉ, and JOSEPH S. LoCASTRO. 1983. "Claims that Retirement Improves Health." *Journal of Gerontology* 38: 231–236.

EKERDT, DAVID J., BARBARA H. VINICK, and RAYMOND BOSSÉ. 1989. "Orderly Endings: Do Men Know When They Will Retire?" *Journal of Gerontology* 44: 528–535.

ERIKSON, ERIK. 1963. *Childhood and Society.* New York: W. W. Norton.

ESTES, CARROLL L., and PHILIP R. LEE. 1986. "Health Problems and Policy Issues of Old Age." In *Applications of Social Science to Clinical Medicine and Health Policy,* edited by L. Aiken and D. Mechanic, 335–355. New Brunswick, NJ: Rutgers University Press.

ESTES, CARROLL L., STEVEN P. WALLACE, and ELIZABETH A. BINNEY. 1989. "Health, Aging, and Medical Sociology." In *Handbook of Medical Sociology,* 4th ed., edited by H. Freeman and S. Levine, 400–418. Englewood Cliffs, NJ: Prentice-Hall.

EVANS, ROBERT G. 1986. "Finding the Levers, Finding the Courage: Lesson from Cost Containment in North America." *Journal of Health Politics, Policy, and Law* 11: 585–616.

FAIRBANK, JOHN KING. 1989. *The United States and China.* 5th ed. Cambridge, MA: Harvard University Press.

FARLEY, REYNOLDS. 1984. *Blacks and Whites: Narrowing the Gap?* Cambridge, MA: Harvard University Press.

FEATHERSTONE, MIKE, and MIKE HEPWORTH. 1990. "Images of Ageing." In *Ageing in Society,* edited by J. Bond and P. Coleman. London: Sage.

FEIFEL, HERMAN, and ALLAN B. BRANSCOMB. 1973. "Who's Afraid of Death?" *Journal of Abnormal Psychology* 81: 282–288.

FENNELL, GRAHAM, CHRIS PHILLIPSON, and HELEN EVERS. 1988. *The Sociology of Old Age.* Philadelphia: Open University Press.

FENWICK, RUDY, and CHARLES M. BARRESI. 1981. "Health Consequences of Marital-Status Change Among the Elderly: A Comparison of Cross-Sectional and Longitudinal Analyses." *Journal of Health and Social Behavior* 22: 106–116.

FERRARO, KENNETH F. 1980. "Self-Ratings of Health Among the Old and Old-Old." *Journal of Health and Social Behavior* 21: 377–383.

—————. 1988. "Double Jeopardy to Health for Black Older Adults." *Journal of Gerontology* 42: 528–533.

—————. 1989. "Widowhood and Health." In *Aging, Stress and Health,* edited by S. Markides and C. Cooper, 69–90. New York: John Wiley.

—————. 1993. "Are Black Older Adults Health-Pessimistic?" *Journal of Health and Social Behavior* 34: 201–214.

FERRARO, KENNETH F., ELIZABETH MUTRAN, and CHARLES M. BARESSI. 1984. "Widowhood, Health, and Friendship Support in Later Life." *Journal of Health and Social Behavior* 25: 245–259.

FILLENBAUM, GERDA G. 1979. "Social Context and Self-Assessments of Health Among the Ederly." *Journal of Health and Social Behavior* 20: 45–51.

FILLENBAUM, GERDA G., LINDA K. GEORGE, and ERDMAN B. PALMORE. 1985. "Determinants and Consequences of Retirement Among Men of Different Races and Economic Levels." *Journal of Gerontology* 40: 85–94.

FISCHER, DAVID H. 1978. *Growing Old in America.* Expanded Edition. New York: Oxford University Press.

FONER, ANNE. 1974. "Age Stratification and Age Conflict in Political Life." *American Sociological Review* 39: 187–196.

—————. 1986. *Aging and Old Age: New Perspectives.* Englewood Cliffs, NJ: Prentice-Hall.

FONTANA, ANDREA. 1977. *The Last Frontier: The Social Meaning of Growing Old.* Beverly Hills, CA: Sage.

FRIES, JAMES F. 1980. "Aging, Natural Deaths, and the Compression of Morbidity." *New England Journal of Medicine* 300: 130–135.

GALVIN, MICHAEL L., and MARGARET FAN. 1975. "The Utilization of Physician's Services in Los Angeles County, 1973." *Journal of Health and Social Behavior* 16: 75–94.

GARRETT, THOMAS M., HAROLD W. BAILLIE, and ROSELLEN M. GARRETT. 1989. *Health Care Ethics: Principles and Problems.* Englewood Cliffs, NJ; Prentice-Hall.

GECAS, V. 1982. "The Self Concept." *Annual Review of Sociology* 8: 1–33.

GELFAND, DONALD E. 1982. *Aging: The Ethnic Factor.* Boston: Little, Brown.

GEORGE, LINDA K. 1989. "Stress, Social Support, and Depression over the Life-Course." *In Aging Stress and Health,* edited by K. Markides and C. Cooper, 241–268. New York: John Wiley.

GEORGE, LINDA K., GERDA G. FILLENBAUM, and ERDMAN PALMORE. 1984. "Sex Differences in the Antecedents and Consequences of Retirement." *Journal of Gerontology* 39: 364–371.

GIBSON, ROSE C. 1986. "Blacks in an Aging Society." *Daedalus* 115: 349–371.

GIDDENS, ANTHONY. 1989. *Sociology.* London: Polity Press.

GILLEARD, CHRISTOPHER J., and ALI A. GURKAN. 1987. "Socioeconomic Development and the Status of Elderly Men in Turkey: A Test of Modernization Theory." *Journal of Gerontology* 42: 353–357.

GIRARD, CHRIS. 1993. "Age, Gender, and Suicide: A Cross-National Analysis." *American Sociological Review* 58: 553–574.

GLASER, BARNEY G., and ANSELM M. STRAUSS. 1965. *Awareness of Dying*. Chicago: Aldine.

————. 1968. *Time for Dying*. Chicago: Aldine.

————. 1971. *Status Passage*. Chicago: Aldine.

GOFFMAN, ERVING. 1959. *The Presentation of Self in Everyday Life*. New York: Anchor.

————. 1961. *Encounters*. Indianapolis: Bobbs-Merrill.

————. 1963. *Stigma*. Englewood Cliffs, NJ: Prentice-Hall.

————. 1967. *Interaction Ritual*. New York: Anchor.

GOVE, WALTER R., SUZANNE T. ORTEGA, and CAROLYN BRIGGS STYLE. 1989. "The Maturational and Role Perspectives on Aging and Self Through the Adult Years: An Empirical Evaluation." *American Journal of Sociology* 94: 1117–1145.

GRAEBNER, WILLIAM. 1980. *A History of Retirement*. New Haven: Yale University Press.

GREMBOWSKI, DAVID, DONALD PATRICK, PAULA DIEHR, MARY DURHAM, SHIRLEY BERESFORD, ERICA KAY, and JULIA HECHT. 1993. "Self-Efficacy and Health Behavior Among Older Adults." *Journal of Health and Social Behavior* 34: 89–104.

GUBRIUM, JABER F. 1975. *Living and Dying at Murray Manor*. New York: St. Martin's.

GUILLEMARD, ANNE-MARIE. 1986. "State, Society and Old-Age Policy in France: From 1945 to the Current Crisis." *Social Science and Medicine* 23: 1319–1326.

HABER, CAROLE. 1978. "Mandatory Retirement in Nineteenth-Century America: The Conceptual Basis for a New Work Cycle." *Journal of Social History* 12: 77–96.

————. 1983. *Beyond Sixty-Five*. Cambridge, UK: Cambridge University Press.

HAFFERTY, FREDERIC W. 1988. "Cadaver Stories and the Emotional Socialization of Medical Students." *Journal of Health and Social Behavior* 29: 344–356.

HARPER, MARY S. 1992. "Elderly Issues in the African-American Community." In *Health Issues in the Black Community*, edited by R. Braithwaite and S. Taylor, 222–238. San Francisco: Jossey-Bass.

HATTORI, HIROYUKI, STEPHEN M. SALZBURG, WINSTON P. KING, TATSUYA FUJIMIYA, YUTAKA TEJIMA, and JUNJI FURUNO. 1991. "The Patient's Right to Information in Japan—Legal Rules and Doctor's Opinions." *Social Science and Medicine* 32: 1007–1016.

HAUG, MARIE, LINDA LISKA BELGRAVE, and BRIAN GRATTON. 1984. "Mental Health and the Elderly: Factors in Stability and Change." *Journal of Health and Social Behavior* 25: 100–115.

HAUG, MARIE R., and STEVEN J. FOLMAR. 1986. "Longevity, Gender, and Life Quality." *Journal of Health and Social Behavior* 27: 332–345.

HAVIGHURST, ROBERT A. 1963. "Successful Aging." In *Processes of Aging*, edited by R. Williams, C. Tibbitts, and W. Donahue, 299–320. New York: Atherton.

HAVIGHURST, ROBERT A., and RUTH ALBRECHT. 1953. *Older People*. New York: Longmans, Green.

HENRETTA, JOHN C., and RICHARD T. CAMPBELL. 1976. "Status Attainment and Status Maintenance: A Study of Stratification in Old Age." *American Sociological Review* 41: 981–992.

HERMALIN, ALBERT L. 1995. "Aging in Asia: Setting the Research Foundation." *Asia-Pacific Population Research Reports* (April): 1–20.

HILDRETH, CAROLYN J., and ELIJAH SAUNDERS. 1992. "Heart Disease, Stroke, and Hypertension." In *Health Issues in the Black Community*, edited by R. Braithwaite and S. Taylor, 90–105. San Francisco: Jossey-Bass.

HOCHSCHILD, ARLIE RUSSELL. 1973. *The Unexpected Community*. Englewood Cliffs, NJ: Prentice-Hall.

HOGAN, DENNIS P., and DAVID J. EGGEBEEN. 1995. "Sources of Emergency Help and Routine Assistance in Old Age." *Social Forces* 73: 917–936.

HOUSE, JAMES S., JAMES M. LEPKOWSKI, ANN M. KINNEY, RICHARD P. MERO, RONALD C. KESSLER, and A. REGULA HERZOG. 1994. "The Social Stratification of Aging and Health." *Journal of Health and Social Behavior* 35: 213–234.

HUDSON, ROBERT B. 1988. "Social Policy in the United States." In *North American Elders*, edited by E. Rathbone-McCuan and B. Havens, 55–68. New York: Greenwood.

HUGMAN, RICHARD. 1994. *Ageing and the Care of Older People in Europe*. New York: St. Martin's.

IKLES, C. 1991. "Aging and Disability in China: Cultural Issues in Measurement and Interpretation." *Social Science and Medicine* 32: 649–665.

JOHNSON, ROBERT J., and FREDRIC D. WOLINSKY. 1993. "The Structure of Health Status Among Older Adults: Disease, Disability, Functional Limitation, and Perceived Health." *Journal of Health and Social Behavior* 34: 105–121.

KAMMERMAN, JACK B. 1988. *Death in the Midst of Life*. Englewood Cliffs, NJ: Prentice-Hall.

KAPLAN, GIORA, VITA BARELL, and AYALA LUSKY. 1988. "Subjective State of Health and Survival in Elderly Adults." *Journal of Gerontology* 43: S114–S120.

KAPLAN, HELEN SINGER. 1974. *The New Sex Therapy*. New York: Quadrangle.

KART, CARY S., EILEEN K. METRESS, and SEAMUS P. METRESS. 1988. *Aging, Health and Society*. Boston: Jones & Bartlett.

KASTENBAUM, ROBERT J. 1971. "Age: Getting There." *Psychology Today* 5: 53–54, 82–83.

——————. 1981. *Death, Society, and Human Experience*. 2d ed. St. Louis: Mosby.

——————. 1992. *The Psychology of Death*. 2d ed. New York: Springer.

KAUFMAN, SHARON R. 1987. *The Ageless Self*. Madison: University of Wisconsin Press.

KEITH, JENNIE, CHRISTINE L. FRY, ANTHONY P. GLASCOCK, CHARLOTTE IKLES, JEANETTE DICKERSON-PUTMAN, HENRY C. HARPENDING, and PATRICIA DRAPER.

1994. *The Aging Experience: Diversity and Commonality Across Cultures.* Thousand Oaks, CA: Sage.

KENT, D. P. 1971. "The Negro Aged." *Gerontologist* 11: 48–51.

KII, TOSHI. 1984. "Asians." In *Handbook on the Aged in the United States,* edited by E. Palmore, 201–217. Westport, CT: Greenwood.

KING, DONALD WEST, NEELA PUSHPARAJ, and KATHLEEN O'TOOLE. 1982. "Morbidity and Mortality in the Aged." *Hospital Practice* 17: 97–109.

KITANO, HARRY H. L. 1991. *Race Relations.* 4th ed. Englewood Cliffs, NJ: Prentice-Hall.

KITE, M., K. DEAUX, and M. MIELE. 1991. "Stereotypes of Young and Old: Does Age Outweigh Gender?" *Psychology and Aging* 6: 19–27.

KLEMMACK, DAVID L., and LUCINDA LEE ROFF. 1984. "Fear of Personal Aging and Subjective Well-Being in Late Life." *Journal of Gerontology* 39: 756–758.

KOBAYASHI, Y., and M. R. REICH. 1993. "Health Care Financing for the Elderly in Japan." *Social Science and Medicine* 37: 343–353.

KORTHASE, K. M., and I. TRENHOLME. 1982. "Perceived Age and Physical Attractiveness." *Perceptual and Motor Skills* 54: 1251–1258.

KRAUSE, NEAL. 1986. "Social Support, Stress, and Well-Being Among Older Adults." *Journal of Gerontology* 41: 512–517.

——————. 1988. "Stressful Life Events and Physician Utilization Among the Elderly." *Journal of Gerontology* 43: 553–561.

KRAUSE, NEAL, and THANH VAN TRAN. 1989. "Stress and Religious Involvement Among Older Blacks." *Journal of Gerontology* 44: 54–63.

KRONENFELD, JENNIE J. 1978. "Provider Variables and the Utilization of Ambulatory Care Services." *Journal of Health and Social Behavior* 19: 133–149.

KÜBLER-ROSS, ELIZABETH. 1969. *On Death and Dying.* New York: Macmillan.

LARSON, REED. 1978. "Thirty Years of Research on the Subjective Well-Being of Older Americans." *Journal of Gerontology* 33: 109–125.

LARUE, ASENATH, LEW BANK, LISSY JARVIK, and MONTE HETLAND. 1979. "Health in Old Age: How Do Physicians' Ratings and Self-Ratings Compare?" *Journal of Gerontology* 34: 687–691.

LEE, DAVID Z., and KYRIAKOS S. MARKIDES. 1990. "Activity and Mortality Among Aged Persons over an Eight-Year Period." *Journal of Gerontology* 45: S39–S42.

LEVIN, JACK, and WILLIAM C. LEVIN. 1980. *Ageism: Prejudice and Discrimination Against the Elderly.* Belmont, CA : Wadsworth.

LEVKOFF, SUE, PAUL D. CLEARY, and TERRIE WETLE. 1987. "Differences in the Appraisal of Health Between Aged and Middle-Aged Adults." *Journal of Gerontology* 42: 114–120.

LEVKOFF, SUE E., IAN MACARTHUR, and JULIA BUCKNALL. 1995. "Elderly Mental Health in the Developing World." *Social Science and Medicine* 4: 983–1003.

LEVY, JUDITH A. 1988. "Intersections of Gender and Aging." *Sociological Quarterly* 29: 479–486.

LIANG, JERSEY. 1986. "Self-Reported Physical Health Among Aged Adults." *Journal of Gerontology* 41: 248–260.

LIANG, JERSEY, EDWARD JOW-CHING TU, and XIANGMING CHEN. 1986. "Population Aging in the People's Republic of China." *Social Science and Medicine* 23: 1353–1362.

LICHTER, DANIEL T. 1988. "Racial Differences in Underemployment in American Cities." *American Journal of Sociology* 93: 771–792.

LICHTMAN, RICHARD. 1982. *The Production of Desire: The Integration of Psychoanalysis into Marxist Theory.* New York: Free Press.

LINDESMITH, ALFRED R., ANSELM L. STRAUSS, and NORMAN K. DENZIN. 1988. *Social Psychology.* 6th ed. Englewood Cliffs, NJ: Prentice-Hall.

LINN, BERNARD S., and MARGARET W. LINN. 1980. "Objective and Self-Assessed Health in the Old and Very Old." *Social Science and Medicine* 14: 311–315.

LOCAYO, CARMELA G. 1984. "Hispanics." In *Handbook on the Aged in the United States,* edited by E. Palmore, 253–267. Westport, CT: Greenwood.

LONGINO, CHARLES F., JR. 1988. "A Population Profile of Very Old Men and Women in the United States." *Sociological Quarterly* 29: 559–564.

LOPATA, HELENA Z. 1973. "Social Relations of Black and White Widowed Women in a Northern Metropolis." *American Journal of Sociology* 78: 1003–1010.

LUND, DALE A. 1987. "Gerontology Update on Bereavement." *In Gerontology Updates,* edited by J. Borup, 27–35. Washington, DC: U.S. Department of Health and Human Services.

LUND, DALE A., MICHAEL S. CASERTA, and MARGARET F. DIMOND. 1986. "Gender Differences Through Two Years of Bereavement Among the Elderly." *Gerontologist* 26: 314–320.

LUND, DALE A., MICHAEL S. CASERTA, MARGARET F. DIMOND, and ROBERT M. GRAY. 1986. "Impact of Bereavement on the Self-Conceptions of Older Surviving Spouses." *Symbolic Interaction* 9: 235–244.

LÜSCHEN, GÜNTHER, WILLIAM COCKERHAM, JOUKE VAN DER ZEE, FRED STEVENS, JOS DIEDERIKS, MANUAL GARCIA FERRANDO, ALPHONSE D'HOUTAUD, RUUD PEETERS, THOMAS ABEL, and STEFFEN NIEMANN. 1995. *Health Systems in the European Union: Diversity, Convergence, and Integration.* Munich: Oldenbourg.

LUSKY, RICHARD A. 1986. "Anticipating the Needs of the U.S. Aged in the 21st Century: Dilemmas in Epidemiology, Gerontology, and Public Policy." *Social Science and Medicine* 23: 1217–1227.

MCAULEY, WILLIAM J., and GREG ARLING. 1984. "Use of In-Home Care by Very Old People." *Journal of Health and Social Behavior* 25: 54–64.

MCCRAE, R. R., and P. T. COSTA, JR. 1982. *Emerging Lives, Enduring Dispositions: Personality in Adulthood.* Boston: Little, Brown.

MCDANIEL, SUSAN A. 1986. *Canada's Aging Population.* Toronto: Butterworth.

MCGOLDRICK, ANNE E. 1989. "Stress, Early Retirement and Health." In *Aging, Stress and Health,* edited by K. Markides and C. Cooper, 91–118. New York: John Wiley.

MCGOLDRICK, ANNE E., and CARY L. COOPER. 1989. *Early Retirement.* Aldershot, UK: Gower Press.

MCTAVISH, DONALD G. 1971. "Perceptions of Old People: A Review of Research, Methodologies, and Findings." *Gerontologist* 11: 90–101.

MacNeil, Richard D., and Michael L. Teague. 1987. *Aging and Leisure*. Englewood Cliffs, NJ: Prentice-Hall.

Maddox, George L. 1962. "Some Correlates of Differences in Self-Assessment of Health Status Among the Elderly." *Journal of Gerontology* 17: 180–185.

Maddox, George L., and Elizabeth B. Douglass. 1973. "Self-Assessment of Health: A Longitudinal Study of Elderly Subjects." *Journal of Health and Social Behavior* 14: 87–93.

Manton, Kenneth G. 1980. "Sex and Race Specific Mortality Differentials in Multiple Cause of Death Data." *Gerontologist* 20: 480–493.

Manton, Kenneth G., and James W. Vaupel. 1995. "Survival After the Age of 80 in the United States, Sweden, France, England, and Japan." *New England Journal of Medicine* 333: 1232–1235.

Markides, Kyriakos S., ed. 1989. *Aging and Health*. Beverly Hills, CA: Sage.

Markides, Kyriakos, and Cary L. Cooper, eds. 1987. *Retirement in Industrialized Societies: Social, Psychological and Health Factors*. New York: John Wiley.

——————. 1989. *Aging, Stress and Health*. New York: John Wiley.

Markides, Kyriakos S., and Charles H. Mindel. 1987. *Aging and Ethnicity*. Beverly Hills, CA: Sage.

Marshall, T. H. 1964. *Class, Citizenship, and Social Development*. Chicago: University of Chicago Press.

Marshall, Victor W. 1975. "Socialization for Impending Death in a Retirement Village." *American Journal of Sociology* 80: 1124–1144.

Martin, Linda G. 1988. "The Aging of Asia." *Journal of Gerontology* 43: S99–S113.

Mason, Evelyn P. 1954. "Some Correlates of Self-Judgments of the Aged." *Journal of Gerontology* 9: 324–337.

Massey, Douglas S., and Mitchell L. Eggers. 1990. "The Ecology of Inequality: Minorities and the Concentration of Poverty, 1970–1980." *American Journal of Sociology* 95: 1153–1188.

Masters, W., V. Johnson, and R. Kolodny. 1992. *Human Sexuality*. 4th ed. New York: HarperCollins.

Matt, Georg E., and Alfred Dean. 1993. "Social Support from Friends and Psychological Distress Among Elderly Persons: Moderator Effects of Age." *Journal of Health and Social Behavior* 34: 187–200.

Mead, George H. 1934. *Mind, Self, and Society*. Chicago: University of Chicago Press.

Mead, Lawrence M. 1985. *The Social Obligations of Citizenship*. New York: Free Press.

Mechanic, David, and Ronald J. Angel. 1987. "Some Factors Associated with the Report and Evaluation of Back Pain." *Journal of Health and Social Behavior* 28: 131–139.

Meyer, Bernard C. 1991. "Truth and the Physician." In *Taking Sides: Clashing Views on Controversial Bioethical Issues*, edited by C. Levin, 82–91. Guilford, CT: Dushkin.

Mezentseva, Elena, and Natalia Rimachevskaya. 1992. "The Health Profile of the Population in the Republics of the Former Soviet Union: An Analysis of the Situation in the 70s and 80s." *International Journal of Health Sciences* 3: 127–142.

MIROWSKY, JOHN, and CATHERINE E. ROSS. 1992. "Aging and Depression." *Journal of Health and Social Behavior* 33: 187–205.

MONTEIRO, LOIS. 1973. "Expense Is No Object . . . : Income and Physician Visits Reconsidered." *Journal of Health and Social Behavior* 14: 99–115.

MOODY, RAYMOND. 1976. *Life After Life.* New York: Bantam.

MORGAN, S. PHILIP, and KIYOSI HIROSIMA. 1983. "The Persistence of Extended Family Residence in Japan: Anachronism or Alternative Strategy?" *American Sociological Review* 48: 269–281.

MORRISON, MALCOLM H. 1986. "Work and Retirement in the Aging Society." *Daedalus* 115: 269–294.

MOSSEY, JANA M., and EVELYN SHAPIRO. 1982. "Self-Rated Health: A Predictor of Mortality Among the Elderly." *American Journal of Public Health* 8: 800–808.

MUTCHLER, JAN E., and JEFFREY A. BURR. 1991. "Racial Differences in Health and Health Care Service Utilization in Later Life: The Effects of Socioeconomic Status." *Journal of Health and Social Behavior* 32: 342–356.

MUTRAN, ELIZABETH. 1985. "Intergenerational Family Support Among Blacks and Whites: Response to Culture or to Socioeconomic Differences." *Journal of Gerontology* 40: 382–389.

MUTRAN, ELIZABETH, and KENNETH F. FERRARO. 1988. "Medical Need and Use of Services Among Older Men and Women." *Journal of Gerontology* 43: S162–S171.

MUTRAN, ELIZABETH, and DONALD C. REITZES. 1981. "Retirement, Identity and Well-Being: Realignment of Role Relationships." *Journal of Gerontology* 37: 733–740.

————. 1984. "Intergenerational Support Activities and Well-Being Among the Elderly: A Convergence of Exchange and Symbolic Interaction Perspectives." *American Sociological Review* 49: 117–130.

MYLES, JOHN F. 1978. "Institutionalization and Sick Role Identification Among the Elderly." *American Sociological Review* 43: 508–521.

————. 1984. *Old Age in the Welfare State.* Boston: Little, Brown.

————. 1988. "Social Policy in Canada." In *North American Elders*, edited by E. Rathbone-McCuan and B. Havens, 37–53. New York: Greenwood.

National Center for Health Statistics. 1986. "Aging in the Eighties." Preliminary Data from the Supplement on Aging to the National Health Interview Survey, United States, January–June 1984. No. 115. U.S. Department of Health and Human Services.

————. 1987a. "Use of Nursing Homes by the Elderly." Preliminary Data from the 1985 National Nursing Home Survey. No. 135. U.S. Department of Health and Human Services.

————. 1987b. "Aging in the Eighties, Ability to Perform Work-Related Activities." No. 136. U.S. Department of Health and Human Services.

————. 1989. "Physical Functioning of the Aged, United States, 1984." *Vital and Health Statistics*, Series 10. No. 167. U.S. Department of Health and Human Services.

——————. 1995. *Health United States 1994.* Washington, DC: U.S. Government Printing Office.

——————. 1996. *Health United States 1995.* Washington, DC: U.S. Government Printing Office.

NATIONAL INSTITUTE OF MENTAL HEALTH. 1994. *Mental Health, United States, 1994.* Washington, DC: U.S. Government Printing Office.

NAVARRO, VICENTE. 1986. *Crisis, Health, and Medicine: A Social Critique.* New York: Tavistock.

NEUGARTEN, BERNICE. 1964. *Personality in Middle and Later Life.* New York: Atherton.

——————. 1970. "The Old and Young in Modern Societies." *American Behavioral Scientist* 14: 13–24.

——————. 1971. "Grow Old with Me. The Best Is Yet to Be." *Psychology Today* 5: 45–48.

NEUGARTEN, BERNICE L., and DAIL A. NEUGARTEN. 1986. "Age in the Aging Society." *Daedalus* 115: 31–50.

NOVAK, MARK. 1993. *Aging and Society: A Canadian Perspective.* Scarborough, Ontario: Nelson Canada.

NOYES, RUSSELL, JR. 1972. "The Experience of Dying." *Psychiatry* 35: 174–184.

OKEN, DONALD. 1961. "What to Tell Cancer Patients: A Study of Medical Attitudes." *Journal of the American Medical Association* 175: 1120–1128.

OLSHANSKY, S. JAY, BRUCE A. CARNES, and CHRISTINE CASSEL. 1992. "In Search of Methuselah: Estimating the Upper Limits to Human Longevity." *Science* 250: 634–640.

OLSON, PHILIP. 1988. "Modernization in the People's Republic of China: The Politicization of the Elderly." *Sociological Quarterly* 29: 241–262.

O'NEILL, J. 1985. "Role Differentiation and the Gender Gap in Wage Rates." In *Women and Work,* edited by L. Larwood, A. Stromberg, and B. Gutek, 50–75. Beverly Hills, CA: Sage.

ORY, MARCIA G., and KATHLEEN BOND. 1989. *Aging and Health Care.* London: Routledge.

OTTEN, MAC W., JR., STEVEN M. TEUTSCH, DAVID F. WILLIAMSON, and JAMES S. MARKS. 1990. "The Effect of Known Risk Factors on the Excess Mortality of Black Adults in the United States." *Journal of the American Medical Association* 263: 845–850.

OWEN, J. P., and D. BELZUNG. 1967. "Consequences of Voluntary Early Retirement: A Study of a New Labour Force Phenomenon." *British Journal of Industrial Relations* 5: 162–189.

PALMORE, ERDMAN. 1968. "The Effects of Aging on Activities and Attitudes." *Gerontologist* 8: 259–263.

——————. 1969. "Sociological Aspects of Aging." In *Behavior and Adaptation in Later Life,* edited by E. Busse and E. Pfeiffer, 33–69. Boston: Little, Brown.

——————. 1971. "Attitudes Toward Aging as Shown by Humor." *Gerontologist* 11: 181–186.

—————————. 1975a. "The Status and Integration of the Aged in Japanese Society." *Journal of Gerontology* 30: 199–208.

—————————. 1975b. *The Honorable Elders*. Durham, NC: Duke University Press.

—————————. 1981. *Social Patterns in Normal Aging*. Durham, NC: Duke University Press.

—————————. 1985. *The Honorable Elders Revisited*. Durham, NC: Duke University Press.

PALMORE, ERDMAN B., LINDA K. GEORGE, and GERDA G. FILLENBAUM. 1982. "Predictors of Retirement." *Journal of Gerontology* 37: 733–742.

PALMORE, ERDMAN, and KENNETH MANTON. 1974. "Modernization and Status of the Aged: International Comparisons." *Journal of Gerontology* 29: 205–210.

PAMPEL, FRED C. 1981. *Social Change and the Aged*. Lexington, MA: Lexington Books.

PAMPEL, FRED C., and MELISSA HARDY. 1994. "Status Maintenance and Change in Old Age." *Social Forces* 73: 289–314.

PAMPEL, FRED C., and SOOKJA PARK. 1986. "Cross-National Patterns and Determinants of Female Retirement." *American Journal of Sociology* 91: 932–955.

PAMPEL, FRED C., and JANE A. WEISS. 1983. "Economic Development, Pension Policies, and the Labor Force Participation of Aged Males: A Cross-National, Longitudinal Approach." *American Journal of Sociology* 89: 350–372.

PAMPEL, FRED C., and JOHN B. WILLIAMSON. 1985. "Age Structure, Politics, and Cross-National Patterns of Public Pension Expenditures." *American Sociological Review* 50: 782–799.

PARADIS, LENORA FINN, and SCOTT B. CUMMINGS. 1986. "The Evolution of Hospice in America Toward Organizational Homogeneity." *Journal of Health and Social Behavior* 27: 370–386.

PARKER, S. 1982. *Work and Retirement*. London: Allen & Unwin.

PARSONS, TALCOTT. 1951. *The Social System*. Glencoe, IL: Free Press.

PENCE, GREGORY E. 1995. *Classical Cases in Medical Ethics*. New York: McGraw-Hill.

PESCOSOLIDO, BERNICE A., CAROL A. BOYER, and WAI YING TSUI. 1985. "Medical Care in the Welfare State: A Cross-National Study of Public Evaluations." *Journal of Health and Social Behavior* 26: 276–297.

PETERSON, MERRILL. 1970. *Thomas Jefferson and the New Nation*. New York: Oxford University Press.

PHILLIPS, DAVID P., and KENNETH A. FELDMAN. 1973. "A Dip in Deaths Before Ceremonial Occasions: Some New Relationships Between Social Integration and Mortality." *American Sociological Review* 38: 678–696.

PHILLIPS, DAVID P., and E. W. KING. 1988. "Death Takes a Holiday: Mortality Surrounding Major Social Occasions." *Lancet* 87: 728–732.

PHILLIPS, DAVID P., and DANIEL G. SMITH. 1990. "Postponement of Death Until Symbolically Meaningful Occasions." *Journal of the American Medical Association* 263: 1947–1951.

PIFER, ALAN, and D. LYDIA BRONTE. 1986. "Introduction: Squaring the Pyramid." *Daedalus* 115: 1–12.

PILCHER, JANE. 1995. *Age and Generation in Modern Britain*. Oxford, UK: Oxford University Press.

PILGRIM, DAVID, and ANNE ROGERS. 1993. *A Sociology of Mental Health and Illness*. Buckingham, UK: Open University Press.

PINKNEY, ALPHONSO. 1984. *The Myth of Black Progress*. Cambridge, UK: Cambridge University Press.

POSNER, RICHARD A. 1995. *Aging and Old Age*. Chicago: University of Chicago Press.

PRESTON, CAROLINE E. 1967. "Self-Reporting Among Older Retired and Non-Retired Subjects." *Journal of Gerontology* 22: 415–418.

———. 1968. "Subjectively Perceived Agedness and Retirement." *Journal of Gerontology* 23: 201–204.

PRESTON, CAROLINE E., and KAREN S. GUDIKEN. 1966. "A Measure of Self-Perception Among Older People." *Journal of Gerontology* 212: 63–67.

PRUGH, D. G., E. M. STAUB, H. H. SANDS, R. M. KIRSCHBAUM, and E. A. LENIHAN. 1953. "A Study of the Emotional Responses of Children and Families to Hospitalization and Illness." *American Journal of Orthopsychiatry* 23: 70–106.

QUADAGNO, S. JILL. 1982. *Aging in Early Industrialized Society: Work, Family, and Social Policy in Nineteenth Century England*. New York: Academic Press.

———. 1984. "Welfare Capitalism and the Social Security Act of 1935." *American Sociological Review* 49: 632–647.

———. 1988a. *The Transformation of Old Age Security: Class and Politics in the American Welfare State*. Chicago: University of Chicago Press.

———. 1988b. "Women's Access to Pensions and the Structure of Eligibility Rules: Systems of Production and Reproduction." *Sociological Quarterly* 29: 541–558.

RASMUSSEN, CHRISTINA, and MARK JOHNSON. 1994. "Spirituality and Religiosity: Relative Relationship to Death Anxiety." *Omega* 29: 313–318.

RILEY, MATILDA WHITE. 1971. "Social Gerontology and the Age Stratification of Society." *Gerontologist* 11: 79–87.

———. 1987. "On the Significance of Age in Sociology." *American Sociological Review* 52: 1–14.

RILEY, MATILDA WHITE, and ANNE FONER. 1968. Vol. 1, *Aging and Society*. New York: Russell Sage Foundation.

RILEY, MATILDA WHITE, ANNE FONER, and JOAN WARING. 1988. "Sociology of Age." In *Handbook of Sociology*, edited by N. Smelser, 243–290. Beverly Hills, CA: Sage.

RILEY, MATILDA WHITE, MARILYN JOHNSON, and ANNE FONER. 1972. Vol. 3, *Aging and Society*. New York: Russell Sage Foundation.

RILEY, MATILDA WHITE, and JOHN W. RILEY, JR. 1986. "Longevity and Social Structure: The Added Years." *Daedalus* 115: 51–75.

RING, KENNETH. 1980. *Life at Death: A Scientific Investigation of the Near-Death Experience*. New York: Coward, McCann & Geoghegan.

ROMAN, PAUL, and PHILIP TAIETZ. 1967. "Organizational Structure and Disengagement: The Emeritus Professor." *Gerontologist* 7: 147–152.

ROSE, ARNOLD M. 1965. "The Subculture of Aging: A Framework for Research in Social Gerontology." In *Older People and Their Social World*, edited by A. Rose and W. Peterson, 3–16. Philadelphia: Davis.

ROSENFELD, ALBERT. 1985. "Stretching the Span." *Wilson Quarterly* 9: 96–107.

ROSENWAIKE, IRA. 1985. "A Demographic Portrait of the Oldest Old." *Milbank Quarterly* 63: 187–203.

ROSOFF, ARNOLD J. 1981. *Informed Consent: A Guide for Health Care Providers*. Rockville, MD: Aspen.

ROSOW, IRVING. 1967. *Social Integration of the Aged*. New York: Free Press.

————. 1974. *Socialization to Old Age*. Berkeley: University of California Press.

ROSTOW, WALT W. 1978. *The World Economy: History and Prospect*. Austin, TX: University of Texas Press.

ROWLAND, DIANE. 1992. "A Five-Nation Perspective on the Elderly." *Health Affairs* (Fall): 205–216.

RUDMAN, DANIEL, AXEL G. FELLER, HOSKOTE S. NAGRAJ, GREGORY A. GERGENS, PARDEE Y. LALITHA, ALLEN F. GOLDBERG, ROBERT A. SCHLENKER, LESTER COHEN, INGE W. RUDMAN, and DALE E. MATTSON. 1990. "Effects of Human Growth Hormone in Men Over 60 Years Old." *New England Journal of Medicine* 323: 1–6.

SCHEUCH, ERWIN K. 1987. "Entwicklung der Bevolkerungsstruktur und unser Gesundheitswesen." *Mensch Medizin Gesellschaft* 12: 135–143.

————. 1989. "Theoretical Implications of Comparative Survey Research: Why the Wheel of Cross-Cultural Methodology Keeps on Being Reinvented." *International Sociology* 4: 147–167.

SCHWARTZ, ARTHUR, and ROBERT W. KLEEMEIER. 1965. "The Effects of Illness on Some Aspects of Personality." *Journal of Gerontology* 20: 85–91.

SELIGMAN, MARTIN E. P. 1974. "Submissive Death: Giving Up on Life." *Psychology Today* 7: 80–85.

SELTZER, MILDRED M., and ROBERT C. ATCHLEY. 1971. "The Concept of Old Age: Changing Attitudes and Stereotypes." *Gerontologist* 11: 226–230.

SHER, ADA ELIZABETH. 1984. *Aging in Post-Mao China: The Politics of Veneration*. Boulder, CO: Westview.

SHI, L. 1994. "Elderly Support in Rural and Suburban Villages: Implications for Future Support Systems in China." *Social Science and Medicine* 39: 265–277.

SHKOLNIKOV, VLADIMIR. 1995. "Recent Trends in Russian Mortality: 1993–1994." Moscow: Institute for Economics.

SIMONS, JOHN. 1992. "Europe's Ageing Population—Demographic Trends." In *Social Europe*, edited by J. Bailey, 69–50. London: Longman.

SKOCPOL, THEDA. 1994. *Social Policy in the United States*. Princeton: NJ: Princeton University Press.

SMITH, KEN R., and PHYLLIS MOEN. 1988. "Passage Through Midlife: Women's Changing Family Roles and Economic Well-Being." *Sociological Quarterly* 29: 503–524.

SORLIE, PAUL D., ERIC BACKLUND, NORMAN J. JOHNSON, and EUGENE ROGOT. 1993. "Mortality by Hispanic Status in the United States." *Journal of the American Medical Association* 270: 2464–2468.

SORLIE, PAUL, EUGENE ROOT, ROGER ANDERSON, NORMAN J. JOHNSON, and ERIC BACKLUND. 1992. "Black-White Mortality Differences by Family Income." *Lancet* 340: 346–350.

SPACAPAN, SHIRLYNN, and STUART OSKAMP, eds. 1989. *The Social Psychology of Aging*. Beverly Hills, CA: Sage.

SPINETTA, JOHN J. 1974. "The Dying Child's Awareness of Death: A Review." *Psychological Bulletin* 81: 256–260.

SPINETTA, JOHN J., DAVID RIGLER, and MYRON KARON. 1974. "Personal Space as a Measure of a Dying Child's Sense of Isolation." *Journal of Consulting and Clinical Psychology* 42: 751–756.

STOKES, GRAHAM. 1992. *On Being Old: The Psychology of Later Life*. London: Falmer Press.

STOLLER, ELEANOR PALO. 1984. "Self-Assessments of Health by the Elderly: The Impact of Informal Assistance." *Journal of Health and Social Behavior* 25: 260–270.

STREHLER, BERNARD L. 1977. *Time, Cells, and Aging*. 2d ed. New York: Academic Press.

STREIB, GORDON F. 1965. "Are the Aged a Minority Group?" In *Applied Sociology*, edited by A. Gouldner, 311–328. New York: Free Press.

———. 1976. "Social Stratification and Aging." In *Handbook of Aging and the Social Sciences*, edited by R. Binstock and E. Shanas, 160–188. New York: Van Nostrand Reinhold.

———. 1984. "Socioeconomic Strata." In *Handbook on the Aged in the United States*, edited by E. Palmore, 77–92. Westport, CT: Greenwood.

STREIB, GORDON F., and CARROLL J. BOURG. 1984. "Age Stratification Theory, Inequality, and Social Change." *Comparative Social Research* 7: 63–77.

STREIB, GORDON F., and CLEMENT J. SCHNEIDER. 1971. *Retirement in American Society*. Ithaca, NY: Cornell University Press.

SUDNOW, DAVID. 1967. *Passing On*. Englewood Cliffs, NJ: Prentice-Hall.

SUZMAN, RICHARD, and MATILDA WHITE RILEY. 1985. "Introducing the Oldest Old." *Milbank Quarterly* 63: 177–186.

TAYLOR, ROBERT J., and LINDA M. CHATTERS. 1986. "Patterns of Informal Support to Elderly Black Adults: Family, Friends, and Church Members." *Social Work* 31: 432–438.

THOMAS, ELIZABETH C., and KAORU YAMAMOTO. 1975. "Attitudes Toward Age: An Exploration in School-Age Children." *International Journal of Aging and Human Development* 6: 29–40.

THOMPSON, P., C. ITZIN, and M. ABENDSTERN. 1991. *I Don't Feel Old: Understanding the Experience of Later Life*. Oxford, UK: Oxford University Press.

TORRES-GIL, FERNANDO. 1986. "The Latinization of a Multigenerational Population: Hispanics in an Aging Society." *Daedalus* 115: 325–348.

TURNER, BRYAN S. 1987. *Medical Power and Social Knowledge*. London: Sage.

——————. 1988. *Status*. Milton Keynes, UK: Open University Press.

U.S. Census Bureau. 1987. *An Aging World*. Washington, DC: U.S. Government Printing Office.

——————. 1988. *Aging in the Third World*. Washington, DC: U.S. Government Printing Office.

——————. 1995. *Statistical Abstract of the United States, 1995*. Washington, DC: U.S. Government Printing Office.

VEGA, WILLIAM A., and HORTENSIA AMARO. 1994. "Latino Outlook: Good Health, Uncertain Prognosis." *Annual Review of Public Health* 15: 39–67.

VERBRUGGE, LOIS M. 1982. "Marital Status and Health." *Journal of Marriage and Family* 41: 267–285.

——————. 1985. "Gender and Health: An Update on Hypotheses and Evidence." *Journal of Health and Social Behavior* 26: 156–182.

WAECHTER, E. H. 1971. "Children's Awareness of Fatal Illness." *American Journal of Nursing* 71: 1168–1172.

WALLERSTEIN, IMMANUEL. 1983. *The Capitalist World Economy*. New York: Cambridge University Press.

WALLIMANN, ISIDOR. 1986. "Social Insurance and the Delivery of Social Services in France." *Social Science and Medicine* 23: 1305–1317.

WAN, THOMAS T. 1982. "Use of Health Services by the Elderly in Low Income Communities." *Milbank Quarterly* 60: 82–107.

WAN, THOMAS T., and SCOTT J. SOIFER. 1974. "Determinants of Physician Utilization: A Causal Analysis." *Journal of Health and Social Behavior* 15: 100–108.

WARD, RUSSELL. 1979. *The Aging Experience: An Introduction to Social Gerontology*. Philadelphia: Lippincott.

WARE, JOHN E., JR. 1986. "The Assessment of Health Status." In *Applications of Social Science to Clinical Medicine and Health Policy*, edited by L. Aiken and D. Mechanic, 204–228. New Brunswick, NJ: Rutgers University Press.

WATANUKI, JOJI. 1986. "Is There a 'Japanese-Type Welfare Society'?" *International Sociology* 1: 259–269.

WEBER, MAX. 1958. *From Max Weber: Essays in Sociology*. Translated and edited by H. Gerth and C. Mills. New York: Oxford University Press.

WEBSTER, MURRAY, JR., and JAMES E. DRISKELL, JR. 1983. "Beauty as Status." *American Journal of Sociology* 89: 140–165.

WEINBERGER, MORRIS, JEFFREY C. DARNELL, B. L. MARTZ, SHARON L. HINES, PEGGY C. NEILL, and WILLIAM M. TIERNEY. 1986. "The Effects of Positive and Negative Life Changes on the Self-Reported Health Status of Elderly Adults." *Journal of Gerontology* 41: 114–119.

WEISMAN, AVERY D. 1985. "Thanatology." In *Comprehensive Textbook of Psychiatry,* Vol. 2, 4th ed., edited by H. Kaplan and B. Sadock, 1277–1286. Baltimore: Williams & Wilkins.

WELLS, NICHOLAS, and CHARLES FREER, eds. 1988. *The Ageing Population*. London: Macmillan.

WHITE, LYNN K. 1988. "Gender Differences in Awareness of Aging Among Married Adults Ages 20 to 60." *Sociological Quarterly* 29: 487–502.

WILLIAMSON, JOHN B., LINDA EVANS, and LAWRENCE A. POWELL. 1982. *The Politics of Aging: Power and Policy.* Springfield, IL: Thomas.

WILSON, WILLIAM JULIUS. 1987. *The Truly Disadvantaged.* Chicago: University of Chicago Press.

WIRTH, LOUIS. 1945. "The Problem of Minority Groups." In *The Science of Man in the Modern World*, edited by R. Linton, 67–92. New York: Columbia University Press.

WITT, DAVID D., GEORGE D. LOWE, CHARLES W. PEEK, and EVANS W. CURRY. 1980. "The Changing Association Between Age and Happiness: Emerging Trend or Methodological Artifact." *Social Forces* 58: 1302–1307.

WOLINSKY, FREDERIC D., RODNEY M. COE, DOUGLAS K. MILLER, JOHN M. PRENDERGAST, MYRA J. CREEL, and M. NOEL CHAVEZ. 1983. "Health Services Utilization Among the Noninstitutionalized Elderly." *Journal of Health and Social Behavior* 24: 325–337.

WOLINSKY, FREDERIC D., and ROBERT J. JOHNSON. 1992. "Perceived Health Status and Mortality Among Older Men and Women." *Journal of Gerontology* 47: S304–S312.

WOLINSKY, FREDERIC D., RAY R. MOSELY II, and RODNEY M. COE. 1986. "A Cohort Analysis of the Use of Health Services by Elderly Americans." *Journal of Health and Social Behavior* 27: 209–219.

WONG, MORRISON G. 1984. "Economic Survival: The Case of Asian-American Elderly." *Sociological Perspectives* 27: 197–218.

YAMORI, YUKIO, YASUO NARA, KATSUMI IKEDA, SATORU TSUCHIKURA, TETSUYA EGUCHI, MASAYUKI MANO, RYOICHI HORIE, and TSUTOMU SUGAHARA. 1989. "Recent Advances in Experimental Studies on Dietary Prevention of Cardiovascular Diseases." In *New Horizons in Preventing Cardiovascular Diseases*, edited by Y. Yamori and T. Strasser, 1–11. Amsterdam: Excerpta Medica.

YIN, PETER, and KWOK HUNG LAI. 1983. "A Reconceptualization of Age Stratification in China." *Journal of Gerontology* 38: 608–613.

AUTHOR INDEX

SUBJECT INDEX